REALITY AND RELEVANCE

REALITY AND RELEVANCE

Commentaries on Abundant Life

Robert L. Grupp

Library of Congress Number: 2001117461
ISBN #: Softcover 1-4010-1549-2

This book was printed in the United States of America.

To order additional copies of this book, contact:
Xlibris Corporation
1-888-795-4274
www.Xlibris.com
Orders@Xlibris.com

CONTENTS

ADVENT AND CHRISTMAS

LENTEN SEASON AND EASTER

THE DAY OF THANKS

Reality and Relevance

is lovingly dedicated to
SUSAN ELIZABETH GRUPP,
my wife and helpmate for
more than 50 years. I am richly
blessed by her Christian Faith, love,
patience and encouragement. Our
greatest happiness is found in the
Abundant Life we share, as promised
and given by our Lord and Savior.

I am come that they might have life, and
that they might have it more abundantly.

(John 10:10 KJV)

PREFACE

Since January of 1983 I have written and produced brief commentaries for a daily radio segment of 90 seconds on Radio Station KLEM. 1410 AM, in Le Mars, Iowa.

The topics have not all been "religious." I speak about psychological problems, family concerns, national and international issues—as well as seeking to apply the Word of God to common and uncommon life situations. The aims have been reality, relevance and inspiration.

My background includes graduate work in radio, film and television. For seven years I was privileged to direct the Egypt programing for Radio Voice of the Gospel, which was beamed throughout much of Africa and the Middle East.

Radio has always been part of my ministry—mainly the broadcasting of worship services and teaching sessions.

In January of 1983 I approached the late Paul Olson, owner of Radio Stations KLEM and KZZL in Le Mars, Iowa. Paul did not know me except by name, but listened with courtesy as I proposed to produce daily 90 second commentaries, titled *Insights,* for airing on KLEM during early morning prime time.

For all he knew I could be a flaming, pulpit pounding religious nut, with little credibility and shallow material. But Paul decided to do it, and we reached an agreement. Within weeks the broadcasts began going out over the airwaves, and they continue. I am grateful to Paul Olson for his trust.

Five times a week during all these years have resulted in many commentary scripts. With the hope that they might be helpful to readers from every walk of life, I have selected more than four hundred of these commentaries for this book. My prayer is that the

81-GRUP

result will be life changes and enrichment because of their influence.

Robert L. Grupp—Le Mars, Iowa—February, 2001

A CERTAIN CONFIDENCE

Confidence is trust—a trust that is faith in combination with experience—whether it is trust in ourselves, in others or in God. The question is insistent: "In whom or what should we place our confidence?"

Confidence in ourselves is important, but it cannot stand alone. Eventually it breaks down and fails us.

The same is true of confidence in others. Most of us have learned that there are severe limits on the trust we might place in other persons. Some of us have learned that important lesson to our great sorrow.

Confidence in God is the only trust that never fails us, and that will take us all the way through this life and into immortality—eternal life in the presence of God.

Psalm 71:5 is an exquisite verse from the Word: "For You have been my hope, O Sovereign Lord, my confidence since my youth."

Faith in God finds its reality and possibilities only through Jesus Christ. Paul wrote in Ephesians 3:12: "In Him and through faith in Him we may approach God with freedom and confidence."

Faith in ourselves and in others takes us only so far. Faith in God through Jesus Christ takes us all the way to our eternal home.

GOOD ALWAYS CARRIES A SHADOW

Quite often I hear well meaning persons lamenting the evils that characterize the internet. And yes, they are to be lamented—and battled.

But we also need to keep in mind that every good produced by well intentioned persons carries a shadow, by which I mean the possibilities and even probabilities of that good element being turned to evil purposes.

Solomon stated that there is nothing new under the sun—and he was not talking about inventions. His lament was that evil manages to intrude, to do its dreadful work of hijacking, spoiling and ravaging.

But even so, the good is to be celebrated and promoted, not diminished in a timid reaction to evil's intrusions.

The printing press was a marvelous invention. But while persons of good intentions had Bibles and great writing in mind, evil forces got busy printing smut and rancor.

The shadow of evil falls on all accomplishments and fields of endeavor, including politics, business, government, religion, education, art and entertainment. Radios came into being, and quickly became a mix of good and bad. The same with television and the telephone.

So the mix of the bad, the ugly and the good in computers and the internet should not surprise us.

Fight the evil—promote the good.

BAD NEWS AND GOOD NEWS PERSONS

Sometimes we call certain persons "bad news." That's no compliment, and nobody wants to be known as a "bad news person!"

We don't even like to get chummy with a person who is "bad news"—such as those who seem to carry everywhere a kind of aura that makes for gloom, turns joy into sadness, breaks up parties and spoils the fun.

But what does it mean to be a "good news" person? Rarely have I heard anyone referred to as "good news."

A "good news' person benefits us; creates a happy atmosphere; solves some of our problems; alleviates our suffering; shares our troubles, and also our times of happiness.

Some people are like that almost constantly. We sense a change of atmosphere when they enter the room. Laughter becomes more spontaneous and genuine. Wallflowers start to bloom. They bring out the best in others, these "good news" persons.

And it is not that they are the life of the party! More often than not they are too busy listening to others to do much talking themselves. They don't necessarily tell the best jokes, but they help make others feel that they have made a real hit!

A good question for all of us: "Am I mainly 'bad news'—or 'good news'?"

KEEPERS OF THE FAITH

I'd like to challenge all churches and their congregations and staff to begin thinking through the definitive roles of church members—both in their church and in our culture.

Other than being a pew potato, what is their main calling?

Here's a start: First and foremost church members are called to be keepers of the faith.

From Christianity's beginnings believers in community were conscious of that very calling: to be keepers of the faith.

The Sacred Scriptures have been translated, interpreted and maintained—often at the risk of terrible penalties, including death. Heretics, agnostics and atheists have been resisted, along with all who would twist and distort God's Word to the end that it be man's word, in stark opposition to the revelation of God's ways and will.

In our era of a truly universal Church and a very intrusive world, the call to be keepers of the faith is more urgent than ever. The world in general, with all its paganism and screwball ideas, does not want the Church to be the Church, but to be the world.

In the thinking of some pagan zealots, one should be able to see few if any differences between the Church and the society and culture in which it exists. In your discussions of these serious matters, start with the call to be keepers of the faith.

IT'S NOT FAIR!

I've heard many exclaim in the face of life's calamities, "It's not fair."

And you know, they usually are right! Life can be terribly unfair—dishing out horrible and extended times of suffering—and ripping beloved family members out of this life through accidents, illness and murder.

Life is not fair because so many have more wealth than they could use in 20 lifetimes, while others barely eke out an existence in grinding poverty and deprivation.

It is a primary fact of life: Life is not fair!

But the worse thing we can do as we face those times of unfairness is to allow them to weaken our faith. Some have been so discouraged and disheartened in the midst of trouble that they begin to question their faith—to doubt and even discard the very God Who comes to us in special ways in the times of life's unfairness.

The truth is, we need a strong faith in God precisely because so often life is unfair.

A realistic and authentic faith gives us the needed options that take the sting out of life's unfairness. Faith responds to all our troubles with a big "Yes, but"—giving us sweet assurance that there is meaning and good that are generated even through the worst of times.

"INHERITED" PREJUDICE

Recently I had a long phone conversation with a gentleman in another state who had refused to attend his daughter's wedding because she married a young man who happens to be mulatto.

Handsome, smart, successful and socially gracious—all those things did not matter. Prejudice again has had an ugly and destructive victory.

I chided him for not being at the wedding, telling him how disappointed we all were. His response: "Well, Bob, I was raised by my grandfather who was a real bigot and I guess it stuck."

"Well, my friend," I told him, "You don't inherit prejudice. You have made a bad decision to stick with stupid and harmful influences from out of your past. Your grandpa was wrong, and you are simply perpetuating his unjustified and hateful notions."

We are wrong to justify our continuing red neck attitudes as "inherited" when they are ours by our own deliberate choice. The blame lies with us, not our forebears.

To all who would trace their bigotry to their parents or others, let's be clear: You don't inherit prejudice.

There is a time to grow up and away from the fallacies and foolishness of hateful impressions foisted on your childhood.

A SENSE OF DESTINY

I once heard a counselor telling some needy soul that the way to higher self-esteem is to look at the beautiful trees and flowers, and imagine they were all made just for you—and that will help you realize just how worthwhile you are.

Frankly, I find no satisfaction in imagining that the birds, flowers and trees love me. They are impersonal forces—and anyway, they are too busy looking after their own interests to love the likes of me.

Nor will my self-esteem benefit from thinking about how all the trees and flowers were made for me. After all, God made them for others, too! I have to share them with a lot of people.

The point is, you and I need much more than sappy psyching to raise our personal morale and improve our self-image.

We all are faced with eventual deterioration and death. It would help our self-esteem immensely if we could be sure we are not destined for the garbage heap—that the local cemetery is *not* the end of the line!

Assurance for sense, meaning and love in this life *and* in the life to come is found in and acquired from one Person. His Name is "Jesus."

Not the trees and flowers. Jesus.

A SENSE OF FUTILITY

Life just never adds up to meaning and contentment for a lot of folks. In their darkest moments they view it as senseless, and hardly worth all the effort.

Shakespeare's character Macbeth mourns the futility of life:

> "Life's but a walking shadow,
> A poor player
> That struts and frets his hour upon the stage,
> And then is heard no more.
> It is a tale Told by an idiot,
> Full of sound and fury,
> Signifying nothing."

Perhaps Macbeth spoke for a lot of people in Shakespeare's time and ours—persons who long for meaning and destiny. They want assurance that life is not "a tale told by an idiot, full of sound and fury, signifying nothing."

Jesus came to assure us that life is more, much more, than "a tale told by an idiot." He came to give us the joy and assurance of His companionship in this life—and the certainty of life to come.

But there are two sides to that coin of His realm. One side is the exquisite joy of knowing that life does indeed follow death. The other side is the sobering realization that God holds us accountable for our daily living.

It is our responsibility to fill life with meaning. Only then do we really avoid a sense of futility.

A SENSE OF HUMOR

Somebody asked this question: "If there really are people from other galaxies watching us, how come we don't hear them giggling?"

Hopefully whoever might be watching from out there has a good, healthy sense of humor.

Far too many people live out their lives in grim determination not to see the hilarity in much of life. They are blind to the humor in their own personalities and in their personal adventures and misadventures.

Aside from faith in Jesus Christ the most valuable asset you and I can have is a sense of humor. Life without it would be grim indeed! One writer commented: "A sense of humor . . . is not so much the ability to appreciate humorous stories as it is . . . the capacity to recognize the absurdity of the positions one gets into from time to time."

There is a big difference between humor that amuses, builds and makes people feel good—and humor used to cut down and destroy. Some people are masters of the art of putting others down—and often with crude humor. They think they're funny, when the truth is they are probably somewhat sadistic. Their sick humor masks an aggressive, destructive spirit.

Let your humor entertain and build others up, not hurt and destroy!

A STRONG PERSON

Some men think that being strong is being mean, stubborn, and quick to anger. They form a kind of macho image in their mind, that sometimes is close to being a gangster or a thug in one's own home. But those are qualities of weakness, not strength.

What most women want is a man who leads in the family without being domineering, one who is assertive in the face of difficulties, is able to offer help and comfort from a position of strength, and helps the whole family to feel greatly loved and protected.

This is not true only of the male role in a marriage—men often look for such characteristics in their wives, too.

A strong person, man or woman, is secure in his or her identity. He or she is facing life with truth and honesty, having expectations that are reasonable and attainable.

A strong person does not live by fantasies, does not exploit the weaknesses of others, rejoices when loved ones achieve success, and is enormously comforting in times of failure, deprivation and other hassles of life.

We require a good model for our images and fulfillment of personal strength. There is no better than Jesus Christ. Follow Him and learn the ways of strength tempered by compassion, caring and serving.

81-GRUP

COMING OF AGE

In the main, the phrase "coming of age" has to do with children growing up—reaching an acceptable and somewhat useful level of maturity.

Coming of age is not always the result of pleasant life experiences. Many youngsters get caught in a maelstrom of nightmarish abuses as they become victims of adult pedophiles, molesters, pimps and unbelievably cruel persons for whom these young lives are little more than trash.

Asked how she reacted to being kept for years as a slave prostitute, a sixteen year old Filipino girl, Pia Augustin Corvera, responded: "I felt like garbage."

Did Pia come of age when her aunt sold her into prostitution at age 9 at $3 an encounter—or at age 12 when she was sold to a visiting pedophile from Germany?

Or did she really come of age when she entered a therapeutic community for child victims of sexual abuse, and is learning that there is another and infinitely better side to life?

Do you suppose that while there is a world of monstrous depravity in which many came of age in very negative and life degrading ways, there is also the possibility and hope of a magnificent and healthy coming of age when one leaves that darkness and comes in contact with goodness, truth, caring and compassion in life?

A TRIBUTE TO CARDINAL O'CONNOR

I was saddened by the death of Cardinal John O'Connor some years ago. I met him just once, and it was a powerful experience. He was a man who had come of age in the highest sense of the phrase. His life orientation was toward God's best, and even in his terrible sufferings he had learned to identify with God's suffering on Calvary's cross.

That is fantastic enlightenment—and perhaps is the ultimate coming of age. It echoes the Apostle Paul's declaration in Colossians 1:24, "Now I rejoice in my sufferings for your sake, and in my flesh I complete what is lacking in Christ's afflictions for the sake of His Body, that is, the Church." (RSV)

So long as one exhibits indifferent tolerance toward predators and their evil exploitations of victims of any age, one has not come of age where it counts, in the realms of goodness, truth and light. There is no divine credit or approbation for permissive tolerance of hideous evil—but only judgment.

Could this be what is meant in Hebrews 4:13?

> **Nothing in all creation is hidden from God's sight. Everything is uncovered and laid bare before the eyes of Him to Whom we must give account.**

The pointed lesson: "Don't face God's judgment without coming of age."

ABOUT A GREAT WORK

The highest form and meaning about coming of age is when someone moves from the darkness of evil into the light that yields enormous blessings for all. That move calls for significant life sacrifices on behalf of the good, and in doing serious battle with the forces of darkness.

Father Shay Cullen certainly has come of age in the highest sense as he gives himself to a ministry with significant risk factors, including death threats from those whose evil doings he has thwarted.

An article published April 13, 2000, by the Philippines News Service tells us: "Known throughout the world for the work combating child sex tourism, Father Shay Cullen, a missionary from Ireland, has been nominated for the prestigious Nobel Peace Prize. {The nomination recognizes} the risks and threats endured by the priest and his Filipino helpers in their 26 years of effort to help exploited youth and children. They have persevered against death threats and opposition from local politicians and organized pedophile and sex tour agents."

We live in an age in which coming of age can mean being brutalized.

Then along comes a person such as the Rev. Shay Cullen, who gives us lessons on the real coming of age, as we move into God's light—and get involved in battling evil.

ALL IN THE FAMILY

Family ties are very important—especially in these days of stress and strain on all our human relationships.

When young parents live far from their own parents, it's tough on all concerned. The human family cries out for closeness.

One of the things I love about the Church of Jesus Christ is that it provides for all concerned an extended family. There is caring, love and lots of help and hope generated in the extended family of the church. Some amazing acts of love and service take place between the members and their families.

When one suffers, all suffer. When one rejoices, all rejoice. There is high meaning and helpfulness in the concepts of Christian Fellowship and being brothers and sisters in Christ.

As with any family there are always a few people who don't understand what God's grace, forgiveness, compassion and calls to reconciliation are all about. But in a healthy church such folks must be the exception—and certainly not the rule.

Now think about your church—and what you are doing to make it an extended family. Think also about what might be done to make those church family ties even stronger. That's what God intends, you know—and that's the reason why Christians are called "children of God." We're family!

ANTICIPATIONS

Some of the most delectable and heartening aspects of life are the anticipations we develop over neat events that lie just ahead.

In the early summer of the year anticipation is keen in many homes as vacations, reunions and various outings and celebrations are planned.

With each passing year I become more aware of the importance of having good things in the offing. Life in its sameness can be dreadfully dull. It's when we have something to look forward to that we are at our psychological and quite likely physical best.

Oh, yes—it's true that experiencing such special times usually leaves us exhausted, and so glad to be home, and back to more routine matters. But nonetheless the experiences are productive of good health and psychological wellbeing. Renewed appreciation for the common and ordinary home scene is just one aspect of the therapy of anticipation and fulfillment.

Another way to keep young and involved is creating anticipation for others, and of course, the joyful completion of those expectations. While one should be very thoughtful and careful about making promises to children and grandchildren, their lives light up when they are given some future adventure to which they can look forward.

Anticipations are at their best when loaded with love and thoughtfulness about what creates happiness for others.

BEAUTY AND THE BEAST

In spite of all the sin and ugliness in this world, there may be some truth in that old expression, "Beauty is in the eye of the beholder." God sees in His creation a beauty that sometimes escapes us. Surely to the Holy God we are not attractive, not appealing. And yet He loves us, cherishes us, gave His all for us to make our personal world beautiful.

The world becomes beautiful as we make it so. We bring beauty to situations, along with joy and peace.

We feel miserable in some situations precisely because misery is what we bring to them—what we expect of them. Our bad attitudes are always self fulfilling.

Ask yourself what you bring into any gathering of people. A complaining, gloomy, depressed, ugly spirit? Or do you bring freshness and vitality, humor and optimism, beauty and peace? Are you a creator of beauty?

To a great extent the world is what each of us makes it. If you are determined to be gloomy and see only ugliness—that is what you will experience!

As you move through your small world today, be determined to see and do the good. You'll be absolutely amazed at the difference it will make—both to you and to others!

BECOMING

The word "becoming" can be used in several senses. As a verb form it means to be changing, to grow or to be transformed in various ways—to be in process. That meaning applies to the young people who are graduating this spring.

They have become what they are today—but they are still in process, and that state of becoming will be even more intense as they move into new phases.

There's another sense of becoming—when it is used as an adjective. When we say that something is becoming for or to us, it means that it goes with us, it enhances our appearance or demeanor. This also is applicable to our graduates.

Both senses of "becoming" are especially applicable for Christians. We are people who are becoming in the sense that we are growing, maturing and changing as we walk with Jesus Christ. And we are to be becoming to Him—to be persons who go well with Jesus—making sure we make the best match possible with our Lord.

All human beings are meant to keep growing psychologically, intellectually, morally, emotionally and spiritually until disease or disablement makes it impossible to continue growing.

Christians should be even more aware of the Creator's intent, and make sure that our lives stay on the growing edge.

BEING MISSED

Have you ever experienced being away on a week or so vacation, then return home—and people act as though you were never gone? Some even ask, "Oh, have you been away?"

A four-year old child was playing in his yard when a grown-up friend of the family came by, and asked: "Hi, Mike! Where's your big brother, Jason?" Mike answered, "He's away for the summer."

"Oh?" said the man, "Don't you miss him?"

Mike thought about the number of times Jason had been mean to him, and then replied emphatically, "Yes. But I like missing him!"

One of the most important things we do in life is to make our presence felt in ways that are meaningful to others—such as being a good listener, or offering occasional words of encouragement, or sharing in someone's problems or troubles in helpful ways.

To be missed when absent is one of the highest compliments of life. But it is reserved for people who make an effort to be meaningful and helpful in the lives of others—for persons who have taken the time and trouble to learn how to praise and affirm, to be cheery and uplifting, to laugh with some and weep with others.

It is a sobering question, but we all need to ask it: "How much are *you* missed?"

BOAT ROCKERS

There is a time to rock boats—but needless boat rocking works destructively in relationships and organizations.

Boat rockers go to work when they aren't getting their way, when the relationship or organization is not paying enough attention to them and to their notions. So they clamor for undeserved attention and sometimes bizarre changes.

Persons who are first class enablers for boat rockers learn to their sorrow that most boat rockers have no real concern for the group, but only for their own egos—so all attempts to satisfy them simply encourage their obstinate attempt to sabotage what's going on.

Granted, sometimes the boat needs to be rocked in any relationship or organization. Changes are needed, and people don't change without a certain amount of boat-rocking. But that kind aims for improvement, for specific changes. It doesn't deal in generalities but specifics. It has a concrete program for adjustment for the better.

Destructive boat-rocking is usually vague, accusatory, not solution-oriented, and calls on the other person or group to satisfy the boat-rocker—to pander to his or her whims, no matter the cost.

For such personalities, the best approach is never to yield to their emotional blackmail and self-seeking gripes.

CHRISTIANITY "LITE"

The worst times of my life are when I have indulged in what I call "Christianity Lite."

There are many ways in which we try to take the heft out of our faith—sometimes diluting it right out of existence.

When we compromise on morality, avoiding or denying the clear teachings of God's Word, we are indulging in "Christianity Lite."

When we disclaim responsibility for the lives of others we are creating our own version of "Christianity Lite."

Our lack of concern for social justice, along with our easy tolerance of hateful prejudice offer us only the vapid and essentially lifeless qualities of "Christianity Lite."

Authentic Christian Faith can never be "Christianity Lite." We either have it or we do not. We cannot "adjust" and "condition" our faith to the silly vagaries of crazy making activities and imagine that somehow we remain secure and safe in the company of Jesus Christ.

Some find it easy to joke about their lack of attendance at worship, thereby evidencing their "Christianity Lite." We can be sure that such neglect is not humorous in God's eyes.

This is a good time, as we begin the fall season in our churches, to weigh our Christianity and see if we have not obliterated it with various forms of "Christianity Lite."

COMEUPPANCE

There are some who are convinced that our common, ordinary life carries with it no experiences of God's judgment—of persons getting what amounts to their comeuppance, their just desserts—punishment and retribution for their wrong doing, foolishness and sin.

I cannot agree with that assessment of life. I believe that God has instilled into the fabric of creation certain inevitable consequences for the follies of sin and rebellion against our Creator. I also believe that there is a judgment in life after death that will be a real corker.

Have you ever felt that you have received a comeuppance that you well deserved—and perhaps were the better for it? That is the intent, you know—not just that we be punished, but that we turn from the stupidity of our out of control behaviors and lives.

We've all watched while certain elected officials got their comeuppance for improprieties in office. We may have thought of their retribution as too mild or too severe—but the important thing is that they got their comeuppance.

Youngsters who are indifferent and lazy toward school assignments will get their comeuppance when the report cards come out—and when their poor grades keep them from entering the college of their choice.

Believe it—comeuppances are a main feature of life—sometimes slow in coming, but inevitable.

HUMANOIDS

Our imaginings about space and other realms of existence have given us new words—one of which is "humanoid."

"Humanoid" means having the appearance of a human being. We have a lot of people in our society who are humanoids—meaning they just have the shape and appearance of human beings, but they are more like animals in their attitudes and behaviors.

The highest concept of being human is to show the image of God in which we all have been created. That image gets pretty marred and even shattered in a lot of lives. It's at that point such persons are mere humanoids—not truly human.

A humanoid is a person without grace, compassion, love, caring and social sensitivity and responsibility. Humanoids tend to be conceited, self-centered and devoid of elements of self-giving and self-control for the sake of others.

Part of Christ's work in us is to restore the image of God. This means we are to show the qualities of the Divine Creator in our living—in our attitudes and actions. Jesus is out to make us human in the highest and best sense of the word: God's image-bearers.

Humanoid is never enough. Just resembling a God-imaging human being through physical traits does not mean we are human. We just look like it.

COMPLIMENTS

There are folks who have a tough time giving compliments. With some it's fear of misunderstanding. Others think they will sound phony.

And—let's face it—a lot of people are stingy with the compliments because they themselves have rarely received them. Or they are grudging about the accomplishments of others when theirs are so meager! They are more inclined to put down and disparage, than to affirm and praise.

So they hold back on the affirmations and compliments to the very people who are looking toward them for encouragement. They want to hear words of encouragement because of their respect and love for you

There are people in your life who look to you for encouragement. So don't disappoint them by holding back on the affirmation and encouragement. In chapter 2 of Philippians Paul tells us:

> Rivalry and personal vanity should have no place among you, but you should humbly think of others as better than yourselves. You must look to each other's concerns and not merely to your own. Let your bearing toward one another arise out of your life in Christ Jesus.

Compliments. affirmation and encouragement of others come much easier when we understand the Bible's counsel to be concerned for the needs of others, not just our own.

I HAVE TO FORGIVE—

Some time ago, Oprah Winfrey had a program on severe child abuse.

One horrific story was of two boys who were repeatedly tortured by their mother's boy friend. His vicious brutality toward those two children was unimaginable, and apparently the mother offered little if any protest.

The youngest boy of 5 died one morning after being left all night hanging upside down in a closet. The other boy of 9 managed to survive—and later was adopted by a loving couple. The boy friend and mother are in prison for life.

Oprah introduced that survivor—now 19 years of age, and a student in college. It was a powerful moment when the lad sat down and responded to questions from Oprah.

When she asked him if he hated his mother for permitting such terrible things to happen to him and his brother, the young man replied: "I can't hate her. I have to forgive her because I am a Christian."

I almost jumped out of my chair with delight and celebration! I've heard far too many say with smug self pity, "I'll never forget and I'll never forgive!"

That young man has found a maturity and faith that all of us would do well to heed and develop in our own lives.

USER FRIENDLY

There's a designation that computer companies like to use: "User friendly." They intend to convey the idea that their particular computer and its programs are easy to use. They do not hassle the purchaser with endless things to figure out, codes to memorize and mysterious combinations to get the job done.

For some people life is not particularly user friendly. That's because life is even more complex than a computer—and people, generally, are much more complicated than any computer or computer program.

We're wise when we don't relax too much with user friendly computers. It's good to be on your guard, to back up your data, do some praying, and to let your trust have some hefty reservations.

We need to approach life in the same way. Even though life is "Maker friendly," meaning that God the Creator cares about us and loves us, living out our days can have some hassles, heartaches and even calamities. Life is meant to be user friendly, but because of human perversity things often go awry.

Our Maker has given us a great manual for life: The Holy Bible. There's also a prayer line, and a users group called, "The Church"—full of knowledgeable and helpful people whose purpose is to make life more user friendly.

THE FACTS OF LIFE

I wonder how many parents are really making an effort to teach their children the facts of life. I wonder even more about what most parents *include* in the facts of life.

The facts of life include matters of sexuality, to be sure. But there's much more.

One such fact is the existence of raw evil in the world—that certain persons have turned their lives over to devilish forces—resulting in terrorism, brutal murders, and all sorts of evil happenings in the world.

We need to be wary of such persons. To teach our children a kind of Pollyanna attitude toward life, as though all is good and beautiful, is to prepare them for disillusion and even tragedy.

Another fact of life is personal accountability. Parents need to teach their children the hard lessons about their responsibility before God and humankind for their actions in life.

Have you ever heard the word "impunity?" It means doing things with no backlash, with no consequences. Some parents unwittingly communicate to their children that they can live with impunity: that there is no accounting for their behavior; that no one will ever call them to account for their living.

By all means teach your children the facts of life—but be sure you teach all of them!

STEER CLEAR OF IMBROGLIOS

A good word to know is imbroglio, with a silent "g." It means a tangled mess of human interaction, a confused situation, a complicated disagreement.

There are many ways in which we make a tangle of our lives, creating confusion and conflict, often with a lot of hurt for ourselves and for others.

Whenever we ignore the demands of full reality, an imbroglio pops into being. And what a huge imbroglio we make when we turn our backs on God, and ignore His laws and ways.

The Ten Commandments and all the other laws of God are intended to keep our lives and societies free of devastating entanglements. Men and women who break their marriage vows and engage in what we call "affairs" with others find themselves in an awful tangle.

Greed, pride, avarice, hate, prejudice and all types of lawlessness are the makings of the awesome entanglements of imbroglios. For sure the cutting tongues of gossipers and tale bearers set imbroglios in motion.

The very opposite of an imbroglio is the order, purity, peace and contentment of a person dedicated to simple good—to being and doing the right, and speaking and listening to the truth.

By all means steer clear of imbroglios, the destructive entanglements of life.

SHARED PASSAGES

Not long ago I was privileged to share in the funeral service for my brother, Roger Grupp. As you can well imagine, it was not an easy thing to do.

The impact of the loss of a brother is severe because we have shared so many important passages. This is compounded by all the other loved ones who also have shared in passages—some the same, some different.

Birth, the various stages of maturity, illnesses and losses, marriage and children, jobs and vacations, along with church, faith and celebrations all make up passages which we have traversed together—sometimes closely, and sometimes from afar—but the commonality of experience, affection and concern are all there.

Then there is that final passage through which Roger and many other dear ones have preceded us—the passage from this mortal life to the life of immortality, from living by faith and hope to an eternal life of certitude and full understanding.

Our faith assures us that the final passage is also one of reunion with loved ones who have gone on before. There will be a wonderful welcome home to the Kingdom where we originated in the mind and heart of our Heavenly Father.

One thing I know—while facing such loss is difficult and disheartening, without my faith in Christ it would be horrendous.

SANCTIFICATION OF SELFISHNESS

One of the more negative and destructive aspects of our current western culture are the efforts to popularize selfishness. "Look after yourself, and offer not a whiff of apology for self focused attitudes and behaviors. If others are too dumb to understand the logic and benefits of this stance, that's their problem." The trend seems to be the dethronement of idealistic service and self sacrifice, and putting in its place a smug self-centeredness that is considered lofty and wholesome for self and society.

The greatest accomplishments of any age have been rooted in self deprecation and attitudes of self giving service. Greatness has always been the product of self-expenditure.

But more and more these days I hear people declaring the virtue and even sanctity of looking out for "number one"—and it's just tough if others get in the way.

In Luke 14:11 Jesus teaches: "For everyone who exalts himself will be humbled, and he who humbles himself will be exalted."

In Ephesians 4:2 the Apostle Paul gives this counsel: "Be completely humble and gentle; be patient, bearing with one another in love."

And Peter advises us in his first letter, Chapter 5: "All of you, clothe yourselves with humility toward one another, because, 'God opposes the proud but gives grace to the humble.'"

GOD NOTIONS

Have you ever heard something like this: "I have my own ideas about God—no matter what the Church teaches."

Many insist on creating God in their own image. If they don't like the character and personality of God as given in His Holy Word, they will make up their own! I call these "God notions."

Sometimes we do this in regard to our human relationships. We define their character, sometimes because of gossip. "That's the way he is, all right!" This is not only unfair—it's plain foolish.

We need to examine our notions about God's Person, making sure that we are truly tracking His real Personality. He is either loving or not, full of Grace or ruthless toward His Creation, compassionate and merciful or vengeful and hateful. He cannot be all of these and more just because some folks might think so.

And where do we go to fill in the God picture and to get our notions straight? To the Bible, the Word of God, and especially as it tells of Jesus Who made the fantastic claim: "If you have seen Me, you have seen God. If you get to know Me, you've become acquainted with God."

God notions are often silly, and sometimes dangerous. Get it straight from His revealed Word.

HAPPINESS

A pastor had just married a couple, and the best man handed him an envelope, with a check and a note, which read: "Thank you for working so hard to bring our happiness to such a beautiful conclusion."

Words do sometimes come out wrong!

But it's true that many people in effect "conclude" their happiness prematurely and needlessly. And I suspect that there also are many who never quite reach a state of mind and being in which they can honestly say: "I'm happy!"

Happiness is also very hard to define! But try this definition on for size: "Happiness is a state of being content, with overtones of satisfaction, amusement, and delight." With that definition, contentment becomes the key factor. And this means that if our expectations are always beyond our reach and even beyond reality, we will never gain happiness!

Another pitfall in the quest for happiness is when we make our happiness dependent on the actions or attitudes of others. In effect, we permit others to determine and control our happiness. True contentment is developed from within, often in spite of the bitter and destructive ways of others.

Happy, contented responses to life rise out of a state of mind that is determined to find good and make the best of all circumstances.

HOSTILE TERRITORY

It's sometimes fun to watch movies in which people deal with hostile territory. But in real life it is not enjoyable at all to find one's self in hostile territory and circumstances—among people who hold hostility toward others for whatever reasons, good or bad—and sometimes for no reason at all.

The home can become hostile territory, and so can your work place, your vacation resort—and believe it or not, even your church!

Hostility sometimes develops when a person has unsettled business from the past. They got burned in earlier days and never really dealt with it. So when anything comes up that slightly resembles that earlier experience, they express the anger they've repressed over the years, and become aggressive and even belligerent. Their loved ones are usually amazed!

And sometimes they themselves are astounded. They have little or no understanding why certain experiences or situations can make their blood boil, and cause them to lash out with reactions not really justified by the present circumstances.

We need to learn why we develop hostilities, and then offer them up to Christ with a plea that He help us get them under solid Christian control. Nobody, no matter how much he or she loves us, enjoys living in hostile territory!

PEOPLE WITHOUT GOD

I am not very patient with people who do not have God in their lives. There are so many opportunities to open the door for God to come into one's life. If people steer clear of the Almighty it is because of a kind of prideful, even arrogant choice. But I also feel very sorry for people without God.

Someone wrote:

> People without God:
> They laugh, but there is no lasting joy.
> They exist, but they are not living.
> They cry, but there is no comfort.
> They die—and there is no Heaven!

I wonder how people without God react when told they have just a few months to live.

I wonder how people without God feel and react when a close loved one dies—someone who is very dear and precious to them.

I wonder how people without God face life's big tests and trials—what goes through their minds when life tumbles in around them.

Do people without God bull their way through adversity with a stoical stance—a stiff upper lip, and a show of bravado? Do they for one moment imagine that nothing in life makes sense without God? Do they have any inkling of what they are missing, and of how barren their lives are without God?

PEREMPTORY

The word "peremptory" denotes quick or sudden acts of authority that allow neither contradiction nor refusal.

When a person gives a peremptory command there is no discussion. It is intended to be final and is not to be challenged.

It's usually hopeless to argue with a peremptory person.

Granted, there are some people who act in a peremptory manner when they should not. They do not really carry the kind of authority and know-how that commends their being peremptory. They need more tentativeness, more caution, less imperiousness and a much less commanding demeanor.

Frankly there are not many people in the world who have the credentials for being peremptory. Such persons come under subdefinition of the word "peremptory," which means being "offensively self-assured; dictatorial." Authoritarian dictators such as Hitler and Stalin were peremptory—not because they merited being so, but because they had the force to back them up.

When you get right down to it, there is only one Being Who has the right to be and act in a peremptory manner with which we cannot and dare not argue—and that is God.

God does not dote on discussion and argument. He expects us to obey, and be quick about it.

LOVE'S ABUSE

The abuse of love reached a new low a few years ago with an enormously destructive computer virus or worm bearing the title "I love you."

When first opened it seized on the recipient's list of E-mail addresses, and sent the fateful messages to everyone listed—and then it went to work on files in the recipients' computers. It destroyed graphics, music and more as it rampaged through the world, including our nation. The estimated cost to business, agencies and government will run into billions of dollars.

Aside from the criminal destruction in this matter, it is noteworthy that the lure was an expression of love—hard for most persons to resist. At the very least it arouses curiosity, and in some persons, hope.

Love is one of the highest concepts of the human family. While it may mean different things to various persons and groups, everyone agrees that the word "love" carries connotations of helpfulness, admiration, encouragement and deep affection—not the kinds of destructiveness unleashed by forces with evil intent.

In expressing love some may be too emotional, too mushy, too unrealistic and too hopeful—but the intent always must be for the good of others, not their hurt.

Maybe that is one of the best lessons to be learned from that terrible invasion.

WARINESS

Wariness is what keeps us from being naive, from being taken in. When people tell us some juicy bit of gossip, or propose a questionable course of action, or try to sell us something that resembles the Brooklyn Bridge, it's definitely in order to be wary.

One of the dictionary definitions characterizes wariness as "prudent care to foresee and to guard against evil."

For sure we ought to be wary about following religious thrusts of the New Age Movement—and about the kooky cults that seem to proliferate in our culture.

The Apostle John in his first letter tells us to be wary of religious forces that are in conflict with the Christian faith. John wrote:

> Dear friends, do not believe every spirit, but test the spirits to see whether they are from God, because many false prophets have gone out into the world. This is how you can recognize the Spirit of God: Every spirit that acknowledges that Jesus Christ has come in the flesh is from God, but every spirit that does not acknowledge Jesus is not from God.
>
> (I John 4:1-6)

If you are a committed follower of Jesus the Christ, trusting Him as your personal Savior and Lord, then be wary of any who would tamper with your beliefs.

Wariness is an essential concept for steadiness in life.

INTIMIDATION

Intimidation takes place when someone does or says things that result in our feeling fear, hesitation, or discouragement. To deliberately intimidate is to work by whatever means to cause others to feel timid and afraid.

Bullying, bulldozing, browbeating and all kinds of verbal assaults are used by intimidators to make us compliant and afraid to act. Threats are sometimes made or implied—sometimes even the threat of violence.

Intimidation is both forerunner and companion to extortion and blackmail. For whatever reasons, certain persons want their way with us.

Being non-assertive is an open invitation to intimidators. Parents, peers, children, spouses and relatives of all kinds know our weaknesses. The husband who browbeats his wife; the teenager who outyells the parents and threatens to leave home if they don't stop bugging him or her; the bully who insinuates threats if we don't back off—these are typical examples of deliberate intimidation.

Intimidators are successful only when we allow it, instead of standing firm. Most persons who use intimidation are basically cowards. But they have learned that they can get their way because of weaknesses in others. When we yield, we encourage the continuation of their evil behaviors.

The best response to any kind of intimidation is to stand firm, call their bluff and let the chips fall where they may.

ONE OF LIFE'S MYSTERIES

I've discovered that wherever I go the most contented and happy people are not those for whom much is done and to whom much is given. Quite often those folks are the most miserable!

The most contented are people who are on the giving end—even to the point of making significant sacrifices. They are the builders of others' lives, the movers and shakers who are willing to expend themselves to make things happen.

This phenomenon is not a mystery for the Christian. Jesus taught that the way to abundant living is through self-expenditure. He said: "If a man seeks to save his life, he will lose it; but the man who loses his life for My sake will find it and preserve it."

Self-centered life preservers most often are unhappy people. They worry as to whether they have enough—and, of course, they never do. They get paranoid about what other people think about them and whether others are after them and their money. They turn sour on life.

Jesus talked about treasures in heaven. The implication is clear: we will take out of this life, into the world to come, only what we have given and done for others.

When it comes to abundant full life, the key is in our expenditures.

IS ANYBODY HOME?

In one of the most beautiful passages in the Book of Revelation Jesus tells the church at Laodicea:

> **Behold, I stand at the door and knock; if any one hears My voice and opens the door, I will come in to him, and will dine with him, and he with Me.** (Revelation 3:20)

This is nothing less than an offer of a personal, warm relationship with the Lord of the universe. He has taken the initiative to make that possible—but we have to open up.

A cartoon shows a couple peeking out the curtains of the front window, hiding from unwanted visitors. In the meantime the visitors entered through the back door, which they found unlocked. The next panel shows the shock and embarrassment of the home owners when caught trying to hide.

Isn't that a kind of portrayal of how we resist Jesus coming into our hearts and homes?

Jesus wants a personal relationship with us—but He respects our rights and our freedom, and waits for our invitation to enter.

Jesus stands outside the door of every life and knocks. The most important act of our lives is to open the door to the living Lord, and invite Him in—and not just for a visit, but as a permanent resident.

KEEPING UP

A mother commented on her teenage daughter's careless hairdo: "Your hair looks like a mop!" To which the girl innocently replied: "What's a mop?"

Well, times do change, and we find ourselves using new words, dealing with new circumstances, having to figure out new frames of reference—often because there are no personal experiences with the old. An unwillingness to change is a real handicap in this futuristic world.

Manual typewriters were a great invention, and electric typewriters a marvelous improvement, but now we deal with amazingly powerful computers and word processors.

A nursery rhyme once fantasized a cow jumping over the moon, but we have put people there, and sent our space craft far out into our galaxy.

But there is a philosophical con game that accompanies all these technological changes, trying to persuade us that basic morals and values also have to roll with the times—that there are no absolutes—no long-lasting, dependable and unchangeable moral frames of reference. Because so much changes over time, bedrock values and morals must also change.

The Bible talks about Jesus Christ and all He stands for being the same—yesterday, today and forever. It's good to move with the times, and make the needed changes in technology.

But don't get caught in the moral con game!

A FAMILY MISSION STATEMENT

Corporations, agencies, churches and various businesses usually develop mission statements to describe their overall purpose, values and reasons for being. Such statements declare origins, identity and intentions with clarity.

If we are serious about the family being the most important institution in society, why not a mission statement that provides guidance for family awareness, planning and goals—along with setting the tone for appropriate conduct, attitudes and relating?

Here are a few of the components of what I consider to be a vital and meaningful "Family Mission Statement."

• Our family members are committed to the best for each other, believing that we are intended to be "family" by Almighty God—from Whom we come and to Whom we someday shall return. This conviction has powerful implications for each of us.

• We exist as "family" because of God's grace and love, and we know that we are at our best as a family and as individuals when we demonstrate God's grace and love to each other.

• Our overall family purpose is to encourage each family member to live meaningfully and purposefully, with a strong sense of identity, worth and destiny—in accord with the values and standards set forth in the Holy Scriptures. The Bible is our main guide book for family matters.

FAMILY GOALS—1

In the previous commentary I suggested a Mission Statement for the family. The statement read in part: Our overall family purpose is to encourage each family member to live meaningfully and purposefully, with a strong sense of identity, worth and destiny, in accord with the values and standards set forth in the Holy Scriptures.

Now we turn to basic goals that jibe with a full reality Statement of Mission for the Family.

Goal 1: We are committed to refrain from destructive attitudes and behaviors toward each other, rejecting all that discourages and degrades, and embracing all that lifts up and affirms. We understand this to be the foundation for contentment and happiness.

Goal 2: It is each member's responsibility to avoid all that is destructive to self, to others and to family unity and purpose. Ignoring or walking away from problems are not options, and violence in speech or behaviors in our home is unthinkable.

Goal 3: Because effective family life requires cooperation, we will share work responsibilities in and outside the home. We will strive to excel in all endeavors.

Goal 4: We will listen carefully, speak with love and clarity, and be there for each other in times of emotional stress, problems and troubles. Total respect for each other is always our aim.

FAMILY GOALS—2

In the segment just prior I offered four basic family goals that mesh with a full reality mission statement for the family. Here are three more for your consideration.

Goal 5: As individuals or as a family, we will not assess or judge our success, worth or meaning by superficial cultural trendiness, by the opinions of others, or by the examples set by other families or individuals. We will not take our cues for attitudes and actions from outside forces. Our family is instituted by God, and we submit to our Creator's standards for worth, morality and success.

Goal 6: We commit ourselves to participating in the extended and larger family of grandparents and other relatives—and especially the family of Christ, which is His Church. We intend to worship and pray together in our church as well as in our home.

Goal 7: We will be mindful of the evils of prejudice, divisiveness and hate, and will not tolerate expressions of contempt for persons in or outside our family, for any reason.

Whether you are a single, a couple, or a family with children, try writing your own Family Mission Statement and some basic goals.

Educational aims for the family might be the subject of a goal—and also issues of health, friendships and other concerns.

A FULL DECK

I remember an exam as a student at Hamline University, in which the professor asked what was wrong with the statement of a noted philosopher: "Faith is betting your life on God."

For the life of me I couldn't find anything wrong with it. So after the exam was handed in I approached the professor and asked him what was wrong.

His answer: "It's the language of the race track and casino, and so is unfit for applying to God and our relationships to Him."

Well, frankly—I still don't see anything wrong with that assertion that "Faith is betting your life on God"!

So I'll use another illustration from gambling—this one from a deck of cards. Trying to play the game of life without faith in God is like playing without a full deck.

In my childhood I learned that there are 52 cards in a regular, full deck. I learned this from one of my brothers who asked me if I would like to play a game called "52 Pickup." He caught me just once.

The point of all this: we are bound to lose big time in the game of life if we are missing a bunch of cards from the deck. For sure, the game won't even make sense!

31-GRUP

BAD PARTIES

Nearly everyone loves a party.

Granted, some irritating personalities tend to be party spoilers or party poopers. Then there are the determined loners who would rather die than enjoy themselves in interaction with other persons.

It's interesting that evidently Jesus loved a good party, and was even accused of being a little too strong in that department. It's on record that He enjoyed being with people and sharing in their celebrations.

Most of us know the difference between a good party and a bad party. Good ones are conducive to healthy relating and enjoyments. Bad ones prey on others, sometimes steal away one's dignity, offer too much booze and sometimes even drugs.

Another kind of bad party is the pity party. We throw a bash in honor of how sorry we feel for ourselves. We may try to invite and include others, but if they're smart, they will decline our invitation—thereby avoiding listening to our recitation of woes.

Much more attractive are gossip parties, in which we get together with one or two others to dissect and roast some person known to all. Of course, that poor soul is not there to defend himself—but that would spoil the fun.

Attend all the good parties you can, but avoid the bad ones!

BREVITY'S COUNSEL

How often have you said it? "Life is so short. It goes so fast!"

As we grow older, life seems to speed by at a much faster rate.

To be sure, the brevity of life has some important lessons to teach us.

The first is that we need to be in a hurry to discover and hold to our hearts all the faith, meaning and purpose that we can possibly find. It's never wise to postpone the acquisition of these essential ingredients of life.

I am amazed by parents who are in no hurry to introduce their children to the indispensable matters of faith, hope, high values and eternal verities.

The second lesson we should learn from brevity is that if there are some important things we need to do, get at them! Don't wait. Opportunities seem to evaporate with the passing of time. Too often we find ourselves lamenting and regretting our delay. Get at whatever of good you feel should be accomplished—before it's too late!

The third lesson of brevity is simply the enormous value of time. The supply is not great. It goes so fast. An old adage cautions us: "Time is treasure, spend it wisely."

Time seems to be in a hurry—and so should we be in a hurry about the truly important matters of life.

CHILDREN WRITE TO GOD

Recently I came across some charming notes that children wrote to God.

Dear God, Instead of letting people die and having to make new ones, why don't you just keep the ones You have? Sally

Dear God, Maybe Cain and Abel would not kill each other so much if they had their own rooms. It works with my brother. Ben

Dear God, I bet it is very hard for You to love everybody in the whole world. There are only 4 people in our family and I can never do it. Todd

Dear God, I read the Bible. What does "begat" mean? Nobody will tell me.—Love, Allison

Dear God, thank you for the baby brother, but what I prayed for was a puppy. Joyce

Dear God, I went to this wedding and they kissed right in church. Is that okay? Danny

Dear God, Did You really mean "do unto others as they do unto you?" Because if You did, then I'm going to fix my brother.—Darla

Dear God, My brother told me about being born but it doesn't sound right. They're just kidding, aren't they?—Marsha

CONSTRUCTS

For the most part it is a blessing to have an active imagination—as long as we don't let it get out of hand and make frequent departures from reality—and we use it to serve healthy, helpful pursuits.

Sometimes an overactive imagination can get us into trouble. This has to do with the human tendency to make constructs—to fashion ideas and notions that we then believe are true. And they may or may not be.

For example, imaginations that are steeped in poor self-images and a certain level of paranoia may create a construct that "everybody is against me," "nobody likes me," and even "people want to hurt me."

Those are harmful constructs, and the moment they pop into our minds we need to fight them and subdue them—lest they become dominant and dictatorial in our thinking and actions.

Healthy constructs are what we need. An example: "Others are responsible for their bad manners and hateful ways. I am not. They can hurt me only if I allow it." That is a construct related to truth and reality.

Another healthy construct: "I will be and become what I think—so I must be very careful of what my mind produces."

We all need to watch our personal constructs, lest overactive and dark imaginings lead us into difficulties.

CONTESTS AND COMPETITIONS

Metaphors about life being like a game or sports contest are often used in popular expressions—and in God's Word. We're not sure of the identity of the author of Hebrews, but he or she used the sports metaphor.

Hebrews 12 instructs us:

> Therefore, since we are surrounded by such a great cloud of witnesses, let us throw off everything that hinders and the sin that so easily entangles, and let us run with perseverance the race marked out for us. Let us fix our eyes on Jesus, the Author and Perfecter of our faith, Who for the joy set before Him endured the cross, scorning its shame, and sat down at the right hand of the throne of God. Consider Him Who endured such opposition from sinful men, so that you will not grow weary and lose heart.

One of the comparisons is in the matter of a contest—in which there will be winner and losers.

There are folks who object to the contest element in today's games. They recommend win-win rules, in which all win and nobody loses.

If we're talking about fantasy, they have a point. But if we are talking about reality, there is competition in every aspect of life—with some winners, and many losers.

HOLD THEM CLOSE

One of the outcomes of the killing sprees and other violence in the schools of our nation is the increased awareness and tenderness that loved ones show toward each other—and especially toward their children.

Here in America we are experiencing a surge of concern for the family unit and its essential meanings. And we mourn the loss of homes that teach the highest values and the best in discipline, respect and responsibility.

There is a hymn that sings out:

> O give us homes with godly fathers, mothers,
> Who always place their hope and trust in Him;
> Whose tender patience turmoil never bothers,
> Whose calm and courage trouble cannot dim;
> A home where each finds joy in serving others,
> And love still shines, though days be dark and grim.

Parents everywhere: Hold them close and closer. Speak to your children of God's Being, truth and redemption. Let them know that while there is enormous evil in the world, there also is an abundance of good. And instruct them in the ways of choosing good over evil, and passing on the good.

Yes, indeed—hold them close! And one of the best ways to do that and make it last is to make Christ the center and focus of your home.

HERD MENTALITY

I well remember my parents' intolerance of the herd mentality. The argument that "everybody's doing it" was useless. They wanted their children to make decisions on the basis of more important convictions and standards.

Herd mentality has always been the main driving force for too many human beings. It is the notion that if others are approving of it and doing it, then it must be OK.

The herd mentality honestly but wrongly believes that the majority opinion is always the right one. So if enough people are convinced about something, no matter how dead wrong they are in the eyes of the minority, then it must be so. "Majority rules"—or so some think!

It's not easy to shuck the herd mentality and take on the freedom in Christ to which we are called.

The herd seems to be the only place some people can find security and comfort. Never mind that the herd is heading for the cliffs. Don't let it bother you that the herd listens to its leaders with rapt devotion, even though their leaders are heading in the wrong direction..

One of the most unrelenting, uncompromising and meaningful commands of Jesus is this: "Follow Me!" There is no way we can do that, and still maintain our herd mentality.

IDENTITY CUES AND CLUES

In your search for personal identity and a valid sense of worth, what clues assure you—what cues do you seek and recognize?

Will you find that assurance in the historical records of a humanity that more often than not degrades itself with wars, crimes and unspeakable acts toward one another?

Will you find it in the violence among us that has become so horrific that we casually and "legally" take the lives of unborn children as they lie within their mothers' wombs?

Will you find it in humanity's easy tolerance of prejudice, greed, and exploitation?

There also is much that is noble in the records of our human adventure. But how will we be sure as to which camp is ours? Do we belong with the good or with the evil—with the builders or with the destroyers?

For worth, for dignity, for stature and for status, we must seek both clues and cues in the One Who made us—and in His stance toward us. It is God Who endows our lives with meaning. He salvages us to eminent perfection with His costly redemption. He declares us to be His sons and daughters.

The truth is plain—unless and until we find and value our Creator and Redeemer, we cannot find and value our own beings.

GOD AND PARENTING

We call God "Father" because He is our heavenly parent. It is amazing how well this metaphor jibes with human parenting.

Throughout history God has raised His children, His human family, with patience, tenderness and love. He has stayed with us while we weathered the confusions and dependencies of infancy and young childhood.

As we moved into older childhood, God expects more of us—as does any good parent. The requirements and disciplines take on an insistence and persistence that grow less and less tolerant of our childishness, our self focus, and our mulish reluctance to do what is best.

Increasing maturity automatically calls for more dependability, self discipline and responsibility. That is what parenting aims for—bringing the child to the age of discretion and discipline, where the necessities of an ordered life are understood by the son or daughter, and they buy into them—without being told or constantly cajoled.

Many times parents face calamitous meanderings of their children from the ways of right and health. Forgiveness is granted time after time, as they plead with their children to walk in the ways of common sense, truth and righteousness. And so with God.

Small wonder that the most wondrous thing to be said of us is that we are children of God.

LATE LEARNING

One of the most plaintive declarations a human can make is "I wish I had known." For all of us there are areas of ignorance about the lives and accomplishments of others. Later, when we are finally told about them, we say sometimes with anguish, "I wish I had known."

Often it is a need on the part of a person close to us, that we could have met with ease if we had only known. But we were not curious enough, not loving enough, not patient enough to hear them out and find the truth that they perhaps longed to share—but were afraid of being misunderstood. "I wish I had known!"

To understand the lives of loved ones we have to get close and stay close.

It takes a listening ear and extraordinary patience that spring from genuine, loving concern. When late learning is too late, there is little to be done—except to apply the learned lessons to others around us.

Recently a distant cousin died in England. I had met him, but did not probe, and listened little. I wish I had known of his lifelong pursuit of the good, his devotion to Mother Teresa and his many years of sacrificial participation in her marvelous work among the poor. I learned of them only after his death at the age of 90.

For many reasons, I wish I had known.

LIFE'S BEST LESSON

Here's a good question: What is the best, most relevant and helpful lesson for any person to learn in life?

This is a tough question, because there are many good lessons—such as lessons about love, joy, hope, peace and compassion. There are lessons about taking care of ourselves, steering clear of trouble, and how to live longer and better lives.

But the lesson that must be learned for the sake of eternity's destiny and outcomes is the lesson of forgiveness.

It is a wild thing we pray in the Lord's Prayer, when we ask God to forgive us as we have forgiven others. What a dreadful qualification! Any forgiveness from God is conditional on our forgiving others. That makes it the supreme lesson to learn and practice in our living.

Alexander Pope wrote that powerful saying: "To err is human, to forgive divine." It is at the points and times of our forgiveness toward others that we most show our nature to be close to the nature of God.

The argument that in some cases, forgiveness is just too costly is an empty one. Ultimate forgiveness by God cost Him dearly—and so it is for us. If forgiveness is easy, the act of pardon cheap—then where is the virtue, the good of it?

MADE FOR GOD

There are certain matters which we must face and resolve as early as possible in life—and one of the most basic is the question of our reason for being.

Are we made for obliteration, for eradication? Are we made for our own self pursuits—made for rampant egotism? Or are we made for God—to express the glory of His creative powers, to serve Him all the days of our lives, and finally to go and be with Him in His heavenly Kingdom?

Which of those three options best describes your day to day mindset? Oblivion and obliteration? A brief ego-centered existence? Or made for God, and to be with God in fellowship forever?

I would have to be pretty nutty to choose any but the third. I am made by God and for God. I am His creature, but through Christ He has made me to be His child. I am bound to Him and bound for Him.

If I am made for God then I cannot possibly serve the causes of evil, the aims and devices of Satan.

The implications of my being made for God are vast and complex. I am here on earth to do God's will—to carry out His assignments.

Which descriptor have you chosen?

MALICE

Malice means desiring to harm others, enjoyment over the sufferings of others, and the holding of attitudes of hate, meanness and spite.

Malice produces actions toward others that result in harm or even death—and they are performed with no just cause—just the orneriness of the malicious person.

Obviously, under no circumstances can malice be considered a virtue. It is one of the worst of vices, and has the potential to do a great amount of crazy making destructiveness. Malice is the very opposite of love or charity—and worse.

If we know that someone is acting out of sheer malice, it is eminently wise and sensible to break off any kind of relationship. Nobody, but nobody needs malicious persons in their lives.

There are some who seem to make a lifelong career of malice and malicious actions. They never have a kind thought or word for anyone. Their tongues seem full of venom as they speak of how detestable others are.

Paul describes them in Romans 3:13 ff: "The poison of vipers is on their lips." "Their mouths are full of cursing and bitterness." "Ruin and misery mark their ways, and the way of peace they do not know."

God's Word is clear: malicious persons are the truly detestable persons of life. Avoid them, and and don't buy into their attitudes and actions of malice.

RAISING PAGANS

Recently I commented to the prosperous father of a large family, "I wonder if your children are perhaps being raised as materialistic pagans. They have so much to live with, and so little to live by."

That father was not happy with me. He was on the outs with his church, and refused to take his kids to Sunday School. And he was compensating with loads of playthings that would delight the heart of any child.

We raise pagans when we teach that having things is more important than having faith and doing good.

We raise pagans when we deprive children of opportunities to learn the essentials of faith in company with others.

We raise pagans when we confuse expressions of home religion with the enticements of toys and entertainment.

We raise pagans when we fail to teach children how to cope with and avoid the hedonistic and materialistic ways of the world in which they will live as adults—and eventually be the parents of their children.

When I hear children lamenting that activities much more important than play are "not fun," and occasionally yelling their heads off because they can't have what they want in the mall—then I have more than a suspicion that the parents are busy raising a tribe of pagans.

RELATIONAL HEALING

The closeness that must characterize a healthy marriage, at the same time make the persons involved extremely vulnerable. Their defenses normally are down, which means the typical husband and wife are psychologically and emotionally naked before each other. Sadly, they have learned what can hurt the most.

Thoughtlessness, slights and criticisms are never minor matters. Disloyalty is devastating, and infidelity horrendous. We need more than words. What could be a rationale for making genuine, whole-hearted attempts at healing and restoration?

There exists just one rationale that is sufficiently powerful for healing and health in marriage. It comes straight from God. Its symbol is the cross. Its imperatives are articulated in the concepts of forgiveness, reconciliation, redemption and restoration—all motivated by love that is more a matter of the will than emotions.

It is the rationale of selfless love, of 70 times 7 forgiveness, of all we have in common as sinners—along with all we share as human beings made in God's image and redeemed by the loving sacrifice of Jesus Christ.

When *both* marriage partners have committed themselves to the cross as their model for relating and their resource for healing and health, there is hope for diminished warfare, fewer wounds and greater health and joy in the relationship.

SINGULARITY AND PLURALISM

We live in a pluralistic society. There's no question about that.

Pluralism in these United States of America means diversity and differences, big time. That diversity shows up all around us. We cannot avoid it.

Our aim should be to honor and respect diversity with a healthy level of tolerance—but not to fall into the trap of imagining that every way has equal value and equal truth. Equality before the law does not mean equality before the God Who has spoken and related to humanity, and declared Himself to be the One and only God Who has no rivals.

Anyone who accepts the designation of "Christian" must learn that tolerance of others does not mean acceptance of their views that conflict with the teachings and standards of the Christian faith. Such persons have equality with us as American citizens, but this does not mean that every idea of every person is equally right and true.

We can become hopelessly enmeshed in a web of deceit, lies, falsehoods and fantasy when we declare that everybody is right, and nobody is wrong. That is not tolerance—that is foolishness and stupidity of the worst kind.

Our responsibility in this world is to maintain a strong and healthy singularity, while respecting the pluralism that surrounds us.

SOME FACTS ABOUT GOSSIP

One of the strange phenomena of life is that persons who gossip do it without realizing they are doing so. I was surprised one time when I heard a certain person denounce gossip, gossiping and gossipers with a passion—when we all knew that person to be one of the most talkative and mean-spirited gossips in Northwest Iowa, if not the entire state of Iowa!

In Leviticus 19:16 God commands: "Don't gossip. Don't falsely accuse your neighbor of some crime, for I am Jehovah."

Proverbs 20:19 gives this wise counsel: "Don't tell your secrets to a gossip unless you want them broadcast to the world." *(The Living Bible)*

And Romans 1:29 puts gossip with the worst of evil and sins: "Their lives became full of every kind of wickedness and sin, of greed and hate, envy, murder, fighting, lying, bitterness, and gossip."

Thomas Fuller wrote that "gossiping and lying go together." And there is a Spanish proverb that lays it on the line: "Whoever gossips to you will gossip of you."

Gossip totally lacks the will and love to make the world better. The gossip never speaks with kindness and compassion. His or her tales are filled with spite and meanness, subtle and overt, bland and blatant. Their intent is to destroy, not build.

STAY ALIVE!

I remember with keen appreciation what a friend once advised me: "Stay alive all your life." I have often thought of the wisdom of that counsel. There is a possibility of dying before our time, and yet continuing to exist. A tombstone in a New England cemetery reads: "Died at 30—Buried at 80." Someone felt that life petered out before they did!

The Bible speaks of being dead in one's sins. In chapter 2 of the book of Ephesians we read:

> As for you, you were dead in your transgressions and sins, in which you used to live when you followed the ways of this world and of the ruler of the kingdom of the air, the spirit who is now at work in those who are disobedient.

And a verse later Paul declares the good news of our resurrection from this dreadful state of spiritual death:

> But because of His great love for us, God, Who is rich in mercy, made us alive with Christ even when we were dead in transgressions—it is by grace you have been saved.

We also die early when we fail to maintain vital interests in the meaningful matters of life. Cynical, bored, disinterested persons are dead and don't know it.

Good advice: "Stay alive all your life!"

TESTS OF THE HEART

In the Bible the heart is considered to be the seat of intelligence and wisdom. This is in contrast to today's world, in which speaking of the heart has more to do with emotions than with wisdom. We talk about loving from the heart, when we would be much smarter to speak of love as a product of the will and mind.

According to God's Word the heart is the center for our intentions, our deliberations and decisions. The heart has to do with will power and discretion, with intelligence and wisdom. The heart is where we deliberate and make up our minds about attitudes and courses of action.

Proverbs 17:3 counsels us: "The crucible for silver and the furnace for gold, but the Lord tests the heart."

What is the Lord testing about our hearts? I'm sure that He wants to know our level of devotion and loyalty, our faith and trust in Him.

Hebrews 4:12 assures us:

> For the word of God is living and active. Sharper than any double-edged sword, it penetrates even to dividing soul and spirit, joints and marrow; it judges the thoughts and attitudes of the heart.

We can be very sure that from time to time God tests our hearts.

THE BEST COMPANION

One of the constants of life is the need for decisions about who will share it with us. Spouse and children make for easy decisions. But what about friends and acquaintances?

From childhood on we are pressured to decide on whom to pull close and share with—and whom to avoid, push away and close off.

Sometimes we fear for our teenagers in their choices for peer relationships, friends and companions. We want them to choose persons who will exercise a healthy influence in their lives, and not persuade or drag them into destructive ways.

But when we adults really think hard about our own selections for companions, we just might discover that we often make poor choices—drawing persons into our close circle who have little of good to offer.

This is a good time to choose and hold close the best of all life's companions—One Whose will and provisions for our lives are excellent and to our best interests.

The Name of that best of all companions? Jesus. Get related to Him through belief and commitment, and then hang on for dear life!

No other person earth can offer us the joys, possibilities and life fulfillments that Jesus gives to us every moment of our lives.

THE CROSS AND MARITAL HEALING

The Cross is more than an emblem of faith. It also stands for healing and health in our most treasured relationships, including marriage.

The Cross is the only rationale sufficient to sustain a relationship and to restore a marriage when matters go awry. Life begins anew when our behaviors and attitudes are driven by faith, love and grace grounded in the theology of the cross.

Most of us have never thought of the Cross as the fitting symbol of what it takes to make a marriage whole and lasting—as well as a powerful resource for relational healing and health. We tend to think of redemption, salvation and reconciliation as one-time occurrences—and that they have no relevance to the limitless demands of real life, including marriage challenges, hurts and hassles. But these forces, generated by God's redemptive love, are applicable to all of life.

Christ-inspired love knows the necessity and meaning of repentance: A strange blend of sorrow for what has hurt and alienated, and high intentionality to cease the destructive behaviors that cause the problems.

The cross is God's final and only way of drawing us back to a relationship with Him. We are at our best in all our relating when we act on its principles.

Marriages may falter because we haven't been to the cross.

WORLDLINESS IN THE CHURCH

I'm sure that a lot of pastors get some strange requests concerning weddings held in their churches. Marriages are occasions when some folks go a bit weird and worldly—sometimes making demands that are way out of touch with what the church is all about.

I remember a mother of the bride who wanted us to remove the Bible from its prominent location in the chancel area. She thought that it "spoiled the decor" for her daughter's wedding service. She did not get her way.

In preparations for another wedding I was asked by the bride and groom, "Do we have to have all this religious stuff in our wedding?" I responded quietly: "No, you do not. But you will need to hold your marriage event somewhere else—not in this or any church—and you'll need to find another officiant."

So many couples these days have such loose or non-existent connections with the church, they have a tough time understanding that the marriage service is a worship service—not a high fallutin' ego trip for them and their dear relatives. If you want to "stage it" in a church, expect to find God mentioned in the words of the pastor—and yes, even in the music.

Church leaders need to do their part in making sure people understand where the line is drawn that differentiates between genuine church activities and pagan doings. Some wedding celebrations are way out of place in church precincts.

WHY WORSHIP?

Whenever I mention the need for worship in a church of our choice, some person who is full of it will tell me that we don't need to be in a church to worship God. "I can worship on the golf course, or in my jaccuzi, or out on the lake in my fishing boat.—and even in front of my television set," he tells me.

My gentle but pointed reply: "Let's be honest. Yes, you can. But the truth is, you don't."

I then explain that fellow worshipers are not on the golf course, not in his fishing boat, not sitting with him and his television set—and certainly not in his jaccuzi!

Another thing that won't happen is the passing of the offering basket on the lake, golf course, before his TV or in his jaccuzi. He will not present his offerings for the mission of Christ and the needs of the world in company with God's congregation.

Another missing element in this dream world of worship avoiders is they won't be exposed to hymns, prayers, the reading and interpretation of the Word, confessions and affirmations unless they worship in church. And those matters are critical to our spiritual growth.

Sad but true—a lot of people "pagan out" Sunday after Sunday.

WHEN WE GO ROGUE

The word "rogue" carries some fascinating implications. In modern parlance it can be used to describe a person as playful and impish. But it also may convey the descriptors of unreliability, deceitfulness and being unprincipled.

When a person goes against everything he or she is supposed to stand for, we call him or her "a rogue." We say they've "gone rogue."

The fireman who some time ago fired shots at his comrades as they came to his home to put out a fire is aptly described as "a rogue fireman." A judge who turns to criminal activity is "a rogue judge." We may also speak of rogue mothers, rogue fathers, rogue teachers, rogue ministers, rogue priests and rogue scientists.

In recent years a number of scientists have been accused of doctoring their research and falsifying their findings. They went rogue.

Judas Iscariot became a disciple of Jesus, and then went rogue. So did Peter—although he repented and stepped back from his roguishness.

A lot of church members could possible be described as "rogue Christians." They have left any semblance of commitment and discipleship, and have gotten into ways of thinking and behaving that mark them as rogue.

Avoid being roguish. Stick with loyalty and principles, with devotion to God and faithfulness.

WHEN OTHERS DISAPPOINT US

A lot of otherwise nice folks have some pretty nutty ideas about God and what they can expect from Him. Naturally, they are very disappointed when He doesn't come through.

We also need to talk about the times when loved ones and friends disappoint us.

Could it be that more often than not we have some unreasonable expectations about others? I've known parents who want their children to fulfill parental expectations that are nothing less than a surrogacy trip. "I could not become a doctor (or whatever) so you become one in my place. It's your calling and responsibility to fulfill my unfulfilled hopes."

Sometimes expectations of friends are plain dumb. There are folks who place demands on friendship that nobody in their right mind would even attempt to meet. Even stranger is the fact that those who hold those expectations have never lifted a hand to help anybody.

Children often are disappointed in their parents because they don't come though as they think they should when it comes to dishing out money, or holding a high and really silly level of tolerance for their offspring's repeated wrong doing.

It's certainly true that we can have some outrageous expectations about others and what they ought to do for us—including God. Small wonder we are disappointed. And guess whose fault that is!

1-GRUP

WE ARE WHAT WE THINK

The notion that "You are what you eat" is a sobering thought to me. There is truth in that assessment.

But an even more important concept for us to ponder is this: "You are what you think." Our minds, our emotions, our values and our behaviors are all impacted by what enters the mind. This includes everything we see, read, and listen to—good or bad, nonsensical or profound, lofty or base.

The stuff that flows into our heads will affect us regardless of our concentration or the lack thereof.

Isn't it a sobering thought that all the mayhem, silliness, violence and shabby morality that we watch for hours on television become us? We are in real danger of blending with the garbage taken in by our eye and ear gates.

It all enters and mixes with our minds and emotions in a thousand subtle ways.

Most of the current television entertainment erodes the values, morals and ethics we once thought were the best to live by—for individuals and for society as a whole.

Every time we take up a trashy book or magazine, or sit mesmerized by a violent and raunchy television program, we should consider this solemn fact: "I am and will become what I think."

THE DIRECTION OF OUR FEELINGS

Far too many people focus on their feelings just about every waking moment. They may grow angry quickly because their feelings alert them to the putdowns or criticisms of others. They weep for themselves, they smile and laugh for themselves. They pity themselves, often feeling very sorry for "me, myself and I."

That multitude of persons whose feelings are always turned inward are plain pathetic. They live and die to themselves. They feel for no one else. They weep for no one else. They smile and laugh and have pity for no one else. What desperate souls they are!

Feelings are a gift from God, to be used in our relating, serving and loving others. With high intentionality we must turn our feelings and emotions away from our own conditions, to concern and helpfulness toward others.

I once lived in an area of the world where poverty and stark suffering were the lot of most people. I feared that such a deluge of poverty before my eyes would dull my feelings of caring, sympathy and yes, indignation. And so my daily prayers included petitions to God that I not lose care and feelings toward those who suffered so terribly and consistently.

Our feelings must turn outward, more than inward.

THE FUTILITY OF WORRY

Two powerful verses from the New Testament speak of the futility and needlessness of worry.

Jesus, in Matthew 6:27: "Will all your worries add a single moment to your life?" *(The Living Bible)*

Paul, in Philippians 4:6: "Don't worry about anything; instead, pray about everything; tell God your needs, and don't forget to thank Him for His answers." *(The Living Bible)*

The message is clear: Worry less and pray more. And be sure to thank God when He answers your prayers—whether or not it's the answer you want. A prayerful and thankful heart is a treasure indeed. Get hold of that and your worries can be whistled away.

We've all had the experience of worrying and fretting, only to have everything turn out just fine. A few have had experiences in which they placed it all before the Lord, enjoyed a trouble free mind, and no matter what the outcomes there was peace and contentment—for God was in the picture.

In fact, verse 7 of Philippians 4 tells us: "And the peace of God, which transcends all understanding, will guard your hearts and your minds in Christ Jesus."

A medical doctor commented on the destruction of worry by saying, "Worry is sand in the machinery of life."

He's absolutely right! Worry is a destructive force.

THE GLORY AND JOY OF HOPE

An old English proverb states: "If it were not for hope, the heart would break." Hope is the need of every life—for it gives us the will to live and endure.

Thomas Fuller wrote that "Great hopes make great men."

And yes, there are false hopes. But the Bible describes genuine hope as confidence in what we may not now see, but because our confidence is based on God's promises and assurances, our hopes are true and dependable reality.

The prayer of the 25th Psalm states: "Lead me; teach me; for You are the God Who gives me salvation. I have no hope except in You."

And in Psalm 40:11 we have this plea: "O Lord, don't hold back Your tender mercies from me! My only hope is in Your love and faithfulness." *(The Living Bible)*

And here is a verse that holds so much for us: "Lord, when doubts fill my mind, when my heart is in turmoil, quiet me and give me renewed hope and cheer." That's from Psalm 94:19. *(The Living Bible)*

The most apropos question of life is this: "Where and in what or whom is your hope?" All our hopes ultimately must center in God and His will and provisions for us. All things of worth and endurance have trace lines to Him.

A POROUS MIND

There is a condition of open mindedness that is neither truthful nor helpful. Simply put, such a mind is too porous for conviction.

While we abhor all intolerance that leads to harm for others, we simply cannot build or sustain a society or civilization, on the foundations of subjectivity and relativity, dubbing every conflicting opinion "right." That view may appeal to many, sounding wise and appearing to offer the noblest of human positions. But it's really a crock.

In the minds of many "tolerance" means full agreement.

I may hold to a belief in monotheism, one God—but to be tolerant in an acceptable form today, I must agree with all who believe in a pantheon of gods.

The makings of greatness are not the easy "everybody's right, nobody's wrong" attitudes—but convictions in the face of differences—and confrontation with those who would deal with truth on the cheap, and wallow in the muck and mire of rotting ideals and corrupt moral nonsense.

In that idiot land of endless, limitless tolerance, human beings become free to call evil good and good evil. It is a cuckoo nest of moral and spiritual relativity that by its nature and logical outcomes prods the sane toward insanity. It really is the ultimate in the theater of the absurd.

A PERSISTENT QUESTION

I always enjoy the Peanuts cartoon strip by the late Charles M. Schulz. There is wisdom there, as well as good entertainment. In one cartoon Linus says to Charley Brown, "I have to write a report on why we're here." And Charley answers: "Who knows?" Linus then walks away saying, "Good. That was easier than I thought."

That is probably the way many of us dismiss that most persistent question about the meaning of our lives—why we are here.

But the question won't go away. God is asking us to discover the correct answers in His Word.

According to the Bible we are not here by accident. There is purpose for our being and existence, these lives we live out on this old earth. And for sure we are not here simply for our own enjoyment.

We are not here to live haphazardly and destructively.

We are all here for basically the same reasons.

We are intended to relate to God through Jesus Christ, to find reconciliation and eternal life through Him, and to give ourselves to Christian discipleship, living out the special calling God has for each of us.

"Who knows?" is not the proper response to the question of life's purpose. Certainly God knows, and He has made it possible for each of us to know.

ALIENATION AND ALIENS

There are some folks who claim that we are surrounded by aliens from outer space who are busy monitoring our crazy activities, occasionally beaming someone up for a closer examination.

But near us all are some genuine aliens and alienation.

Among the correspondence we receive there are some that are extra special. A family we have known for years shared their joy that a daughter who had been caught up in a cult nearly twenty ago finally contacted the family. The alien has returned, and apparently alienation has been resolved.

Another family wrote of the suicide of their 24 year old granddaughter—whom I had baptized as a baby. She was so depressed and felt so alienated from others. She saw no other way out. But, of course there always are other ways out.

One couple wrote sadly that "John is still estranged from the family." I know John well, and it is his choice to remain alienated.

God came to us in Jesus Christ because of our alienation from our Heavenly Father—and from each other. We are aliens until we accept His reconciliation and healing.

The main business of life is to end our alienation from God—and then from all others. We simply dare not live and die with alienation.

AN EMPTY LIFE

I wonder how many of us are living lives we deem full and productive—and how many are living what might be called an empty life.

Empty lives are lonely, non-productive and apparently hopeless. Such persons feel they have no destiny, but only the dread and emptiness of the here and now.

I usually find that their church involvement is nil. Some seem determined to put down the church and its members, as though they are in a kind of envious rage of what others have found while fullness of life has eluded them.

In empty lives there is nothing of community interest, no investments of energy and time in the lives of others, little or nothing that turns a person outward from self to the needs and aspirations of other persons.

In empty lives I find no special relationship with other persons—be they children or grandchildren or other relatives or friends. They seem determined to turn sour on humanity, and even themselves.

Someone once wrote that "An empty life is an early death."

Life is too short and too precious to let it lie empty and essentially useless, forlorn and cynical—having no sense of the urgency of the here and now, much less a perspective that embraces an eternity with God.

AUTHENTIC FAITH

Perhaps you have noted my occasional use of the term "authentic faith." As best I can, I want to explain what I mean by that phrase.

Faith that is authentic must be held and practiced on the basis of firm convictions about fuller realities beyond what we know with our ordinary senses—along with information and support drawn from dependable and tested resources.

There is also the essential of a faith community—persons who share their faith, along with the common and extraordinary experiences that derive from their faith. They communicate with a language of faith that expresses not only their subjective reactions, but the objectives of the resources on which faith relies.

Christians firmly believe that faith is resourced dependably by the Holy Scriptures, by the historical verities of the faith community and by the Holy Spirit of God Who dwells among and within believers and their community.

Faith generated from our imaginations and emotions may be satisfying to some, but it has no stamp of authenticity, no dependable resources shared by a community through centuries of history. Its theology springs from egocentricity, and is resourced only by personal imaginings and feelings. Its very nature excludes revelation from the God Who intends to have a people, not just individuals—and Who has revealed Himself in dependable, shared and tested resources.

AUTHORITY IN THE HOME

Who is in charge in your home?

Some parents have allowed their authority to erode on the home scene, in effect surrendering it into the hands of their children. The kids run the home, call the shots, sass the parents, make all sorts of demands, defy all other authority—and in a hundred other ways have the parents wrapped around their little fingers.

It is intended by the Word of God and by the society in which we live that parents be in charge at home. Children must recognize their authority as primary. There is no such thing as a vote. Parental prerogatives are incontrovertible—and while they may be challenged, they must never be surrendered.

That word "authority" bothers a lot of people—mainly because they fill it with meanings of their own concoction.

It's common to equate "authority" with authoritarianism, heavy-handed and heartless discipline—with rigidity and dictatorial qualities bordering on the cruel and thoughtless.

But what we're talking about is recognized and respected leadership in the home. That's the job of parents, and it's not up for grabs or a vote at the whim of the offspring.

Moms and Dads—like it or not, you are in charge. You are to lead. You are to demand respect. Don't waffle.

BOUNDARY STONES

In the land of Palestine stones are really plentiful—and useful. They make up fences, are used in building houses and setting boundaries.

Boundary stones were recognized in Bible times. They marked territory, they signified altars and holy ground. Throughout history the wise have respected boundary stones. The Book of Proverbs, chapter 22, verse 28: "Do not move an ancient boundary stone set up by your forefathers."

Boundary stones were considered sacred because they represented past wisdom and discretion that should be carried over into the present.

There are worthy traditions out of our past history that we ought to regard as boundary stones—and respect what they're trying to tell us. We are slow to learn from our past successes and mistakes. Boundary stones are thoughtlessly tossed aside as we move into the future. Some even buy into the notion that such folly constitutes great wisdom.

When university dorms went coed, we removed a valuable boundary stone. When common respect and courtesy began to exit from our culture, other boundary stones were removed. And another boundary stone was removed when sex before marriage became commonplace, And there are hundreds of others.

One of the main tasks of this and coming generations is to find the important boundary stones, and put them back in place.

CHANGING CHURCHES

It seems that lately I'm getting more communications from distraught pastors and lay persons about how dry, ineffective and even dead their churches have become. Some letters have carried more than a note of despair and discouragement.

One writer commented that his church is marked by "lameness, tameness and sameness."

I have witnessed churches opting to be the voice of the devil in preference to being the voice of God, usually to satisfy the miserable troublemakers in the congregation, rather than satisfying the ways and will of the Lord. There is a tendency to give up and simply flow with the teachings and customs of the culture rather than swimming against the current.

In fashioning responses to all critics of the church, I realize that the first step is that the complainers become part of the solution, and keep from being the real focus of the problem. I have learned that many who complain the most do the least when it comes to encouraging and enabling their church toward healthy activity.

The next bit of counsel is to encourage activities, structures and policies that pressure every board, committee and organization within the church to be first and foremost the *Corpus Christi,* the Body of Christ, in all their decision making, all their activities, all their efforts on behalf of His church.

And mark that—*it is His Church!*

CLOSE TO THE LINE

Have you ever known someone who tried your patience greatly because they insisted on living close to the line?

If there is a rule about something, close to the line persons come as close as they can to breaking the rule, but without actually doing so. They seem to live in a spirit of perpetual defiance, with chips on their shoulders and rebellion in their hearts.

When persons persist in pushing as close to the line as possible, legally they may not be crossing it—but in spirit they are.

We always have folks who want to push God as far back as they can—always looking for reasons why the rules are unfair and the demands of God unreasonable. They are close to the line people in their faith, barely keeping up, and in spirit not really aiming at living their lives in the abundance, exuberance and dedication God expects of them.

In Christians there is a passion for righteousness—not a desire to live close to the line. We want it very evident that heart, mind and soul we belong to Jesus Christ and we have no intention of fudging on His programs and demands.

Also we are aware from the Word that God has little tolerance for close to the line people.

CHURCH ATTENDANCE

For many Sunday is mainly a day of play and recreation. For others the focal point is worship in the church of their choice. Sometimes this means morning and evening, plus an hour or so in Sunday School classes with the whole family involved.

Churches that are savvy emphasize their nature as the extended or larger family of concerned, loving and helping brothers and sisters in Christ.

I read this comment recently: "An empty tomb proves Christianity. An empty church denies it."

In my years of Christian service, I think I've heard every excuse imaginable for not attending worship and relating to the church.

"Too many hypocrites" continues to be the favorite of most people who both shoot and think from the hip, not the brain. A pastor I know is quick to respond to that one with a jovial, "Come on in anyway. There's always room for one more!"

"They're always asking for money," is another favorite. I preached a sermon about giving just once a year. But there were still erring and ornery members who used that excuse to stay away.

Of course the church needs money. Only a dunce could or would imagine otherwise. If church members give as they should no mention of money would be needed.

WOLVES AND SHEEP

A friend was sharing her estimate of a minister, and said: "This pastor won't tolerate the political games and backbiting ways of some church members. They will be met by a firm statement: 'I have so many sheep who really need my pastoral care and skills, I just don't have time for the wolves!'"

That's one of the most delightful things I've heard in years! We all know that many churches have suffered because one or two per cent of the flock are really wolves in sheep's clothing. I admire any pastor who has the courage to draw the line and say "No more! Don't expect my cooperation in your efforts to weaken and even destroy this church."

In his final meeting with the elders of the church at Ephesus, Paul told them:

> **Keep watch over yourselves and all the flock of which the Holy Spirit has made you overseers. Be shepherds of the Church of God, which He bought with His own Blood. I know that after I leave, savage wolves will come in among you and will not spare the flock.** (Acts 20:28, 29)

So while it's not a new phenomenon, it is refreshing to hear of a pastor who so bluntly and rightfully deals with it when the wolves try to make their move.

HANDLING CRITICISM

An old proverb states: "Those who can, do. Those who can't criticize."

The word "criticism" comes from the Greek language, from root words meaning "to judge."

For sure in real life any criticism dished out is a judgment, plain and simple. No matter how critics try to soften and dress up their criticism, they are issuing a judgment—and more often than not in the negative.

Someone once commented that "Animals are such agreeable friends. They ask no questions. They make no criticisms."

Probably among my readers are those who have seen friendships and other relationships damaged—or blown to smithereens by ill-conceived and ill-received criticisms.

Criticism is often meant to be helpful—and often it is. But even so, it usually carries with it some hurtful barbs. No one appreciates the value of constructive criticism more than the one who is giving it. When one is on the receiving end, it is not always perceived as constructive.

I read this recently: "Adverse criticism from a wise man is more to be desired than the enthusiastic approval of a fool."

A good rule for anyone to follow is to receive criticism graciously. Examine it for truth and relevance. Whatever has merit, work on it. What does not, reject it without malice to the critic.

DELIBERATE IGNORANCE

As I grew up and began to learn the ways of the world, I eventually realized that some people do not want to learn. They would even tell me, "Ignorance is bliss." They were proud of not knowing, and quite determined to not learn anything they did not want to.

This was a startling discovery—and to this very day I cannot for the life of me give any good reason about deliberate ignorance.

However, I can give a few *credible* reasons—the first of which is that with increased knowledge comes increased responsibility. Not many want that. They like to stay with the rank and file where responsibilities and blame are spread out. No one seems to have more than another.

Another reason for deliberate ignorance is that others begin to expect more of us. They make demands on our knowledge, our time, our patience and our good nature.

They presume on us, with their expectations being clear that to help them in whatever their problems are we must be willing to drop everything and everyone else.

Who wants that? Some kind of masochist?

In these strange days in which we live, it's beginning to look as though quite a few persons are fighting fiercely to preserve their ignorance. And that is sad.

31-GRUP

ENCOURAGING POTENTIAL

One of the most important gifts we can offer our children in their growing up years is encouragement.

Even what seem to be the most confident of children need honest and warm words of encouragement as they set out on various adventures in learning. Security and confidence are chancy forces, and every child needs lots of encouragement to fulfill their potential.

I like to hear about parents who encourage their children to surpass their own achievements in education and other accomplishments. I am really put off by moms and dads who seem almost resentful about the possibility of their children outdoing them.

Believe it or not, this does happen: Consciously or unconsciously some parents hold their child back from too much achievement with some carefully chosen words of discouragement—even trying to shame the child for wanting more in life than what their mom and dad were able to do.

On the other hand there are parents who lose sight of the realities of a child's potential and intelligence—because they are so determined that their children achieve and reach goals they never could. The end result can be terrible and terrifying discouragement.

Encourage your children to find and then fulfill their potential. That is the best gift you can give to your maturing children.

DRUMBEATS & HOOFBEATS

In chapter 6 of the Book of Revelation there are descriptions of the four horsemen of the end times. The riders and horses all represent end time events that will precede the awesome Judgment before the throne of God.

In these times of faithlessness, sudden death, horrific violence—and the spread of war, disease and famine throughout the earth—one cannot help but wonder if we might be hearing the hoofbeats of the four horsemen of the Apocalypse, meaning the Book of Revelation.

Could it be that they indeed are riding, and that we are closer to the end times than most of us think?

For sure there are great upheavals on this planet—in human affairs, among the nations, ethnic and racial rivalries and a rampant disregard for human rights and aspirations.

I believe we ought to be listening for the hoofbeats—but even more we ought to be listening for the drumbeats that give us God's cadence for our march through this world.

The writer David Thoreau once said that he listened to different drum beats than are heard by most of humanity. I think that is true of every person who longs for his or her life to be in step with the drumbeats of God.

A good question for every person alive: Who is beating the cadence of life for you?

EVIL IN DISGUISE

I have learned that a great many persons find it difficult to think of human beings in terms of evil—of being evildoers.

They prefer to believe that evil is some kind of mental aberration, or maybe a form of insanity. It happens when otherwise good people go over the edge mentally and do terrible deeds.

Insanity may be a form of evil—in the sense that as with all other illnesses, mental illness is not good. It harms and it destroys, so we classify it as an evil.

But persons who do evil may be clear as a bell mentally, and fully in possession of their sense and sanity. They do wrong simply because they enjoy it. Evil acts are a power trip for them. They do evil by motivation and choice.

One of the awesome facts about evil is that it masquerades as good. And what is even worse, gullible human beings buy it. They acquiesce to the deception.

Writing in II Corinthians, chapter 11, Paul makes some pertinent comments about evil: "Satan himself masquerades as an angel of light. It is not surprising, then, if his servants masquerade as servants of righteousness. Their end will be what their actions deserve."

We are wise indeed when we have trained ourselves to be perceptive in recognizing evil—and are determined to avoid it, and when necessary, to do battle in the Name of the Lord.

EXPECTATIONS

In large part life is a matter of directing and controlling our tendencies and wants, our emotions—and our expectations.

There are folks who expect too much from life—and there are those who expect too little. Healthy, contented, productive living requires realism and balance in our expectations of life.

First of all we need to be real in our expectations of ourselves. Many of our disappointments and experiences of depression are the result of our irrational, unreal expectations of ourselves.

Learning to work within the realities of our abilities is important—but always with the realization that those abilities can be stretched, can be improved.

Then we need to be careful about our expectations of others. The tendency is to demand that our loved ones conform to our desires. Rather than expect them to be themselves, we expect them to somehow transform into our image of what they should be. This is both unwise and unfair.

Our expectations of God also can be unreal—not at all like the revelation He has given in His Holy Word and in Jesus Christ. We want God to conform to our whims and fancies—not to be the God Who expects us to shape up to His intentions for His creation.

In all matters, with all persons—watch your expectations!

FAILURE AVOIDANT

Do you know what it means to be failure avoidant?

Failure avoidant people steer clear of risks. They want nothing to do with challenges that might not succeed, and may show them up as inept or incapable.

There are people who always take the easy way, even though it may cost them more, and may yield little or no satisfaction. They are failure avoidant. They always succeed because they never try anything difficult or risky.

Authentic, gutsy Christianity is not for the failure avoidant. Jesus calls us to take up crosses, to witness for Him, to take on the cares and heartaches of the world, to stretch our vision and our reach, and always to be moving on and out to the horizons of our lives.

Failure avoidance in bad enough in ordinary living. It keeps people from being their best, and from some of the most exciting experiences of life.

But in the Christian faith, failure avoidance could keep us from the prize of the high callings we have in Jesus Christ. It could keep us from knowing Him and experiencing Him at our side as we move through this life, and on to the next.

With Christ's help failure avoidant persons can start to change—to begin to take ever increasing risks to which their faith calls them.

WHAT'S IN A NAME?

At a wedding rehearsal recently there was a beautiful 4 year old Chinese girl. I asked her name of the parents who had adopted her, and they said her name was "Winter." I found that just beautiful. "Winter."

In naming children the seasons have all been covered. I've met persons named "Spring," "Summer," "Autumn"—and now for the very first time, "Winter." Delightful!

When it comes to climatic conditions I've found very few. I have a grandchild whose parents named her "Storm." But I don't know anyone named "Thunder" or "Lightning," or "Typhoon" or "Hurricane"—or "Snow," "Rain," "Sleet" or "Tornado." If you know of any such first names, let me know." Humans, mind you—not pets.

There are some cautions concerning what we name our children. Try to avoid names that will inevitably generate derogatory nicknames. Kids have it tough enough without that added burden.

There also are caveats about living up to or down to certain names—and nicknames, too, for that matter. My name, "Robert," means "Bright Hero." Now that's a name to live up to! I've known some guys from South of the Border who are named "Jesus," pronounced "Hesus." Imagine trying to live up to that name. But I'd sure urge them to try!

FRIENDSHIP IN THE DARK

People have some strange notions of friendship—and most of us have felt the sting and sorrow of friends we thought would stick, but who disappeared when the going got rough.

We call them "Fair Weather Friends"—meaning that when the going gets rough, they get going. Usually their departure is not a surprise.

A fable passed down through the years brings true friendship into sharp focus: "Who is a friend like me?" asked the shadow of the body. "Do I not follow you wherever you go? In sunlight or moonlight I never forsake you."

"That is true," replied the body. "You are with me in sunlight and moonlight. But where are you when neither sun nor moon shines upon me? The true friend is with us in the darkness."

The message needs to sink in: Choose your friends. Be wary of so-called "friends" who choose you—and not always for reasons beneficial to you.

Choose friends for their faith, their loyalty, their ideals and strength. None of us needs a friend who is a loser and a user. There's no friendship in such persons—only the potential for grief and sorrow.

Many of us have learned the truth of that little fable the hard way: "The true friend is with us in the darkness."

HOW CONTAGIOUS ARE YOU?

We're all contagious in one way or another. We pass on disease bugs, ideas, fun, humor, gloom, doom, encouragement, hope or whatever.

Some pass on their marvelous wisdom about life. Others seem to be contagious with encouragement, and they lift our spirits.

Some walk into a room, and are absolutely contagious with good will and warmth. Others offer the contagions of sour grapes, bitterness about life, blame toward others and the inflictions and afflictions of neurotic pity parties.

Our personalities are bound to either pollute the environment or enhance it. We will spread good will and laughter or we'll infect the atmosphere with hopelessness, doubts and fears.

Have you ever had the urge to run when negatively contagious people enter your space. You just know they will make your day miserable. On the other hand many of us have stayed in situations and places longer than we intended because the atmosphere was so contagious with hilarity and good conversation, humor and close warmth.

I've been to hundreds of gatherings—and sometimes I have come away disappointed, because the outcomes and atmosphere ranged from neutral to extremely negative. And thankfully, other times I have come away refreshed and renewed. A good question to ponder: Just how contagious are you—and with what?

A CONTAGIOUS FAITH

The previous commentary focused on various contagions of life, and how we pass on negative or positive infections to the people around us.

Willy nilly we will influence and impact our environment and the people in it. Our obligation as human beings is to make a good and healthy impact. This is even more essential if we are persons of faith.

One of the most valuable forces we can offer to others is a contagious faith—a faith that expresses hope and confidence, a faith that understand there is more to life than meets the eye, a faith that is victorious and conquers fear, wrong and adversity.

Doubt is terribly infectious—but the same is true of faith.

Anybody can pollute the scene with words of doubt and discouragement. It's always easier to tear down than to build up.

But when it comes to faith—if you don't have it, you can't pass it on.

As each of us examines our lives to assess the impact we are having on persons around us, check out your faith. Is it grounded in the realities of God's revelation in His Holy Word? Does it bring light to dark places and hope to persons who despair? Just how contagious are you when it comes to faith?

WHEN DINING IS BEGRUDGED

In Proverbs 22 we are counseled:

> **Do not eat the food of a stingy man, do not crave his delicacies; for he is the kind of man who is always thinking about the cost. "Eat and drink," he says to you, but his heart is not with you.**

Now that is fascinating advice! And I also suspect that for some people it brings to mind those painful occasions when tightwads have issued an invitation to dinner or whatever—and then made it clear in subtle ways how much it was costing them! Have you ever had that kind of experience—trying to relate to "the kind of man who is always thinking about the cost"?

During my life I have known people who begrudgingly and intently count the cost of everything—aloud! They brag about their expenditures on themselves, proudly sounding off with the price of everything they buy.

But seldom if ever have I heard such persons declare their joy in spending money on someone else.

I cannot imagine how anyone could enjoy being dined or entertained by a tightwad. The notions of "cheap," "stingy," and "grudging" ring all kinds of alarm bells.

The Bible is clear that generosity is a virtue—and that not even God appreciates a grudging giver.

WHAT IS ACCEPTABLE

The father of a teenager told me of his concern about the wild profanity his offspring was using in E-mail exchanges with friends. His descriptive word about the letters was "saturated"—saturated with profanity and derogatory sexual allusions and statements.

Part of that dad was inclined to go easy, to remember his own teen years, and to offer just a mild suggestion that the youngster tone it down. In other words, meet verbal violence and putridity with a wimpish stance.

Naturally, I urged a much stronger approach—full of expressions of love and caring—but one of zero tolerance for any destructive conduct.

We are too inclined to accept what is unacceptable. We cloak our wimpishness with solemn comments about the differences in generations and how times have changed.

Most of what has changed in our culture has to do with our caving in on healthy, time tested principles, practices and behaviors that are bulwarks of a viable society.

Has human nature changed? No. Have human needs and foundational and healthy societal requisites changed? No.

Only when we consider how we have changed in our permissive attitudes toward wrong and harmful conduct can we begin to appreciate where the damage has been done, and will continue to be done in our families and society.

"IN YOUR FACE"

Most of us have heard the phrase, "In your face." It's used mainly in reference to persons who will criticize, show disrespect, tell you off or make fun of you right to your face. No hidden gossiping here, no talk behind your back. Right to your face they defy, degrade, complain, show hate and put you down.

There are some who maintain that with the loss of moral certainties, with the rise of greed and selfishness, and with the increasing intensity of rage, anger and violence in our society, "in your face" behaviors are becoming more and more common.

The expectation is that others will just take it, put up with it. If ever there was a reason for diminishing self-esteem and increasing arrogance and violence it is this "in your face" phenomenon that is sweeping the world.

It carries with it some heavy baggage—such as a diminishment of respect for persons and institutions, expectations that people will put up with the crassest and most self-focused behaviors—along with the perverse notion that whoever yells the loudest and beats the other down is a winner, no matter what the other variables.

"In your face" is not a healthy attitude, and is a dark minus for personal relationships and societal well being.

HARMFUL PERSONS

We're all familiar with the dangers of toxic materials. They call for careful and intended usage, the wearing of gloves, plenty of fresh air, and if you spill any on yourself, wash it off quickly.

Toxic materials may cause injuries and sometimes even death. Keep them far from the reach of children and labeled properly—and with certain substances, don't keep them in the house at all.

We are right and wise to warn our children about toxic materials. We're also right and wise to warn our children about toxic persons. These are people whose conduct is destructive, who cannot or will not change, and who are extremely manipulative about getting others to follow them and tolerate their hurtful behaviors.

The worst of toxic persons kill with pleasure. Drug dealers are toxic persons. Purveyors of pornographic materials are toxic—and the same for persons who are inclined to violence as the number 1 solution for everything that troubles them.

There also are toxic cheaters who may try to persuade your child to help them cheat on an exam—offering threats or rewards to secure cooperation. There are toxic liars who would not know the truth if it hit them on their noses.

Mean business when you talk to your children about toxic persons. Be blunt and graphic. It may save their lives.

WHAT ARE FAMILIES FOR?

Every couple should sit down from time to time and mull over the question, "What are families for?" Think about these statements of family purpose:

• The family is where love is explained, modeled, interpreted and solidified.

• The family is where respect is learned, experienced and given to others.

• The family is where children are introduced to God and His ways.

• The family is where children learn whom to trust—and whom not to trust.

• The family is where each person is accepted, declared worthy, forgiven time after time, and always urged to do better in all things.

• The family is where values are set, taught, modeled and learned.

• The family is where children learn discipline, responsibility and accountability.

• The family fosters healthy extensions, bringing others of like mind into the family circle.

• The family is a launching pad, sending grown children out into the world well prepared for the rigors of living.

31-GRUP

GRADUATION SENTIMENTS

Have you ever searched for appropriate graduation cards to send to the grads in your family or circle of friends? Many of them express sentiments that are plain sappy. Some make high school graduation seem like the end of life. Go religious and you'll find Bible references twisted beyond what fits the original thrusts of the verses.

Most grad cards wish the recipients happiness—as though happiness is the main aim of it all. None that I saw gave any credit to parents, teachers, and other mentors—and not a mention of the Lord's input.

All you grads and your kith and kin, try this on:

My dear graduate—Thanks to God Who created you, and thanks to the grace and wisdom of all who helped you toward achievement, you are now making a significant passage in your life.

It's fitting that we call graduation "commencement." It has more to do with where you're going, than with where you've been.

I wish you the kind of happiness that comes not from partying and other forms of self-indulgence—but from an inspiring and motivating sense of divine purpose and destiny in your life—a conviction that you are in touch with the Creator, and that He is deeply involved in your life.

Much love!

THE ONE MEDIATOR

One of the interesting facets of the Christian Faith is that Jesus Christ is our Mediator—our one and only Mediator between God and all humanity, including each of us.

Jesus is like an attorney speaking on behalf of his client, seeking exoneration and freedom, reconciliation and redemption.

Only in the case of Jesus the proof He is offering to establish our innocence and to win our acquittal is the sacrifice of His own life, when He went to the cross to bear our sins and to atone for them.

One can imagine all kinds of forces appearing at our trial to tell of our misdeeds, our failures, our sins. The list is long, and we are shamed. Our enemies call for our eternal destruction.

And then the Great Mediator steps forward, shows His hands and side, and tells the Judge: "I suffered in his place, in his stead. His life of sin and destruction has all been canceled. It its place are My perfection, My clean slate, my righteousness and holiness. I gave it to him. He is not guilty."

Wow! All that is summed up by Paul's declaration to Timothy:

> **For there is one God and one Mediator between God and men, the Man Christ Jesus.**
>
> (I Timothy 2:5)

HALLOWEEN QUESTIONS

I have some questions about Halloween. I'm not expecting any feedback. But these are questions that need to be asked and answered by every parent who dotingly and sometimes in a spirit of self-focused surrogacy, involves children in Halloween activities.

The first question: Why would any parent dress up a child to take on the persona and appearance of a person or a force of evil and destructiveness? There is way too much evil in this world, and it seeks our honor and approval. Why would we want our children to offer that obeisance to the devil and his minions? What "good fun" could ever be the outcome?

Another question: Why would any parent dress children as "monsters" in ways that parody, mock and scorn persons who are handicapped, retarded, mentally challenged, malformed or crippled—persons whose losses and struggles merit our concern, compassion and respect, not our humor and ridicule?

And one more question: Why would any parent encourage their children to identify with those who perpetuate myths and horrific attitudes toward the dead—toward persons who have lived their lives in the human family and now have gone on to their reward?

They are not malicious ghouls, ghosts and zombies unless we plant that thought with the ghoulishness of our Halloween costuming and posturing.

HATE CRIMES

These days we hear reports of "hate crimes," in which highly prejudiced and bigoted persons perform acts of violence and even murder on persons whom they have decided to detest and hate. They play god in matters of human worth and human rights and proceed to promote their despicable agendas by committing mayhem and killings. They target children, as well as adults.

A balkanization of our nation is not some far-fetched and outlandish notion. We are a nation of many minorities, all correctly demanding the same rights and opportunities offered to all by this unique nation. Bitter hate and warring factions in our land could make the troubles in Yugoslavia's provinces look picayune.

One of the greatest challenges of life is to understand the rightful and healthful meaning of tolerance—and those matters of life toward which we need to be very intolerant.

Hate of any kind is intolerable—but especially mindless hate that seems to hate for hate's sake.

It is intolerable to express hate and commit violence against persons simply because they differ in various ways. Such mindless, brainless, heartless and hate-filled prejudice is really "the mark of the beast." It defines one's main relationship to be not with God but with the devil, the father of lies, the enemy of God and all good.

Believe it—hate crimes are generated in warped and evil minds. No rationale can justify their evil ideas and actions.

HATRED'S HIGH COST

There are persons who apparently live with a great deal of hatred toward others for one reason or another. I have found that most such persons have no idea at all of the high cost of maintaining hatred in their lives and relationships—in the here and now and for all eternity.

Hate is a luxury that no one can afford. It always causes much greater harm to the person who nurtures it than to the persons at whom it might be directed.

One of the worst features of hatred are its concomitants—the bad things that just naturally accompany hatred.

One such feature is the unwillingness to forgive. That lack of forgiveness will someday be seen for what it is, the highest cost of hatred.

We cannot really deal effectively with hatred without the forgiveness that is needed to destroy hatred. And while any act of forgiveness carries a big price tag, the costs are minuscule when compared with the dreadful, eternal costs of hating.

Someone wrote that "Hatred is a cancer of the intellect." There may be temporary satisfaction in hating, but eventually its destructiveness will be evident.

Hatred also has been described as a boomerang—that when thrown out, whirls around and comes back at the one who threw it.

INDECISION

Some persons are victims of their own indecision. They just can't get off dead-center. They spend all their time examining the alternatives, sitting on the fence, afraid or disinclined to jump one way or the other.

Tycoon T. Boone Pickens, at George Washington University, Washington D.C., gave this sound advice: "Be willing to make decisions. That's the most important quality in a good leader. Don't fall victim to what I call the 'ready aim-aim-aim-aim syndrome.' You must be willing to fire."

Some people seem to be forever getting ready for something—but they never get started. They fuss and fume, go over their preparations again and again, but they never fire. They're always aiming. But they never fire.

In one of the parishes I served there was a man who resigned from the deacons so he could have more time to pursue Bible study in a quite rigorous program. He told me he planned to someday use what he learned as a teacher in our Sunday School. Well, this getting ready—aim, aim, aim—went on for the next six years. Finally I suggested that he could be getting ready all the rest of his life—but we needed teachers right now. As far as I know he's still getting ready.

"Get ready—aim" is good advice. But there comes a time to "fire."

TOUCH

There are few things in relationships as powerful as touch.

When we touch someone we're communicating something, and the physical touch adds emphasis and strength to what we intend to convey.

There is the touch of caring, when we reach out to let a loved one know that he or she is not alone. It may be a clasped hand, a gentle touch of the shoulder, or an arm placed around the other. It could be a hug or a caress—and it speaks powerfully of our caring.

There are touches that communicate shared grief—touches that communicate deep affection and love—touches that give assurance of our continuing presence, that we will be there even when the going gets rough.

But there also are touches that are destructive. There is healthy touching, and there is unhealthy touching.

There is the touch of greed—the touch of lust—touch that communicates selfishness and covetousness. There is the touch of illicit passions, and a vast array of touches that signal potential manipulation and using.

Sometimes touching conveys disdain and recklessness—signaling not love, but a total lack of it.

Touch can be not only inappropriate, but lewd and lascivious. Use touch with great care—and if you are not sure of your motives, don't touch.

IN PRAISE OF COMMON SENSE

Sometimes I wonder if common sense has departed from this earth. Certainly it seems less common in our time and culture..

It's quite true that well educated persons do not necessarily have or use common sense. One writer commented, "It is a thousand times better to have common sense without an education—than to have an education without common sense."

This definition of common sense makes good sense: "Common sense is the knack of seeing things as they are. and doing things as they ought to be done."

In my experience I've found that a lot of people get into deep trouble because they follow their emotions rather than common sense. In all matters of any importance, it's wisdom to make emotions take the back seat to the mind guided by common sense. Letting the emotions lead usually takes us into folly and even disaster.

Wisdom is common sense refined by learning and experience.

The Bible tells us much about the importance of wisdom—especially in the Book of Proverbs. A good summary of wisdom counsel is Proverbs 1:22: "How long, O simple ones, will you love being simple? How long will scoffers delight in their scoffing and fools hate knowledge?"

Ponder *that* important question.

TALKING AND HOLLERING

A nine year old boy was asked if his two year old brother had started talking yet, and he replied: "Why should he talk? He gets everything he wants by hollering!"

Many of us have had experience with persons who work in the same way. They know how to shout others down, bamboozle people, and get their way by intimidating and out-hollering everybody around them.

Such persons rule their families by fear. They get their way by demonstrations of lung power sometimes accompanied by physical gestures, threats and even blows.

These pirates of the home think they have it made—thanks to the cooperation and enabling of people around them.

What happens when we call their bluff—when we simply refuse to respond to their hollering?

Well, the same thing that happens when we refuse to cooperate with the hollering of a two year old. There follows a period of intensification of the volume and other unseemly behaviors.

After that there usually comes a time of sulking, pouting and blaming. But in most cases, the culprits finally adjust to a home scene where getting your way by hollering, tantrums and threats is past history. It no longer works.

The enablers have stopped enabling.

ORIGINS OF LIES

Have you ever pondered the real reasons for lying—as well as the origins of lies? Why does a person tell lies? And where does that obtuse tendency come from?

Lies are nearly always for self-protection. They spring from pride, from an unwillingness to confess wrongdoing, from a motivation to always appear right and good.

Lies are conjured up by a mind that has no respect for truth. Other matters take precedence, such as how we might be perceived by others.

Rationalize all you want, lies are a sign of unseemly and ungodly pride at work.

The origins of lies and lying are found in the devil. Jesus called Satan "the father of lies"—the implication being that liars are his children rather than God's.

Someone commented that "The more you speak of yourself, the more you are likely to lie." And once we get used to misrepresentations, they lead to more and more. It is easy to tell one lie, but almost impossible to tell only one.

One of the most precious goals of life is to seek, find and live by the truth. But lies and lying are enemies of truth, and seek to obliterate it.

Truth telling sometimes may cause temporary discomfort, but lies give pain through all eternity.

TYRANNY IN THE FAMILY

At the playground the other day with my grandchild I witnessed an example of tyranny in the family.

Usually we think of family tyrants in terms of adults or out of whack teenagers. But this was a smaller boy—maybe 4 or 5—who demonstrated that he was king of the hill, the boss of his older sister, and the one whose tantrums were to be feared and his crazy making and domineering ways honored.

I watched while he buffaloed his older sister time after time. I was amazed that the parents accepted his conduct as normal, and made no effort to enforce fairness.

This kid used various techniques to get his way and to shut his older sister out. When she went to another play area, he would follow, stake his claim and force her out.

When necessary he could produce tears and wailing, to which the parents were always responsive and attentive, while ordering the sister to yield to the little monster.

Is this some conduct some kind of weird carryover of parental adoration of the male child? Is it a sign of rigor mortis of the mind on the part of the parents?

Please hear this: Tyranny in the family is not cool, not healthy, not productive of worthy self-images—and should not be permitted.

THE VIRTUE OF PATIENCE

I'm quite likely one of those who occasionally offers the prayer: "O Lord, give me patience—and please hurry up about it!"

Most of us could use lots more patience in our lives.

Many are unaware that one of God's greatest attributes is patience. Romans 2:4 tells us: "Do you show contempt for the riches of His kindness, tolerance and patience, not realizing that God's kindness leads you toward repentance?" You can be very sure that all of us are blessed by the fact that God is patient.

It is a fact of life that impatience creates havoc and ill will among people, while patience offers blessing upon blessing.

The Bible lists patience among the fruits of the Spirit—which means the Christian seeks patience for his or her living. In Galatians 5 we read: "But the fruit of the Spirit is love, joy, peace, patience, kindness, goodness, faithfulness, gentleness and self-control."

A wise person wrote that patience is the art of concealing your impatience. And another: "Patience strengthens the spirit, sweetens the temper, stifles anger, subdues pride, and bridles the tongue."

Patience is often bitter—but its fruit is sweet.

Yes, indeed—we all can use a lot more of patience. Truly, it is a life enriching virtue.

READING PEOPLE

While we don't always read others with accuracy, and occasionally we read them in total error, most persons are read with ease and accuracy by an alert and intuitive mind, and generally fall into four categories.

• The first is egocentrism, in which persons are obsessed with themselves, and give little thought to others. Their first question in the face of any request or suggestion is "What's in it for me?"

• In the second category are persons who send out signals of confusion and uncertainty about almost everything in life. They seem to be adrift in a sea of doubt and ambiguity. They have neither faith in themselves nor faith in God.

• A third category includes persons who have sold out their lives to destructive and even evil forces. Willy nilly they emit signals that the devil has gotten hold of their lives, and they leave a trail of personal damage, hurt and even death wherever they go.

• Then there are the persons whom we read as letters from Christ—who are living testimonials of the best of life. Paul wrote in II Corinthians 3: "And you show that you are a letter from Christ."

Such lives always impact others for good, build relationships with the best of friends and mentors, and offer their communities significant leadership.

MAKING CHOICES

One of the true constants of our living is that we must make choices. Another fact is that we cannot avoid decision making. We do so by default if not by deliberate choice. It is eminently true that choice, not chance, determines destiny.

A certain businessman had a sign displayed prominently on his desk: "My decision is 'Maybe'—and that's final!" He had a lot of fun with that one.

It really was a reminder to him that choices must be made—that fence-straddling could go on just so long, and that he had to make the choice, answer for it and live with it.

Most of us have learned along life's way that snap decisions are rarely good. The more pressure there is to choose, the more we ought to take the time needed to weigh our choices and their possible outcomes.

One of the saddest things that can happen to us is when we find that in almost all the important matters of life, we have allowed others to make choices for us.

We default to them by our refusals to choose, by our hesitations and doubts. It also is a fact of life that even if others have chosen for us, we are still responsible for those choices.

Choose by principle—and conviction.

LOSING HAPPINESS

Think hard about this statement: Through ignorance and carelessness we miss out on more happiness than we could ever find.

Do you agree?

For example, for every 60 seconds you are angry, you lose 60 seconds of happiness.

When we continually gripe about what we do not have, and downgrade what we do, the result is a loss of happiness. When we cannot find kind words for others, when every event of life has its shortcomings and faults, when nothing really pleases us and our horizons are only dark and foreboding, we have lost enormous quantities of happiness.

Ego maniacs and even ego centrists lose happiness by the barrel. When we focus on ourselves and a personal quest for happiness, we not only do not find it—we lose most of what we had. The heart is happiest when it beats for others. The mind is happiest when it concentrates on the needs and happiness of others. Selfishness is always a breeding ground for the most desperate kinds of unhappiness.

To love and serve others generates happiness, while to love and serve only our own selves and our interests generates unhappiness.

For sure we lose happiness when we lack appreciation and gratitude for what we have. Happiness must be found and enjoyed where we are right now.

NEW BEGINNINGS

As I write this I'm about to leave for a wedding at which I will be officiating. It's for an older couple—both of whom have lost their spouses and are now ready to begin again.

The anticipated wedding service set me to thinking about new beginnings—and how Christianity is really a faith of new beginnings.

One of the main purposes in the coming of Jesus to His earth is to enable us to make fresh starts in life—new beginnings with God and with each other.

Every relationship needs new beginnings. Forgiveness and reconciliation always call for fresh starts. A new job, a new church, a new home—all call for new approaches, new beginnings in our lives.

I've known quite a few people who seem to major on endings in life. They live with a kind of dread of terminations and finishes to what have been enjoyable times and relationships. When you think about it, concentrating on endings creates a depressing outlook, whereas focusing on beginnings has elements of excitement, anticipations and even adventure.

So Paul assures us in II Corinthians 5:7: "Therefore, if anyone is in Christ, he is a new creation; the old has gone, the new has come! All this is from God. . ."

And so it is.

LIFE ATTITUDES

It strikes me that the two main groups of persons who need the most to examine their life attitudes are the very young and the very old. Both groups can think and act in pretty ridiculous ways if they are nor careful.

This bit of wisdom is anonymous:

> Age is a quality of mind; If you've left your
> Dreams behind, If hope is cold,
> If you no longer look ahead,
> If your ambitious fires Are dead,
> Then, you are old!

Youth too quickly lose the sense of preparation for adventures yet to come. They tend to ignore or deny their need for mentors—their need to learn from the experiences of others. They say that "Life is now"—and never mind the future, when in reality the "now" is mainly about the future.

As early as possible in life, and as late as possible, we all should ponder Longfellow's incisive words in his poem "A Psalm of Life":

Life is real! Life is earnest!
And the grave is not its goal.

Edwin Hubbell Chapin wrote: "The creed of the true saint is to make the most of life and to make the best of it."

That is good and wise counsel for the very young—and the very old. Heed it well and always.

ATTITUDINAL ADJUSTMENTS

There's not a person alive who has no need of attitudinal adjustments.

We've all known adult pouters and spouters, phony and ersatz friends, the proud and the prejudiced, the calloused and hardhearted—just to name a few of the kinds of folks who are in desperate need of attitude adjustments.

When it comes to healthy attitudes, we do not learn the best from the world around us. We find the worst attitudes expressed in situations where persons are about as far from God as they can get.

Proper, healthy, stable attitudes are learned from God's Word—and many times from the persons who are determined to live in accord with His Word.

In His Sermon on the Mount Jesus gave us what we call "The Beatitudes"—and they really are "BE ATTITUDES." Jesus said:

> **"Blessed are the poor in spirit, for theirs is the kingdom of heaven. Blessed are those who mourn, for they will be comforted. Blessed are the meek, for they will inherit the earth. Blessed are those who hunger and thirst for righteousness, for they will be filled. Blessed are the merciful, for they will be shown mercy. Blessed are the pure in heart, for they will see God. Blessed are the peacemakers, for they will be called sons of God."** (Matt. 5:3-10)

THE FAITH OF OUR CHILDREN

The goals of parental nurturing cannot be adequately measured by the wage and salary figures of our children's earnings. Parental success is assessed in terms of the values by which our children live, by characteristics that mark them as children of God and by the skills needed to cope victoriously with the crisis situations of life.

Our children must have the resources of an authentic faith which is held and practiced on the basis of firm convictions about fuller realities beyond what we know with our ordinary senses—and with information and support drawn from dependable and tested resources.

There is also the essential of a faith community—persons who share their faith, along with the common and extraordinary experiences that rise from their faith. They are able to communicate with a language of faith that expresses not only their subjective reactions, but the objectives of the resources on which faith relies.

Christians firmly believe that faith is resourced dependably by the Holy Scriptures, by the historical verities of the faith community and by the Holy Spirit of God Who dwells among and within believers and their community.

In all our communications of caring and nurture, have we opened to our children what they need the most—an authentic faith?

ODD PERCEPTIONS

A certain 2nd grade boy had never encountered a left-handed person. The first day of school he watched with fascination as his teacher wrote a note with her left hand. Finally, he blurted out: "Mrs. Jones! Do you realize you have your arms on backwards?"

I can remember how a mirror confused me as a child. I was trying to figure out left and right, and the mirror's reversal of everything really disoriented me.

Many in our society have odd perceptions about various matters of life. There are those who maintain that certain evil things are perfectly all right—as long as you *think* they are.

Some folks have perceptions of God that are little better than fantasy and a long list of wants.

One of the oddest perceptions of life that people hang on to is the conviction that they will never have to give an account of their attitudes and behaviors in this world, and that they will simply josh their way into heaven. That's not in the Bible I have.

And not so incidentally—the main reason we should master the teachings of God's Word is to avoid developing those odd, quirky and fantasized notions about our lives and the full reality that surrounds us.

SELF EXPRESSION

The ability to communicate one's ideas and convictions is an essential tool for meeting life fully and realistically. Our children need training and encouragement in self expression.

Healthy self expression does not fish around for what the other person may want to hear. It formulates and then expresses our own mind and heart—and hopefully our children will learn to do that with sincerity, tact, and concern for the other person's feelings.

Self expression that is impelled to use profanity is not healthy. To say the least cussing in derogatory terms straight out of the sewers of life generates misunderstandings along with an accurate perception that the mouth and mind of the speaker are out of control.

There is such a thing as turning our communication behaviors over to the devil. The Apostle Paul referred to these when he wrote in Ephesians 6:12: "For our struggle is not against flesh and blood, but against the rulers, against the authorities, against the powers of this dark world and against the spiritual forces of evil in the heavenly realms."

When we are enslaved to such forces, yielding our communication skills to their control, we can only speak in terms of the dark side of life. And really now, who wants to listen to such sewer talk?

SIBLING RIVALRY

I met two brothers at a wedding rehearsal the other night—one 16 and one 11. What struck me as I watched and listened was their obvious affection and respect for each other. They enjoyed each other's company. In fact, they had a ball together!

I saw and heard no putdowns, no spiteful comments, so signs of typical sibling rivalry. Both showed great respect for their parents, and were not reluctant to show their affection in public.

It was refreshing! And it told me that so-called "sibling rivalry" is not all it's cracked up to be. It is not inevitable. It does not have to be.

I have a suspicion that most sibling rivalry is the result of parental comparisons—of parents pitting the children against each other with remarks such as "Why can't you get into sports like your brother?" or "Your brother (or sister) sure brings home better grades than this."

If parents are not careful they can make arch enemies—indeed, sometimes lifelong enemies out of their children.

This is bound to happen when parents favor one child over another. If there is a great inequity about how they treat their son and how they treat their daughter, they are sowing the seeds of what will be a lifelong battle—called "sibling rivalry."

SINCERITY

While sincerity does not cover every needed factor, it can go a long way.

In 2nd Corinthians 8:8 the Apostle Paul tells his readers: "I want to test the sincerity of your love by comparing it with the earnestness of others."

Paul was asking for sincere love—love that meets all the tests and all comparisons with the love shown by others.

The world knows too much of phony and insincere love. Persons who express that kind of love are mainly interested in looking after themselves.

The word "sincere" has an interesting derivation. From the Latin it carries the literal meaning "without wax."

Back in Roman times they had certain shops where original statuary was sold. Certain pieces were more costly because they had no defects that were covered and smoothed over with wax, in order to hide the mistakes of the artist. So in a special section of the shop there were placed the carvings and statues of greater worth, Near them were signs that read: "Sin Ceros"—"Without Wax."

In other words, the real thing—all of the work pure marble with no wax filling to hide the defects. That ought to help us understand the thrust of "sincere love," "sincere actions," and "sincere faith"—all of which are very critical concerns of life.

STRENGTH FOR DIFFICULT TIMES

Meeting life's ordinary demands may sometimes create hardships for some—but most people handle the normal. day to day matters of life with relative ease.

But when crunch times come—what I call the crucibles of life, where we are tested and tried—where extraordinary resources of strength and will are needed—many persons find they have nowhere to turn, no reserves of strength to draw on, no resources for getting through the crucibles of life.

Recently I came across this verse in Proverbs 24:10: "If you falter in times of trouble, how small is your strength!" That tells me that the power of our lives is not measured by how we handle the easy times—but how we handle the tough times, the crucibles of life.

The Bible is clear that we need God's empowerment in order to cope with all that life throws at us.

In II Corinthians 12, the Apostle Paul wrote about the weaknesses of his own life that needed the strength that only God can give—and how those very weaknesses opened the door for empowerment.

When trouble comes and we are too weak to handle it, with Paul and millions of other Christians, we find in Christ the strength we need.

SUSPICION

One of the most difficult things to do is to live with suspicion. Another difficult if not impossible challenge is to maintain a relationship that is riddled with suspicion.

Suspicion makes trust impossible. The very fact that suspicion has crept into the relationship is an indication that trust no longer exists.

The story of King Saul and the destruction of his wonderful relationship with David is a case in point. At first, all was just wonderful. Then, as David became more popular King Saul began to bristle with jealousy and mistrust. Dark suspicions clouded his mind and his judgment. Soon he was plotting to engineer David's death.

Unfounded and misbegotten suspicions had done their dirty work. I Samuel 20 tells how Saul tried to enlist the help of his son, Jonathan, to kill David. But Jonathan refused.

Instead Jonathan ran to warn David of his father's intentions, and to urge David to flee for his life.

In the end it was Saul who died in disgrace, and David became king in his place.

Someone wrote that suspicion "is like a pair of dark glasses—it makes all the world look dark."

Suspicion thrives on the dark side of life—fostering bleak imaginings and harmful prejudice—all the while ignoring the more positive and valuable features of the situation.

THE MARVELS OF THE TONGUE

In the Bible we find references to the marvels of the tongue—descriptions of how its utterances can be helpful and beautiful on the one hand—and yet how bitter and destructive the tongue can be when it gets out of control.

In II Samuel 23:2 David tells of the blessing a controlled tongue can give: "The Spirit of the Lord spoke through me; His word was on my tongue." Certainly that is the tongue at its best!

In Psalm 5 we read other side of the story—the hateful and destructive doings of the tongue:

> **Not a word from their mouth can be trusted; their heart is filled with destruction. Their throat is an open grave; with their tongue they speak deceit.**

In his 3rd chapter, James tells us that often the extremes of goodness and evil come from the same tongue:

> **With the tongue we praise our Lord and Father, and with it we curse men, who have been made in God's likeness. Out of the same mouth come praise and cursing. My brothers, this should not be.**

You can be sure that God's intent is that we use our tongues for good, not evil! Controlling the tongue should have high priority in all our lives.

RELATING TO CHILDREN

Our topic is "Relating to Children." For sure there are some folks who are surprised and puzzled by the very thought of relating to children as real, genuine persons. Their favorite motto is the old saw, "Children should be seen and not heard."

Forget that motto. It never did make much sense. It's a shibboleth for persons who think they own their kids. They're like property, or servants who must obey without question.

Children respond best when they are treated with respect and affection. Shatter their dignity, and you have tuned them out and turned them off. The same with adults.

"Tolerance," "Understanding" and "Tough Love" are key concepts in dealing with children. Those words point up the need for relating to them not as small adults, but in terms of what they really are: children. They lack maturity. They lack experience. They need guidance. They will fumble and fail, so they need forgiveness. They need tough and unconditional love. They need affirmation and praise. They need guidelines and markers for their behaviors and attitudes. Above all, they need healthy role models.

Someone wrote: "Children are a great deal more apt to follow your lead than the way you point."

One final comment: "The best thing to spend on your children is your time."

THE FINAL WORD

Well, who has the final word at your house? Hopefully it's not the children. Parents should have the final word—but of course, at all times in company with the One Who is The Final Word in all things—Jesus Christ.

John calls Jesus "The Word," and wrote in the first three verses of his Gospel:

> **In the beginning was the Word, and the Word was with God, and the Word was God. He was with God in the beginning. Through Him all things were made; without Him n nothing was made that has been made.**

In the 14th verse of that first chapter, John wrote:

> **The Word became flesh and made His dwelling among us. We have seen His glory, the glory of the One and Only, Who came from the Father, full of grace and truth.**

Without question the Bible lays down the fact that Jesus is The Final Word. He has the final, the last say in all human and divine matters.

He is The Final Word as the Revealer of God. He is The Final Word as the portrayal of the best of humanity. And He is The Final Word as the eternal Judge of all things.

Why is it so important to understand Jesus? Because He is The Final Word.

MONEY CONSCIOUSNESS

Occasionally I run into persons who immediately bring to mind an incident in the life of our Lord Jesus.

A woman who had been rescued from a life of destructiveness entered the room where the Lord and His disciples were dining, and as an act of devotion and gratitude broke open a box of costly perfume and showered Jesus with it.

Some disciples were not impressed. Judas Iscariot protested, reminding everyone that if that costly perfume had been sold in the market, the proceeds would feed a lot of poor people.

John's Gospel comments: "He did not say this because he cared about the poor but because he was a thief; as keeper of the money bag, he used to help himself to what was put into it." (John 12:6)

Jesus rebuked Judas for his unseemly money consciousness, and told the disciples:

> **I tell you the truth, wherever the gospel is preached throughout the world, what she has done will also be told, in memory of her.** (Mark 14:9)

While the Bible teaches us to exercise stewardship in money matters. it never suggests that money be the main value in our living. There is such a thing as being money conscious to the point of paganism—and even evil.

A BIT OF MYSTERY

If our religious approaches lack excitement, spirituality and above all a sense of mystery, the Season of Lent is the time to get it all straight.

A religious faith without mystery is a contradiction in terms. The most beautiful and sensitive relationships and experiences of our human life all contain the mystical and mysterious. Trying to keep them simple and earthy often does more damage than good.

The mystery in lofty human relating is magnified and compounded when we approach God. Words such as "awesome," "mysterious," "magnificent," and "ethereal" are very much in order.

When we enter our churches, the first order of the experience is not to seek out conversation with persons around us—but to humbly bow to the mystery. Silence is the order of that momentous experience—not yakky, trite and gossipy conversation.

We rightly sing such songs as "Our God Is An Awesome God," "Majesty," "Holy, Holy, Holy" and other hymns meant to remind us that we are in the Presence of the Highest Reality, and there is mystery, the unfathomable, the hidden and promising. Psalm 96 captures this: **"Worship the Lord in the splendor of His holiness; tremble before Him, all the earth.** (Psalm 96:6-9)

Only as we seek the mystery will we find God and all that He has to offer us in this life and in the life to come.

A HELPFUL REBUKE

Recently someone told me of the dying of a person known to us. She had suffered a heart attack, and died in her kitchen—all alone.

My response fastened on the "aloneness" of her death, and I said to my colleague: "Oh, how terrible to die that way—all alone."

My colleague quickly responded: "She was not alone. Whether we Christians live or die, we are never alone."

It was a well deserved rebuke. We must not forget the companionship of God—in life and in death, and I apologized for my slip of faith.

For sure it's wonderful to be surrounded by friends and loved ones at the time of one's death. But a more important Person is always present.

Jesus' comments on this are often read at funeral services—and there's a danger of tuning them out.

> **Do not let your hearts be troubled. Trust in God; trust also in Me. In My Father's house are many rooms; if it were not so, I would have told you. I am going there to prepare a place for you. And if I go and prepare a place for you, I will come back and take you to be with Me that you also may be where I am.** (John 14:1-3)

A RETREAT ON COMPASSION

Last weekend my oldest granddaughter went off on a retreat for youth sponsored by a group of Sioux City churches. I asked her dad and mom about the theme of the retreat, and was surprised and pleased to hear that these young people planned to involve themselves in discussions and learning exercises about compassion.

Now that's a self-giving theme. Fits with Lent, too. So often retreats major on self-awareness and self-improvement. Somehow "self" gets major attention.

But compassion? That cannot help but direct the self to move aside, and then concentrate on the woes and problems of others.

I hope they come to understand that pity is not the goal. Feeling sorry for others who face unusual deprivations is not the same as exercising compassion—which means seeking understanding, developing empathy and generating solutions and help—and at no small cost to ourselves.

I am convinced that there is an increasing shortage of compassion in this world. It gets easier to block out the unpleasant plights of millions, to ignore the genocide and ethnocide that plague our world—some call it "compassion fatigue." Proper compassion has the divine elements of justice, righteousness and sacrificial approaches.

I'm looking forward to hearing what my grandchild has learned. Compassion is one of the virtues that I hope will adorn her life.

ACIDULOUS PERSONALITIES

In my reading I occasionally come across words that seem to say what they are intended to say with a special flair—a kind of pizzazz. One such word is "acidulous."

"Acidulous" is an adjective which means just what its first four letters say, "acid"—so it is describing persons or things that are caustic in nature. They are biting or harsh with persons to whom they relate.

Do you now any acidulous personalities—the kind who spill acid on to a relationship—who always come off as harsh, biting and caustic personalities?

Thankfully I don't know very many acidulous persons—probably because I won't even give such people the time of day.

Acidulous persons are hurtful, harmful, destructive personalities, who seem to make a game of trying to be as bitter as they can be. They rain on people's parades, they scorn accomplishments, they major on the minor flaws of others—and otherwise do their best to make life miserable for people around them.

Conversations can be acidulous—and even common greetings. Occasionally I'll run into someone downtown whose manners and outlook seem totally acidulous. It seems there's just no sunshine or hope in their lives.

But be sure to start out at home base, making sure you are not acidulous.

ANGELS UNAWARES

In Friday's Men's breakfast we came to this verse in our current study of Hebrews: "Do not forget to entertain strangers, for by so doing some people have entertained angels unawares—without knowing it." (Hebrews 13:2 RSV)

From time to time it's a good idea to think some sane and sensible thoughts about angels.

Angels and Angelology have become very popular in today's culture, and there's a lot of nonsense floating around out there.

The word "angel" comes from the Greek word "angelos," with the Biblical meaning of "a messenger of God."

Most of us may never run into an angel with big wings and a long gown. But, most of us have entertained angels unawares if we take the broader Biblical view of heavenly visitations, of theophanies or "God appearances" in the unusual and turning point times of our lives.

I believe that God sends us messengers, "angelos," far more often than we realize. They come in the nature and form of events, interventions, happenings and divine resourcing. Maybe the angel of the moment comes to us in a friend or mentor, someone who confronts us in a time of destructive conduct, or comforts us in a time of grief and loss.

Be careful not to miss the event by calling it a "coincidence" or "accident."

ANOTHER DIAMOND IN THE DIRT

At this writing Tami Drenk was a 21 year old student at the University of Iowa, who took a year off to go to Albania and serve as a Christian volunteer in an orphanage. This was just prior to the beginnings of big troubles in the Balkans.

Without warning their small town of 5000 began to receive a flood of refugees from Kosovo. The first day, 300, the next day 500—and they kept coming.

Suddenly this young woman from Apple Valley, Minnesota, found herself working hard with other volunteers to scrape together essentials for people who had been robbed of everything.

Tami commented that the Kosovar refugees are racked "by a constant flow of tears. They're completely exhausted, very depressed—hungry, sad. The children are all crying, saying all they want to do is go home. It's the most heartbreaking thing I've ever seen."

Another diamond in the dirt—an outstanding human being whose faith is compelling her to serve in the midst of the terrible chaos of mass human suffering.

What drives these Christians? Naive idealism? Not for one moment do I believe that.

The motive for such self giving starts with Jesus' words in Matthew 25:40: "I tell you the truth, whatever you did for one of the least of these brothers of Mine, you did for Me."

MORE DIAMONDS IN THE DIRT

Not all Albanians are Muslim—some are Christian.

Some years ago, several Muslim families had made their way out of Kosovo, and across the rugged terrain, hiding frequently from Serbian troops. They finally crossed the border into Albania, and for the first time all 26 of them felt safe. They were without food and shelter, but they were alive. God is good!

An elderly Albanian Christian couple came across them as they rested by the roadside near their home. The man and his wife were struggling to cover their necessities on a pension amounting to $40 per month.

There was barely a moment's hesitation on the part of that Albanian Christian couple. They immediately invited all 26 of their fellow Albanians to come and live in their home, share what they had to share, and feel the security of a roof over their heads—not to mention the love of people who cared.

I believe this happening is akin to an appearance of the resurrected Christ. Surely the Lord is in the hearts of that Albanian couple. What else but the love and compassion of Jesus Christ could drive them to such an extreme of hospitality?

Discovering these acts of heroic and costly kindness are like finding diamonds in the dirt in this world of evil, mindless madness.

BY ROTE OR WISDOM?

Probably we all have come across persons who confuse knowledge with wisdom.

I found this pithy comment on the difference: "Knowledge can be memorized—wisdom cannot."

In our days in the Middle East we battled educational systems that taught and graded and graduated by rote—even in the fields of medicine! They had not caught on to the fact that rote learning has a lot of limitations. Learning to think about our knowledge, reason about it, apply it and deduce from it are the most important features of any worthwhile education.

Knowledge is knowing a fact. Wisdom is knowing what to do and what not to do with accumulated and sometimes related facts. Knowing *how* is one thing. Knowing *why* is even more important.

There are folks who live their lives by rote, and never find the joys and possibilities of wisdom. Their lives are full of facts and lists, opinions and shallow conceptions. The application of their knowledge is severely limited by rote learning and rote approaches to life.

They become terribly uncomfortable in the face of flexibility and change. They protest complexity and complications, and their earnest motto is KISS—"Keep it simple, stupid." And worst of all, they imagine *that* is wisdom!

Are you living your life by rote—or wisdom?

CASTING YOUR MANTLE

A mantle is a cloak. In God's Word it is expressive of what makes up one's personality, of one's basic essence before God and man—be it good or evil.

Psalm 109:29 states: "May my accusers be clothed with dishonor; may they be wrapped in their own shame as in a mantle!" (RSV)

When the great Prophet Elijah had finished his course of life and prophecy, he cast his mantle over the young Elisha. We read in I Kings 19:19:

> **So he departed from there, and found Elisha the son of Shaphat, who was plowing, with twelve yoke of oxen before him, and he was with the twelfth. Elijah passed by him and cast his mantle upon him.** (RSV)

It was a gift to Elisha. But even more it was a conferring of life's meaning and God's calling as expressed in Elijah's life and ministry.

We all have a mantle—the outer garment of who we are at our best, or our worst. And there come times when we cast our mantle over others, as did Elijah.

It prompts the question, "What is it, what do I have in my life that I can pass on to others and thereby extend their honor, their responsibility, their influence and their standing before God?"

CHOOSING LEADERS

When we were kids we enjoyed the game of "Follow the Leader"—and, of course, the leader would do his or her best to lead us into difficult situations. It was good fun.

As we grow older we continue to play "Follow the Leader," sometimes by choice, often by default. There are lots of people out there whose fondest desire is to play Pied Piper to the meek and gullible.

They may have something to sell, or a set of beliefs to coax people into. They may be purveyors of drugs or pornographic materials. They do their best to lure people to follow them, and many who ought to know better are led by the nose right down the proverbial garden path.

Aimless, directionless lives have a tough time choosing a leader. What often happens is that would-be leaders *choose them.*

If we want the very best in life, with good direction and healthy ways of living, among all the would-be leaders of the world, there is none to match Jesus Christ.

Yes, He is out to win us over, to encourage our best, and to give us what only He can give—salvation and life eternal.

Settle it once and for all: The most important and beneficial leader is Jesus.

AVOIDING RAGE

The Bible tells us that anger and rage are never signs of wisdom.

In something of an understatement James 1:19 and 20 tells us: "Take note of this: Everyone should be quick to listen, slow to speak and slow to become angry, for man's anger does not bring about the righteous life that God desires."

And fits of rage are on the list of low-life qualities that can only derive from sinful attitudes.

In Galatians 5 we read: "The acts of the sinful nature are obvious: sexual immorality, impurity and debauchery; idolatry and witchcraft; hatred, discord, jealousy, fits of rage, selfish ambition, dissensions, factions and envy; drunkenness, orgies, and the like. I warn you, as I did before, that those who live like this will not inherit the kingdom of God."

That's pretty blunt. If he were writing today about "fits of rage" the Apostle Paul might have been more specific, citing road rage, sports rage, greed rage, envy rage, prejudice rage, losers' rage and more.

In Colossians 3:8 Paul lays it on the line: "But now you must rid yourselves of all such things as these: anger, rage, malice, slander, and filthy language from your lips."

Note that anger and rage head the list. With God's help and great determination, unload them.

PROVOCATIONS

The teenage girl whisked by her younger brother, and without a word punched him in the back.

Their father saw it, and told his daughter that her behavior was inappropriate, unkind and certainly not called for.

Her response "You don't know what a terrible day I've had!"

And, of course, Papa had to tell her the obvious: "That in no way excuses your taking it out on your brother!"

One of the things we have to cope with in this world are persons who feel it's their privilege in life—and even their mission—to provoke persons around them. And that includes the persons who love them.

I sometimes refer to such persons as "Ahab" personalities. King Ahab was one of the worst kings of ancient Israel. He not only provoked his people—he provoked God! I Kings 16:33 tells us: "Ahab also made an Asherah pole and did more to provoke the Lord, the God of Israel, to anger than did all the kings of Israel before him."

Senseless and irrational provocations, dished out by those who feel that life has. been hard on them, are never to be tolerated. Wimpish toleration is seen by such folks as permission to turn up the heat, and make their provocative behaviors all the worse.

In plain English: Don't put up with it!

EFFORTLESS PERSONS

Probably we all have known a person or two who was so skilled at something, they made doing it seem effortless.

Probably we also have known others who are quite determined that their lives will be effortless. They avoid anything that makes demands on them. Achievement has to come with ease—no sweat, no investment of time and training. Otherwise, forget it.

There are quite a few parents out there who see it as their sacred duty to run interference for their child, and keep demands for effort off his or her back. They will help invent excuses so their offspring can avoid the unpleasantness of work, study and even sports demands. If it makes demands question it, avoid it, run from it.

Can you imagine what this attitude is doing and will do in the lives of their children? It cannot help but bring the worst of troubles and problems in their lives. They rapidly become skilled effort and work avoidant personalities, and they imagine they're living life the best ways possible.

Anything in life that is worthy and productive of good demands effort. There are practice times, special exercises, books to study, lessons to learn and many other disciplining forces to contend with.

Avoid effort and you scuttle your life.

IMPOSITIONS

Others sometimes express expectations of us that add up to crass impositions. Somehow they have developed an idea that for whatever reasons we will tolerate their presumptuous demands on our time, energy and whatever else they can impose on us.

They obtrude, in effect forcing their demands and ideas on some other person without permission and without invitation.

I realize that everyone has to make a living, but it takes a lot of chutzpah to telephone an unknown person with what amounts to a demand that we buy, subscribe, contribute or whatever.

There is a couple from a distant city whom we barely know. One night our doorbell rang, and there was pounding on our door. When I opened the door, here was this couple, yelling "Surprise!"

Without a word of warning or a thought in their head they decided to impose on our time and good nature, and pay us a surprise visit. We were surprised, but neither pleased nor honored. We told them bluntly to go to a motel.

A good and wise use of the telephone would have been a courtesy call to see if we were willing to have visitors.

A good rule of life is to always analyze the intrusive, obtrusive and imposition factors before acting in ways that force ourselves on others.

CULTIVATING HAPPINESS AND JOY

People who complain about their personal unhappiness can be a real pain in the neck. With some, it's like a broken record. Over and over they tell the same people the same story that in summary tells the world "I'm so unhappy." And sometimes we get that inane question, "Don't I have the right to some happiness?"

I am convinced that one has a "right" to happiness only if he or she is concerned about and doing something for the happiness and joy of others.

Happiness and joy are great rarities for self-centered clods. Their self focus manages to sabotage happiness before it has a chance to work on them.

Happiness is like gardening. It's a matter of preparing ground, planting at the right time, tending and cultivating and weeding—and only then comes the harvest.

Those who imagine they have a "right" to happiness make lousy gardeners. They want happiness to happen like a miracle—with no discernible effort on their part. What usually happens is they would not recognize what there is to be happy about if it hit them on the nose and wore a big sign.

And remember: happiness is rarely solitary. It always has to involve others—and your being on the supply end of their happiness.

AGRICULTURE AND LIFE

Harvest time should remind us of the close ties between agriculture and life. These logical and essential connections are as old as humanity. The Bible draws richly on agriculture as it teaches the fullness of life.

In the book of Job, chapter 4 verse 8, we read: "They that plough iniquity, and sow wickedness, reap the same." There you have what we might call "the agriculture of the soul."

Paul wrote this famous line in Galatians 6:7: "Whatsoever a man sows, that shall he also reap."

And in Hosea 8:7 the prophet offers this life and agriculture observation: "They have sown the wind, and they shall reap the whirlwind."

Hosea wrote in his 10th chapter: "Sow for yourselves righteousness, reap the fruit of unfailing love, and break up your unplowed ground; for it is time to seek the Lord, until He comes and showers righteousness on you. But you have planted wickedness, you have reaped evil, you have eaten the fruit of deception."

It seems that there is a close affinity between the sane and sensible use of the land and the sane and sensible agriculture of life.

The prophet James tells us: "Peacemakers who sow in peace raise a harvest of righteousness." (James 3:18)

DOG IN THE MANGER

Have you ever known someone who tries to discourage others from enjoying something because he or she does not enjoy it? They have no desire for it. So why should anyone else?

The expression "dog in the manger" applies to such killjoys. It comes from an old fable about a dog who prevented an ox from eating the hay the dog did not want. The ox was finally convinced that eating hay was not a good thing.

Dogs in the manger rain on the parades of others, and smirk at their enjoyments. They question relentlessly, demanding an explanation as to why someone takes pleasure in something that has no appeal to their questioner.

People who are resistive to dogs in the manger are to be commended. They simply will not give in to the dog's narrow range of interests and needs.

"How can those kids like that kind of music?" they ask. Or, "How can you stand to watch a movie like that?" Or, "Why on earth are you interested in this or that?"

Remember—no answer you give will ever satisfy dogs in the manger. They want you to cave in completely to their narrowness.

The ox didn't eat the hay. The dog smirked with satisfaction and victory. The ox died of starvation.

That fable carries lessons right into the contemporary scene.

CHARACTER

It's not surprising that during these past years we've heard a lot of talk about character—and the lack thereof. Character is an important factor in everyone's lives, and especially those who govern.

Someone once wrote that "Character is what you are in the dark." Character is what we are and what we do when we think no one is looking, when we are alone and unknown.

A person of high and good character has principles by which he or she lives. Those principles include justice, compassion, purity, honesty, integrity, compassion, self-control and responsibility.

Blamers have poor character—as do liars, persons whose word is worthless, and folks who shun responsibility.

Manipulators and users have poor character. Gossipmongers certainly have poor character, as well as jealous or spiteful persons. For sure, people who use foul and abusive language have poor character. And we could add a lot more to the list of qualities that make for bad character. Our attitudes and conduct, our words and even our thoughts, are the ingredients for character that is either good or bad, constructive or destructive.

One might say that the Ten Commandments are character indicators.

Yes, indeed. Character is what you are in the dark—and character tells us and others what and who we really are.

LIFE AT ITS BEST

We learn how to live from Jesus the Christ—and we also learn from Him how to die.

The best things people say about life are traceable back to Jesus—and the same with death and dying.

Our Lord teaches us that we cannot live without truthful meaning, and a sense of participation not only in God's plans, but also in His very nature and Being. Rightly are we taught to call Him Father, for it marks our identity as His beloved children.

We also are meant to die in hope and confidence, not in a kind of desperate despair, as though we are surrendering to inevitable darkness and oblivion.

As we have lived in faith, so should we die in faith. As our faith assures us that God's good is in all things, so in death we know we still are headed for God's best and most abiding and permanent state of mode and being.

Just as Jesus takes the hurts and hassles out of our living, so He takes them out of our dying.

Through and with our Lord we live a conquering, victorious life. Through Him we are overcomers and winners. The same is true of dying. We emerge "on the other side" not bedraggled and crushed, but as conquering sons and daughters of God, joyfully celebrating His triumph that has become ours.

SITUATIONAL LONELINESS

Psychologists estimate that in the course of a typical one month period, between 50 and 60 million Americans have significant and even serious feelings of loneliness.

For a lot of those people, their loneliness is situational. It derives from some fairly recent event or condition in their lives: their marriage has begun to go sour, they have experienced job loss, the family has moved, a friend or loved one has died—and these are only a few.

Young people experience the most pronounced situational loneliness. It is usually fostered by peer and parental expectations, by their own feelings of inadequacy in making productive social contacts, and by unrealistic notions of what friendship means and how many friends they can handle. Also, many teenagers have a hard time handling the rejection thrown at them in those years of early maturing in pretty heavy doses, and their loneliness is compounded.

To cope with situational loneliness, I recommend three modes of action: communication, involvement and self-giving or service.

Communicate with others. Get involved in some type of fellowship or action group. And give of yourself—your time, your energy, your creativity.

You'll be absolutely amazed at how quickly these three approaches can turn the tables on situational loneliness: Communicate; get involved with others; and give of yourself.

A KING INDEED

I first learned of Hussein of the Kingdom of Jordan in 1951. As a young prince he stood by the side of King Abdullah at the entry of El Aqsa Mosque in Jerusalem, and endured the horror of witnessing his beloved grandfather being gunned down by an Arab extremist.

Hussein's father, Talal, succeeded Abdullah. But because of emotional problems Talal was declared unfit to rule.

In 1953 at the age of 19 Hussein took the throne—and has held it ever since. In his final years Hussein became afflicted with cancer and went for treatment to the Mayo Clinic in Rochester, Minnesota. It soon was evident the cancer was winning.

Before he went home to die, and in an act typical of his courage, Hussein left Rochester and piloted his own jet to Maryland to join the Israeli-Palestinian Peace Talks at a time when they seemed to be on the verge of collapse.

On his arrival he told the gathering: "We have no right to dictate through irresponsible action or narrow-mindedness the future of our children or their children's children. There has been enough destruction, enough death, enough waste, and it's time that together we occupy a place beyond ourselves, our peoples, that is worthy of them under the sun: the descendants of the children of Abraham, Palestinians and Israelis coming together"

The words of a king—and a most worthy king indeed. He died a hero not only to his people, but to the world.

A LIFETIME OF LEARNING

There is a great deal of wise counsel in the Jewish Talmud—including this statement: "He who adds not to his learning diminishes it."

Many among us simply do not understand that learning is a lifetime adventure. It's not a chore, mind you, but an adventure. When we stop learning, we stagnate intellectually, and quite likely accelerate the aging process.

I admire persons who work hard to stay on the cutting edge, looking for more knowledge and rejoicing when they find it.

We all have a lot to learn, and when we keep learning our lives are the richer for it.

It takes a certain amount of humility to keep learning. Admitting ignorance on any matter is very difficult for some. So they become great pretenders—professing knowledge they really do not have.

Humility enables us to respond to someone's sharing of information with a grateful "I really did not know that. Tell me more about it." That approach generates enthusiasm on the part of all concerned.

Proverbs 1:5 and 7 tell us: "Let the wise listen and add to their learning, and let the discerning get guidance. . . . The fear of the Lord is the beginning of knowledge, but fools despise wisdom and discipline."

We are intended by God to keep learning—all our lives!

WORDS: CUTTING OR SOOTHING

Persons with even a small degree of common sense know that the words we utter convey much more than the basic meaning of those words. Emotions, convictions and attitudes flow out of our mouths along with the words we have chosen.

And it's also true that when we speak, others hear more than mere words. They hear our emotions, convictions and attitudes—and often add their own to the exchange.

So we have to be clear spoken, doing everything in our power to make sure we are heard correctly—and that the message we intend to convey really is the message received by others.

The Living Bible gives us this translation of Proverbs 12:18: "Some people like to make cutting remarks, but the words of the wise soothe and heal."

Cutting remarks do reveal our attitudes, convictions and emotions. Saying them may yield a certain satisfaction, but it soon turns sour. We cannot be destructive and hurtful toward others and keep feeling good about it. Sooner or later our destructiveness catches up with us and usually we pay a great price for that kind of indulgence.

The question to ask before opening one's mouth is always, "What will my words do—cut and damage, or sooth and heal?"

Soothing, healing words always flow from the wise.

WORDS THAT HELP AND HEAL

Occasionally we need to take stock of our working vocabulary to make sure we know and use words that encourage, help and heal—words of life, courage, peace and hope.

I like the word "irenic"—which means "promoting peace." Irenic persons cultivate a vocabulary that breathes reconciliation and forgiveness—that soothes and calms troubled souls and situations.

Most vocabularies have more than enough "downer" words. Most of us know how to put down, nag, demean, cuss and criticize to beat the band. I've been present when otherwise decent and even pious persons have let fly with a vocabulary that effectively grounds someone into the dust. Most try to keep those attack words under wraps, lest they pop out and do more harm than good.

In many ways our working vocabulary paints a vivid picture of the depths or shallowness of our souls—the intent and stance we bear toward others—the real character of the actual person we are.

I recommend the removal of most first person references from our communication—instead using words of the second person: "You." The more we say "you" the less we sound like an egotist. Some are so preoccupied with "I" and "me" and "mine" they just never get around to "you" and "your."

AN EMPTY VESSEL

There is a popular notion that just being alive gives one worth. A person can be empty-headed and totally bereft of anything of value to others, and still be considered as worthy and worthwhile.

Well, that's a noble ideal—a very democratic statement of human worth. But in the arenas of real life, it just won't wash. It's not acceptable. While it might be a step up from being full of one's self, emptiness is not big in the marketplaces of life—neither in the world of commerce nor in the world of ideas.

The Word of God is emphatic about empty vessels. They translate into empty minds and hearts, and empty talkers—and the most they can offer is empty counsel and consolation. In Zechariah 10:2 we read:

> **For the idols utter nonsense, and the diviners see lies; the dreamers tell false dreams, and give empty consolation. Therefore the people wander like sheep; they are afflicted for want of a shepherd.**

To aspire to be nothing—in effect, to be an empty vessel—is of no value to anyone, neither ourselves nor others.

Part of the genius and glory of living is that we fill our minds, our hearts and our lives with good things—matters that will benefit not only ourselves but others.

IMPORTANCE OF THE CHURCH

I really got a kick out of the sign that appeared in front of a church: "You aren't too bad to come in. You aren't too good to stay out."

Every common, ordinary sinner—and every common and extraordinary sinner—needs the church, simply because the church offers the only answers to the two greatest problems of your life and mine.

The first problem is the sin problem. We are created to be accountable—to live reverently, righteously and productively. But we all have failed, and have committed sins big and little.

Only the church offers the solution to our sin problem. That solution is found in Jesus Christ, Who is the main focus and subject matter of any church worth its salt.

The second problem we all have is the death problem. As wonderful as life might be, we're all heading for its certain termination.

What a waste, what a shame! In Romans 7:24 Paul asks the momentous question: "Who will rescue me from this body of death?" In the very next verse he states the only answer: "Thanks be to God—through Jesus Christ our Lord!"

When anyone has a serious problem, they are pretty foolish to just ignore it. You and I have two life and death problems. We'd best not ignore them.

A SUMMARY OF LIFE

A youngster arrived back home after his first day of Kindergarten. When asked how it went, he described it graphically: "Well, we sang a while. Then we cried a while. Then we sang a while."

That sounds like a pretty accurate summary of life. We do seem to ping pong back and forth between times of joyful song and times of sorrow and trouble—times when we can't help but cry a little.

Psalm 30:5 sums it up: "Weeping may remain for a night, but rejoicing comes in the morning."

I suppose there's a sense in which the world is like a big Kindergarten—a place to ask and learn. For sure we humans are slow learners, individually and collectively. When we are young we ask lots of questions—but as we grow older we think we know it all, and stop searching for the meaning and sense of life.

Maybe this is one of the reasons Jesus put so much emphasis on childlike approaches to God and all of life. In Matthew 18 we read:

> **He called a little child and had him stand among them. And He said: "I tell you the truth, unless you change and become like little children, you will never enter the kingdom of heaven."**

ACTS OF KINDNESS

Most of us have no trouble generating acts of mischief, expressions of criticism, and bushels of gossip and even hatemongering that at best are 10% truth and 90% fiction. We can be sure that eventually these will boomerang on us.

But what about acts of kindness. Have you done any of those today—or maybe in the past week or so?

Psalm 109 is one of what we call "The Imprecatory Psalms," in which the petitioner asks God's judgment on persons who delight in evil. The Psalmist writes of someone who "never thought of doing a kindness, but hounded to death the poor and the needy and the brokenhearted. He loved to pronounce a curse—may it come on him; he found no pleasure in blessing—may it be far from him." Ouch!

The Bible is harsh with those who live without the graces of compassion, mercy and kindness.

God is described as kind. In Isaiah 54 the prophet hears God's words of comfort: "'With everlasting kindness I will have compassion on you,' says the Lord your Redeemer."

That's exquisite! In Col 3:12 we are advised: "Therefore, as God's chosen people, holy and dearly loved, clothe yourselves with compassion, kindness, humility, gentleness and patience."

Are those your main items of clothing? If so, you indeed are well dressed!

BEFORE YOU GROW OLD

My mother must have told me dozens of times, "Bob—some day you'll grow old." She was a very wise woman—and she was right.

In case you should be privileged to grow old—and if that blessing includes keeping your wits about you in the process—listen to some kindly counsel.

The good that you can better do while younger, do it now. Perhaps it cannot be done with advancing age.

Learn the true meaning of love, and express it to your dear ones often. When you are old, you can give it—but folks around you might suspect that you are simply cramming for your finals.

Before you grow old learn the relative value of money and possessions, of friends and friendships, of the hug and laughter of a child, of prayer and worship, of faith and folly, of forbearance and forgiveness.

As you contemplate the latter years, remember that what you have been in the earlier years of your life, you will be in your later years—only a lot more so.

That counsel is in line with a comment of Rip Van Winkle, a character created by Washington Irving: "A tart temper never mellows with age, and a sharp tongue is the only edged tool that grows keener with constant use."

DAYS FOR GRATITUDE

Scattered across our nation are memorials to men and women who died in the service of our nation. They are intended to remind us of enormous sacrifices made for the preservation of our freedoms.

I've never been a bona fide, died in the wool pacifist who believes in peace at any cost—especially if it means meek submission to tyrants. I know human nature too well to believe as a friend of mine did—that if we just lay down all our arms and destroy our defenses, our enemies will be so impressed they'll do the same.

Would that human nature would accommodate such a belief. We have no choice but to side with the prophet Jeremiah, who quoted the Lord's assessment:

> **The heart is deceitful above all things, and desperately wicked: who can know it?** (Jeremiah 17:9, KJV)

Millions have suffered and perished in what are deemed just wars, because the intent was to put tyrants out of business. Other millions have suffered and died in foolish wars, instigated and carried on by the pride and utter stupidity of leaders.

Just or unjust, wise or foolish, the victims of all wars must be honored for their sacrifices and sufferings.

Let all our days—and especially Memorial Days—be days of deep and heartfelt gratitude.

A MATTER OF TASTE

When you think about it, religious faith is mainly a matter of taste.

In the first place, it's tasteful to hang on to convictions that make some sense out of life when nothing else can.

It is extremely distasteful to think that we are like the lowest of life forms—we abide awhile, and then nothing—oblivion.

Secondly, the most worthwhile people I have ever known or read about have been persons with a sense of completeness that only a deep faith can provide. They all had exquisite taste about the meaning and outcomes of life. I'll work and fellowship with them any time.

Mournful futility and empty skepticism are just plain tasteless in my book.

Then there's the invitation of Psalm 34:8: "O taste and see that the Lord is good."

A point of that verse is that until we have truly experienced the glory and beauty of God, we will never know how sweet it is. It goes along with the statement in Psalm 119:103: "How sweet are Your words to my taste, sweeter than honey to my mouth!"

I fear that a great many people come to the end of their lives with a sour, bitter taste in their mouths—simply because they've never discovered the taste thrill of a marvelous faith.

A SCALE OF VALUES

How we operate in any relational area is determined largely by our scale of values.

So, what comes first? Money? Pride? Advantage and power?

Many put economics, tradition, prejudice and pride before any value they might place on respect of other persons and their rights and needs.

Every act of heroism is an expression of a person's scale of values. Jesus told stories or parables illustrating contrasting values. A man was attacked by thieves as he traveled a lonely road. For sure, the thieves were acting on the basis of a certain set of values.

Several individuals came by, saw the injured person, and hurried on their way. Part of the thrust of what Jesus is teaching is that those characters were on about the same value scale or level as the thieves.

Then there came along a person from another culture, another society. By prejudice and tradition he had every reason to avert his eyes and hurry on his way. But he did not. He stopped, even though the attackers might still be lurking about. He tended the man's wounds. He put him on his donkey and took him to an inn—and then paid for the man's stay and care. (Read Luke 10:30-37)

Now—who do you suppose was living by the highest scale of values? "The expert in the law replied, 'The one who had mercy on him.' Jesus told him, 'Go and do likewise'"

CHILDHOOD MEMORIES

What kind of memories do you cherish from your childhood? Who stands out, and what makes up the best of those memories?

The other day I read a line from Gail Grenier Sweet that is very instructive. "Children will not remember you for the material things you provided but for the feeling that you cherished them."

Being cherished and loved certainly are the most prominent of all childhood memories. The setting may be the beach, the fishing or hunting trip, the Christmas celebrations or whatever—but the feelings that prevailed in those situations are what make the memories cherished and wonderful.

What I remember about my grandfather was his studied indifference to his grandchildren. His signals contrasted with those from my grandmother. She doted on us, and made it clear in many ways how much she loved us.

Maybe those memories motivate me. I want to be remembered well by my own grandchildren. I want their memories to be clear about our feelings and attitudes of affection and joyful sharing. We would not try to "buy them" with expensive gifts even if we could afford it.

Gail Sweet's comment is worth a lot of thought by parents and grandparents: "Children will not remember you for the material things you provided but for the feeling that you cherished them."

NO MORE ALONE

Sorting through some old writings the other day, I came across some free verse that I wrote years ago—and which continues to express my faith. I call it, "No More Alone."

I sat alone in the darkness of the night,
My fears and insecurities deviling my soul.
I knew no peace, no hope and little good—
And then He came and changed it all.

I joined with shepherds at His birth,
With disciples hearing wisdom from on high.
I stood in temple courts, and then beneath a cross
And watched as holy sacrifice was made.

I visited an empty tomb, and heard the angel cry:
"He is not here, for He has risen!" And
Wondering, fearing it might all be just a dream,
I stood with His disciples in an upper room—

Waiting for His appearing, His assuring word
That reality still is shaped by God despite
Our unbelief and impudence—our pointless
Striving to become as gods, knowing all.

He came and spoke His words of peace—
Showing wounds of sweet redemption in
His Hands and side, torn for my salvation,
For my eternal destiny—and I no more alone.

AWE AND MYSTERY

Do you know one reason it's good for us to attend worship services regularly? It's because we all need a sense of awe and mystery in our lives. We benefit immensely by getting away from the trite and trivial, and confronting the Presence of the Almighty.

In worship services there are readings, hymns and prayers that pull us out of our ruts, and point us toward eternal truths—to full and complete reality.

We live such partial lives, such a segmented existence. And then we enter the sanctuary of God's Holy Place of Worship, and we feel drawn toward the mysteries of Word, Spirit and Sacrament. It can be one of the most enriching times of the week if we will let it. It fills our lives. It refreshes our souls. It reminds us that we are more than mere animals—that we have been created in the Image of the Holy God—made to reach out for awe and mystery.

The church's offerings of worship draw us back to the adoration of what we do not fully understand, confronting us with complexity and eternity.

So make worship a weekly habit. Let your innermost being come in contact with the awe and mystery from which we all came, and to which we will all someday go.

Ephesians 1:9 puts it well: "For He has made known to us in all wisdom and insight the mystery of His will, according to His purpose which He set forth in Christ as a plan for the fulness of time, to unite all things in Him. . ." (RSV)

BEING SUPPORTIVE

One cannot be on the receiving end of a supportive effort by others without actually being included in that system—so that from time to time one will be called on to bear the burdens of others, to help them through their particular problem, hassle, heartache or whatever. So what does it take?

One has to know the difference between being helpful and taking over.

Being supportive does not mean running the lives of others, and making their decisions for them. There is always a recognition of the dignity and rights of the persons with whom we are relating—along with a determined effort to avoid becoming a long-term crutch.

The aim is not relieving others of their basic, God-given responsibilities to make their own decisions, carry through, and be accountable for them.

We also have to avoid the "quick fix" approach. The last thing people want when they're hurting are the old saws, the pat cliches. Silence is often more helpful than trite verbiage.

Most importantly, we must be there when we're needed.

Have you ever had someone tell you how much they care about you and even love you—then as soon as things got a bit rough they did the old disappearing act? Actions really do speak louder (and much more effectively) than words!

1-GRUP

CHOICES

"Choice" is one of the most beautiful words in the English language, precisely because choice is so closely tied to freedom.

Adam and Eve were given true freedom because they had choices. Granted, it was a perilous option, but so it is with many of our situations of choice today. To be able to choose means we are free. Wise and careful choices keep us free.

People have made some strange choices down through human history. Moses chose to identify with his people, rather than continuing in the royal palaces of Egypt. Judas chose to betray Jesus. Peter chose to deny his Lord.

Our Lord chose the cross. Joan of Arc chose to maintain her stand even in the face of certain death. Martin Luther chose to stick with the Word of God. Dr. Albert Schweitzer chose to work in darkest Africa, when he could have had Europe at his feet.

And then the choices of hundreds of volunteers who fight fires, rescue people from drowning, and take enormous risks for total strangers. Most heroes have made choices that are matters of life and death.

We need to be careful with the small choices, so when the big ones come our way we'll handle them well. Jesus tells us to be faithful in the small choices of life, and then we will be ready for the heroic.

The most significant choice of Christians is to choose Jesus.

CREDITING THE LORD

There is a sense in which we need to be very careful about crediting the Lord with things that happen in our lives.

In my years of working with all kinds of people I've heard the Lord credited with the strangest things. There are persons who have conned others, connived and manipulated, and then credited the Lord for giving them such marvelous success, I think they have their theology screwed on backwards.

I've known high school kids who have gone all the way sexually. Then, in their fear of pregnancy, prayed like the dickens. When they are sure there will be no baby, they give God the credit. But when a pregnancy does result from their folly, they blame God, and wonder why He let them down this time!

People get into the riskiest kinds of business ventures and presume on God's protection and provision. When things do not go well, they wonder: (A) what's wrong with their faith?—or (B) What's wrong with God?

The problem is their faith is not knowledgeable enough to know that God does not bless and sanctify our foolishness!

He expects us to use our heads as well as our hearts, to respond to His guiding principles more than to our own "want list."

EMPATHY

"Empathy" should be one of the most important words in your vocabulary, And it should also be among the very best of your skills.

Empathetic people make the best type of friends, as well as the most helpful of professional persons. They add the essential ingredient of genuine understanding to almost any kind of social situation.

When one can honestly comprehend the feelings of others, and, so to speak, walk in their shoes, then one is empathetic.

The opposite of empathetic is to be unfeeling, and therefore quite likely uncaring.

It may seem cool to be aloof and uninvolved—to deal with others in a very logical and lofty fashion. But that doesn't make a very attractive or helpful personality. Most people want to sense that others feel with and for their problems.

Most deliberately avoid empathy by building walls and drawbridges against the intrusion of feelings and concern for others.

Jesus Christ calls us to lower the drawbridge and break down the walls, to let concern for others work in our lives. Sometimes costly? Yes. But it develops in us the makings of the most beautiful of all earthly beings—a son or daughter of God. When we encourage empathy in our minds and hearts, we're getting very close to the mind and heart of the Almighty.

TRUE FRIENDSHIPS

Jesus gave His greatest compliment and honor to His disciples when He called them "Friends"—not servants, or followers, but friends.

Friends are an important asset to anyone's life. They are people who know us thoroughly, and yet accept us just as we are—and we do the same for them. They do not take advantage of us, but they are there when we need them—and we are there when they need us. Friendship is a two way street. To have friends, one must be a friend.

Someone wrote that the quickest way to wipe out a friendship is by sponging on it! Using, manipulating, selfish people lose potential friends quickly. They want servants, not friends.

I'm not sure it's possible to maintain a great many genuine, close relationships, because real friendships take time and effort. They have to be nurtured and maintained.

Depending on one's energy, time and other resources, two or three friendships may be all that most of us can handle.

But there is one friendship that every one of us ought to seek and maintain: friendship with Jesus. He said, "I have not called you servants, but friends."

Probably most of us would feel honored if some famous personality declared his or her friendship with us. Well, there's none greater than Jesus!

WALKING ON THE WATER!

Jesus did some strange things, and expects us to do likewise.

Remember the time our Lord walked on the sea? He gave the disciples the scare of their lives. The disciples didn't recognize Him at first, and cried out in fear, thinking that He was some kind of ghost. (See Matthew 8:23-27) .

He did other strange things.

He went to a party and changed water into wine when the host ran out.

He went to funerals and raised the dead back to life. He violated the customs of the day, even discussing deep religious matters with a Samaritan lady of ill repute.

Jesus drove money changers from the Temple, told the religious elite that prostitutes would enter heaven, but they wouldn't make it. He confounded everybody by allowing Himself to be crucified—and then coming back to life!

Simon Peter asked Him for the power to walk on water, and Jesus told him to get out of the boat and simply do it. But Peter became frightened, and sank into the waters. Then Jesus rebuked Peter for his lack of faith. (See Matthew 14:25-33)

It takes faith to walk on the stormy waters of life. Ordinarily You step out on the water and you sink! Just that simple! But Jesus says "Do it!' Keep the Faith and you'll walk on water!

VENTING ANGER

Anger is about as close to hate as we should ever get, and when we vent our anger—really unload to someone who has injured us in some way—what really comes out of our system is hate.

The best advice on handling your anger goes something like this: Do your very best to immediately recover some sense of humor about the whole situation, and allow that humor full play.

A man whose boat and motor were stolen placed the following advertisement in the classified section of his local newspaper:

> My boat and motor have disappeared from Martha Lake, Alderwood Manor, since June 10. I send my wishes that the boat breaks in half in mid-lake and that your mother is unsuccessful in attracting help as she runs barking along the shore. (from *Seattle Post Intelligence*)

Revenge becomes our preoccupation when someone wrongs us. Anger and thoughts of retribution against the other person take up just about all of our mental and emotional energy. That is terribly destructive to our own person.

Recover your humor as quickly as possible, use it in dealing with the situation, and then move deliberately and swiftly to the sheer emotional, psychological and spiritual strength that come to those who obliterate anger and its twin brother, hate, with the forgiveness lived and taught by the Christ.

ABUSE

I've known persons who are abusive in their speech, attitudes and actions toward their loved ones—yet blandly declare that they have not been abusive because they never physically struck anyone.

We must learn that abuse is often at its worst when it is psychological—when we batter at the personhood of others with the deadly weapons of meanness, anger and derision.

One father would say to his son with some frequency and no small amount of sarcasm: "If there's a wrong way to do a job, you'll find it!" Can you imagine the life impact of that kind of "fatherly" declaration?

Abuse can also be passive, in which we withhold praise and affirmation. Our silence can hurt and even condemn. Aggressively passive abuse wreaks destructive havoc in the personalities and lives of others.

The call of Jesus Christ is to a warmth and tenderness that recognizes the total scope of abuse, and steadfastly refuses to indulge in either active or passive kinds of abusive behaviors.

The Word of God instructs us: "Love one another." When we love on God's terms—which is the only way to genuinely love—the total wellbeing of the other is our major concern.

Make no mistake about it—so-called "love" that dishes out abuse of any kind, is no love at all.

COPING WITH STRESS

Ordinarily we can divide stress inducing situations into four categories: deprivation—when we need something essential and somehow we are not getting it; frustration—when a situation leads us to feelings of helplessness and of not being in control; conflict—when we have to choose between equally appealing events or persons; and pressures—when we feel hassled by our inner psyche—or by persons, events or standards outside of ourselves.

Two important variables of stress are its time-span and its intensity. If intense stress is experienced over a long time, its affects on our life systems are going to be close to devastating—especially if we just let it ride, and don't counter attack with solution oriented approaches.

But many experience stressful conditions of mild intensity over long periods of time, and because they are fairly low in intensity, persons are able to cope with relative ease.

But it's wise to keep in mind that all distress factors impact us adversely. They are eroding our powers, leading us to feelings of distress, and creating difficulties in a variety of ways.

So it's best to face up to our problems, share them with trusted friends or our pastor, and then move deliberately toward a resolution of whatever problems or difficulties are inducing the stress.

Avoiding reality eventually intensifies stress.

STRESS MANAGEMENT

Stress impacts everyone, and it's essential for healthy living that we be able to handle stress effectively.

Stress is a physical, emotional and mental condition created by demands made on us for adjustment—especially to new and trying circumstances. A stressful condition may arise from stress-inducing factors inside of us, such as illness or needless worry—or from factors outside of us, such as financial troubles, job loss, marriage tensions and other challenges.

Stress symptoms range from loss of sleep to extreme touchiness or depression. We need to deal not just with those symptoms, but with the situations that cause and sustain the stress.

I recommend three main approaches to resolving stress and minimizing its unhealthy impact on our lives.

First, be honest with yourself as to what might be troubling you. Don't kid yourself about it, or repress it for such reasons as pride or fear.

Secondly, talk to someone about it—a trusted loved one, a friend or your pastor. The results of stress often are compounded when we try to carry the load all by ourselves.

The third concern is to be solution-oriented about the matters that are inducing the stress. Most people discover to their immense relief that they have a much greater capacity and potential for solving problems than they ever dreamed.

COVETING

One of the Ten Commandments admonishes, "Thou shalt not covet," and then goes on to list things that belong to others and relationships we should not covet or long for.

Coveting is desiring something for yourself that really belongs to someone else—and you want it so badly, that you would be quite willing that the other person not have it, so you could!

Covetousness can be such serious wanting that it amounts to idolatry. The more one covets, the more one is willing to set aside values and principles in order to get what one wants. Covetousness ultimately means a willingness to compromise all faith principles that derive from true belief in Almighty God in order to satisfy our coveting spirit.

Covetousness also causes us to see people as non-persons, as mere pawns to be manipulated in order that we achieve our desires. Covetousness loses sight of the value and importance of persons, as well as losing sight of the place and role of God.

Covetousness produces some ugly scenes. I have conducted funerals for persons whose wealth the relatives were already squabbling over. They would not even sit together at the funeral, so strong was their greed.

With all the grace, discipline and powers at your disposal, steer clear of this destructive force—the sin of covetousness!

OBFUSCATION

My radio listeners and readers know that occasionally I like to look into unusual words. Here's one: "obfuscation." Just roll that one around a bit. It's one of those words that sounds quite a lot like what it means: that which is obscured, muddled, murky or darkened.

Many persons seem to be good at obfuscating instead of clarifying.

Have you ever heard someone answer a question, and when they finally stopped talking it dawned on you that you knew even less about the matter than before they started out?

The world is full of obfuscators. Politicians are often adept at obfuscating. Many doctors forget that their patients haven't been to medical school, and they obfuscate.

Obfuscation is also the fine art of hedging, avoiding the main issues, making black sound like white or gray.

Jesus had some advice about obfuscation. In Matthew 5:37 He told His disciples, "But let your statement be, 'Yes, yes' or 'No, no'; and anything beyond these is evil." He was warning against obfuscatory practices such as clouding the issue, double speak, avoidance and muddled ideas.

Some years ago there were a lot of bumper stickers around that read, "Eschew obfuscation." "Eschew" means to avoid or shun something. In other words, "Stick to the clear, unvarnished and unclouded truth." Good advice!

DELAYING THE INEVITABLE

Have you ever played the games with yourself along the lines of procrastination—of delaying the inevitable? Procrastination is familiar territory to many persons!

I heard a spoof announcement the other day, that went like this: "The re-scheduled meeting of the Procrastinators Club has been postponed until further notice."

Procrastination is one thing—delaying the inevitable is sometimes quite another. We don't want to do what needs to be done, so we stall. We institute delay tactics that supposedly keep the matter at a distance from us.

Students delay studying for exams because there are other things of greater interest. They putz around, doing this and that—anything but what needs to be done, and must be done.

Some delay going to the dentist. They fear the experience, and while they're stalling, mouth conditions are only getting worse.

Persons also delay the inevitable when it comes to medical check-ups, preparing income tax reports, making a will, cleaning the house, mowing the lawn, answering letters, paying bills—and other inevitable demands on their lives.

Now one thing we know for sure: almost always delay compounds the difficulty—making matters worse, not better. In all truth, delaying the inevitable is a sign of weakness, not strength. It's a mark of the undisciplined life.

PERILOUS PROCRASTINATION

Procrastinating on inconsequential demands is one thing. Procrastination on major matters, such as concerns and time lines that can produce dreadful consequences, is quite another.

There come times in everyone's life when one takes a look at the important things that haven't gotten done. Too many wait until zero hour, when it's too late to do much about it.

I remember vividly the day I had to catch the Rocket, a train running on the Rock Island Line from the Twin Cities to the south. I was headed home for the holidays. But I procrastinated, doing odd jobs in my college room. I finally caught the bus for the train station, ran for the gate and beheld—emptiness. The last train for the day had gone! My procrastination cost me a whole day of my holidays at home.

There is such a thing as "perilous procrastination"—the kind for which we pay an enormous, sometimes dreadful price.

The most important decision we make in our entire lives is the decision to accept or reject Jesus Christ as Savior, and follow Him as Lord.

Procrastination on that matter can be the most perilous, foolish waste of your life. There will come a time when you will hear the horribly sad words, "Too late. You must bear the consequences of your procrastination."

MESSED UP!

It used to be that when someone said they were "messed up" it meant that their clothes were disarrayed, or their hands dirty, or their hair out of place.

But in current usage to be "messed up" means that one's total life is out of whack and in a sorry state.

We can get messed up in many ways: when we don't exercise proper control and discipline in our lives; when emotions and "the wants" take over and rule our minds and actions; when we decide to go against God's will and ways.

We also get messed up when we refuse to face reality—when we insist on living in a make believe world.

Typical messed up scenarios: the person who believes that he or she should be "happy" all the time, and on his or her terms; or someone who believes that marriage ought to be just the way he or she fantasizes it.

And then there are thousands of people every year who manage to clear up the messes in their lives with Christ's help.

Life often demands a big clean-up, clear-up job, and we need all the help we can get. The best help of all is the Lord of life, Jesus.

Messed up? Turn to Him, confess it, tell Him that you're determined to clean it all up, and ask His help.

PART OF THE CURE?

The more thoughtful among us wonder occasionally whether we are part of the curse—or part of the cure! And really, in the specific as well as the general, that is a very good question to ask with some frequency in our lives.

And let's be honest—there are times when very definitely we are part of the curse. We cause problems and pain for others. We impede progress. We inflict grief and heartache. And most often it is inadvertent. We did not intend harm.

When we're "part of the cure" in life we land on the side of healing and building. We are constructive, not destructive. We enhance lives, we don't blight them.

I've known persons who seem determined to be "curse oriented" in their approaches to life and to other persons. Apparently they enjoy rocking boats, raising picayune issues, casting doubts, creating shadows and generally raining on everybody's parade.

The call of Jesus Christ to each of us is to be part of the cure, not the curse! He calls us to heal, forgive, to make our life surroundings more beautiful and to ease the pain and sorrow of life for others.

Our lives are enormously fulfilled and satisfying when we side with the cure in all situations.

A CHILD'S BEHAVIOR

Susan and I were dining in a restaurant in Sioux Falls, and noted the good behaviors of three small children. Their mother was with them—and during the entire meal she did not have to offer one word of instruction or rebuke. Those three children just knew what was expected of them, and behaved accordingly.

As we were leaving, I stopped by their booth and complimented the mother on the fine behavior of her children. She said, "Well it helps when they are hungry." And we all laughed.

But there is a profound truth embedded in what she said. Yes, they were hungry—but they also were being fed what they needed for training in social matters.

The behaviors of children relate to hunger and satisfaction—but not just for food. Children also hunger for attention, for love, for discipline—for signs of acceptance and rewards for doing their best.

It is true that when a child's hungers are being met, his or her behavior is much more in keeping with the training parents have offered. Deny a child who is hungry for basic needs, and orneriness and rebellion quickly appear on the scene.

That woman's children seemed wonderfully relaxed and happy—and we had more than a suspicion that they were well fed, in all ways.

A CHURCH'S REPUTATION

Every church has some kind of reputation. I've heard of "dead churches," "live churches," "friendly churches," "unfriendly churches"—and even "country club churches."

Does the way you live show what your church is like? In some cases that might be a good thing—in others an unmitigated disaster. What would you *want* your church to be known for?

I would want some of these descriptors for my church:

> "They really love people." "They are the most forgiving and redeeming bunch I've ever known." "The people in that church are so sympathetic and helpful!" "They take their faith seriously." "When I'm in that church and among its people I feel that I am in the Presence of Christ."

Can you make any of those assessments about your church?

In I Thessalonians chapter 1 Paul tells that church: "You became a model to all the believers in Macedonia and Achaia. The Lord's message rang out from you not only in Macedonia and Achaia—your faith in God has become known everywhere."

This area has a lot of beautiful churches. But what really counts is the faith and works of the people—how well they express and serve the living Christ. That is how a church gets the reputation it deserves.

A HABITAT OF HABITS

A habitat is what we live in, what surrounds us, our total environment. Habitat is related to habits—meaning the customary ways in which we do things—our regular and unchanging mannerisms.

Whether or not we like it, the habits of our lives make up a great deal of our habitat—the overall milieu of our living.

We all have good habits and bad habits—habits that are uplifting and habits that are downright destructive.

At first habits are matters of choice. But over a period of time, they make the choices for us. They have become the masters and directors of our living.

And it's strange how for the most part we fall into bad habits with a certain ease and even flair—but not so with good habits. They require thought and effort—and sometimes demand changes in old habits that have not served us well. Someone wrote: "Good habits are usually intentionally formed; bad habits, we fall into."

Habits stick with us. I've known a host of people who look forward to a new year so they can get a fresh start on their old habits. A few even succeed!

And the final word—this from a fisherman: "Habits are either bobbers or sinkers, corks or lead. They hold you up or pull you down."

A LETTER FROM CHRIST

When I was just a kid my mother would occasionally say to me, "I can read you like a book." And I believe she could and did.

For the most part we are easily read—which means that persons who know us even casually have a pretty good idea of what's going on in our heads and hearts, what we really are up to, what we are after.

If what they are reading is greed, self-centeredness, hatefulness, pettiness and a vengeful temperament, we had better get our lives straightened out, and put out a new text for people to read.

Paul wrote to the church at Corinth:

> **You show that you are a letter from Christ, the result of our ministry, written not with ink but with the Spirit of the living God, not on tablets of stone but on tablets of human hearts.** (II Corinthians 3:3)

That's a marvelous tribute to place on someone's gravestone. "He Was A Letter from Christ." I suspect that far too many people have so lived that their tribute might read: "He never did anyone any serious harm—but on the other hand he never did anyone any serious good, either!"

A good question for all of us to ponder: "What are people reading as the text of my life?" We're at our very best when the comparisons tend toward the Christ.

A NEW LOOK AT FORGIVENESS

Have you ever heard someone disclaim any thought of forgiveness because there was just too much to forgive? It's a fact that people can do terrible things to each other—to the point where their actions seem unforgivable.

One of the most beautiful things that Jesus did on earth was to give us a new look at this whole matter of forgiveness. In the perspective of all He has forgiven us—plus what He has taught us about forgiveness—not for a moment can I imagine Jesus saying to someone: "You know, you're absolutely right. What that person did to you was so terrible, so hurtful, forgiving him should be the farthest thing from your mind. In this case, forget forgiveness."

Can you imagine Jesus saying such a thing? If you can, then it just might be that the Jesus in your mind and heart is merely an extension of your self—of your hangups, prejudices, wants and needs.

In all truth, the crowning achievement of forgiveness is forgiving when everything argues against it—exactly in the midst of those situations that are so humongous no one would blame you if you said, "I just can't." No one but God.

Paul wrote in Ephesians 4:32:

> **Get rid of all bitterness, rage and anger, brawling and slander, along with every form of malice. Be kind and compassionate to one another, forgiving each other, just as in Christ God forgave you.**

A PSALM OF A RESPONSIVE HEART

Occasionally some Scripture that I may have read many times sort of hits me right between the eyes. It was that way with Psalm 116.

The Psalmist starts right off with personal praise and a declaration of love for the Lord:

> **I love the Lord, for He heard my voice; He heard my cry for mercy. Because He turned His ear to me, I will call on Him as long as I live.**

Note how the Psalmist approached God with a "cry for mercy." I suspect that many of us come with a big want list. But we all need to cry for mercy as we seek the Lord.

Then the Psalmist wrote of his personal peace:

> **Be at rest once more, O my soul, for the Lord has been good to you. For you, O Lord, have delivered my soul from death, my eyes from tears, my feet from stumbling.**

The Psalmist then gave the response of his whole being:

> **How can I repay the Lord for all His goodness to me? I will lift up the cup of salvation and call on the Name of the**

> **Lord. I will fulfill my vows to the Lord in the presence of all His people.**

The 116th is a Psalm for us all!

ABOUT THAT GOLDEN RULE

The Golden Rule comes up quite often among people who are used to treating others shabbily, and then when they get treated that way they suddenly are wise about the implications of the Golden Rule—for their own best interests!

I believe that the Golden Rule suffers misapplication and abuse. Jesus taught: "Do unto others what you would have them do to you"—which simply means we should treat other persons the way we like to be treated.

We abuse the Golden Rule when we regard it as the essence of Christianity, a summation of Gospel meaning and imperatives. It's a good social rule, but minimal Christianity.

The Golden Rule is the rock-bottom minimum for human social conduct. It is not particularly religious or noble—much less Christian! It just makes good sense for all human relationships.

The Christian Faith pushes us much further than the Golden Rule! Authentic Christianity commands us to be concerned for people way beyond what we ourselves might expect from others—urging us to reach out beyond what we perceive as our own needs and to give full consideration to the needs of others as we relate to them.

The Golden Rule holds up a mirror—the Christian faith holds up a very clear window.

ADULTS AND TV

There is an abundance of material warning us about the impact of television on children, but very little about proper adult TV fare.

Some seem to think that as long as one is an adult, what one watches on television is irrelevant. Take in any and everything. It's only the small fry that might be damaged in one way or another.

Of course, this is sheer nonsense. Think about it. Have you ever come away from your television viewing feeling blue or depressed? Or have you come away with feelings of good humor and fun? Have you identified with a hero or victim so much that you had a yearning to be in on the action?

My point is that watching television program offerings has an impact on one's psyche—one's emotions and moods. When we consider the sick violence, trashy morals and inverted values expressed in a great many television programs, it is evident that mature adults ought to do some sifting and eliminating, being very choosy about what they watch.

There is a Scriptural passage that applies well to everything we see and read:

> **. . . whatever is true, whatever is noble, whatever is right, whatever is pure, whatever is lovely, whatever is admirable— if anything is excellent or praiseworthy—think about such things.** (Philippians 4:8)

ARTFUL DODGING— ARTFUL BLAMING

Etched into my memory is the cartoon showing a patient on the psychiatrist's couch. Evidently he has been lamenting about his failures and shortcomings—perhaps laying blame on everyone but himself. Suddenly the psychiatrist turns to him and exclaims, "Maybe you are inadequate!"

We are a culture of artful dodging and artful blaming. At times this may be amusing. But such conduct is ugly as sin—precisely because dodging one's responsibilities and blaming others when we are to blame constitute sin.

If all else fails, blame the devil. I've heard a lot of wailing about how "The devil made me do it."

Satan gets blamed for a lot of bad stuff we manage to do without his help. He approves, he applauds—but we did it without Satan having to lift a finger on our behalf. Too often we make the devil's work easy and convenient.

The societal blame game is really a kind of witch hunt. We are determined to find someone to blame who seems more worthy of evil shenanigans than we are—more capable of obtuseness, destructive behaviors and bad attitudes.

So if we cannot manage to pin our failings on a co-worker or a relative or some cultural bogeymen, we turn to the devil.

In all truth, he has not been in on it at all—the mischief and sins are our own accomplishments. But we can be very sure that our accomplishments cheer his heart!

ATTITUDE

I have noted that in ads offering work opportunities, there often are remarks about the job requiring a good attitude. Whether the ad is for a welder, a clerk, a farm helper or whatever, a good attitude is a requirement.

Why is "a good attitude" such an important character trait? Just a few answers should suffice.

• Attitude includes knowing and striving for the excellent, or it could be that we intend to get by with shoddy workmanship.

•Attitude sends signals about whether or not we have exaggerated ideas of our skills and importance.

•Attitude says everything about how we get along with fellow workers.

•Attitude determines our ability to work as a team in projects that demand cooperation and give and take.

Attitude also covers such matters as aggressive and even paranoid behavior, all kinds of ego problems, touchiness, trustworthiness, tendencies toward impulsiveness, prejudice against persons of other ethnic or racial backgrounds, casualness about cleanliness, respect for others' rights and space, how one handles truth—and more.

We may be a highly skilled worker in our field, but attitude could keep us from getting the job—or cause us to lose it. And often rightly so.

KEEP IN TOUCH!

We sometimes fail to assess the impact of parting on people who move away from friends and loved ones.

Our nine year old granddaughter and five year old grandson had to say goodbye to a host of friends in what had become their hometown just before they set out for their new home in India. I know that it was not easy as they tearfully asked their friends to "Keep in touch!"

As we have made our own moves in life, we learned that it has not been easy for friends and loved ones to keep in touch. We all lead busy lives. We make new friends. And even the most beautiful of memories fade.

But it's worth every effort to keep in touch with persons who have blessed and helped us, cared for and encouraged us.

There is a real sense in which our Heavenly Father urges us to keep in touch.

In the children's time on a recent Sunday I asked the youngsters how we keep in touch with God. They knew.

"Prayer." "Study our Bibles." "Be sure to come to worship." "Talk to others about Him." "Sing about Him and praise and thank Him."

Those children are off to a good start!

For all of us it's an essential of life to keep in touch with God.

YOUR PERSONAL VOCABULARY

We all have a personal vocabulary that speaks volumes about our convictions, our values, our hangups, sins and virtues.

Occasionally I hear someone spouting a vocabulary in which profanity is prominent and frequent. They are among the persons who cannot speak without a proliferation of cuss words. I call that not only a very limited vocabulary, but a dreadfully stupid and destructive one. Amazingly I've been in places of business where the owner spouts off with profanity as naturally as can be. Does he think that endears himself and his business to the customers that he certainly needs in order to stay in business?

Listen to yourself speak in various situations, and be sensitive to what words you seem to use the most often. That is a revealing exercise, and will help you to understand just how revealing your vocabulary is to persons around you—including loved ones, casual acquaintances and business associates.

Our personal vocabulary ought to include a proliferation of words that convey hope, encouragement, conviction, optimism, high values and all the best life has to offer.

In I Peter 3:10 we read, "Whoever would love life and see good days must keep his tongue from evil and his lips from deceitful speech." And that's a very good standard for our personal vocabulary. Would your personal vocabulary measure up to that counsel?

AVOIDING SIN

There is a three letter word that a lot of people like to avoid. The word is "sin." Most prefer "mistake" or "whoops!"

Obviously, we do well when we keep from sinning—but more often than not we simply beg the question when we avoid the word, the concept, the truth about sin.

Highly placed officials of the armed forces of our nation are really dancing around the word "sin." Not committing adultery, especially with men or women of lower rank, is spoken of as a regulation. I have not heard one commentator come even close to mentioning that it is a good regulation because adultery is sin.

We can call it "a breach of regulations," "inappropriate conduct," "bad behavior," "a destructive form of relating"—or anything else our minds might concoct.

But the Bible's word for it is "sin," and that conceptual word covers every other term or phrase we might use to describe it—and in the process obfuscate it.

The word "sin" applies to anything that creates a breach between us and God, between us and others, between us and our responsibilities and commitments in the lives we live. Sin is destructive. While adultery may seem to be a delightful pastime, apparently enriching an illicit, sinful relationship, it is a destroyer of persons, of meaningful and long term relationships, and of institutions.

Call a spade a spade. The correct appellation is "sin."

BALANCE

Balance is one of the key factors in any meaningful relationship.

In marriages or close friendships you can't have it all your way. A person who is fond of telling about his or her experiences at work should expect to be a good listener when the friend of spouse wants to tell about what's happening in his or her life.

Balance is also needed in matters of finance, dining, entertainment, socializing, hobbies and habits good and bad.

While we need to be careful not to force it into a phony 100% tit for tat matter, we all have to work at injecting balance into our relationships. These efforts may initiate some misunderstandings and a few battles, but both parties will come out winners if their aim is balance.

The achievement of workable, healthy balances in all that impacts a relationship requires big doses of patience, a will to understand, an attitude of concentration and interest, and a very forgiving heart and mind.

And obviously achieving balance demands that both parties participate and share in the effort. One spouse or one friend cannot be held solely responsible for the establishment of balance. And when there is slippage and reversion to old ways, the party who is responsible needs to 'fess up, receive forgiveness—and then both can get on with that most noble and essential relational pursuit—achieving balance.

WISDOM AND INVOLVEMENT

Occasionally we who parent and grandparent need reminders to carefully avoid the surrogacy syndrome. This goes into action whenever we want those kids we love to participate in some favorite activity of ours. They may not care for it, but we do—so out of courtesy on their part and coercion on ours, they go for it.

One of the most unfair things folks foist on their children is getting them to do our heart's desire, rather than their own.

Many a child has engaged in special activities out of deference to parents—with the parents getting their jollies from what amount to the surrogate sacrificial offerings of the offspring.

As the youngsters get involved, help them to set priorities for school and other activities. Be alert to possible overloading and over scheduling on the part of your children. Some want to do everything and then some. Sit down with your children and talk about it.

Remember that you may have to give advice and even direction about choices and their relative long term impact, along with the need for balance and variety.

An important part of life is learning to assess and assign values to time and energy involvements. It's just common sense that some are much more valuable and life enriching than others—accompanying the child into the coming years, while others are left behind.

WEATHERED FRIENDS

As far as I know I'm the first to use the phrase "weathered friends." And there are many valid comparisons of weather and friends.

When I was a kid, a sailor relative taught me the song that goes, "Shipmates stand forever, don't give up the ship! Friends in stormy weather, we won't give up the ship!"

I hope everyone has at least one "stormy weather friend." They stand by you in the wildest times. I treasure my stormy weather friends—and I need them.

I found this comment by an unknown writer: "No enemy is more dangerous than a friend who isn't quite sure is he's for you or against you."

There also are fair weather friends—with you when the seas are calm, and the journey smooth. But they are off like a shot when the going gets rough. Obviously a bit cynical, someone wrote: "When you're down and out something always turns up—and it's usually the noses of your friends."

Believe it—fair weather friends are no asset in anyone's life.

Best of all are weathered friends—who have been with you and stood by you through all the storms, calms and journeys of life. They know the value of friendship, and they are bent on being the best of friends. I hope you have an abundance of them.

BREADTH OF SPIRIT

Jesus spoke about breadth of character and personality, and rebuked those whose lives manifested narrowness, haughtiness and pride.

Along that line, when you're on the street, in a place of business or wherever, whom do you greet with warmth and heartiness? Just the people you know—or perhaps only the persons who dress and look like you'd want to know them? They're "your kind" you know.

What characterizes persons who encounter your silence, your turning away—or at best a grudging "Hello"?

In His Sermon on the Mount Jesus taught His followers: "If you love only those who love you, what good is that? Even scoundrels do that much. If you are friendly only to your friends, how are you different from anyone else? Even the heathen do that." And then He sums it all up by stating: "But you are to be perfect, even as your Father in heaven is perfect." (Matthew 5:46-48 RSV)

Could it be that in many ways Jesus regards the Christian life as living outside humanity's most common faults and foibles—that in many, many matters we are to disregard rights and justifications and rationalizations and do what for many is the unthinkable and unpleasant?

And even more remarkably, it sounds very much as though Jesus regards these surprise moves on our part as at least the beginnings of perfection.

BUILDING AN IDENTITY

Think about it—we spend a lifetime building an identity, the real and complete person we want to be known as. Our identity is never perfect. But it can be close to what we want to be known as and known for.

Every choice we make, the ways we spend our money, our work attitudes, our relationships and how we handle them—all these and more go into the identity by which we are known.

The most important elements in one's identity are the values and standards we choose and by which we live. When persons are known mainly for negative factors, it should not surprise them. They have built and maintained that identity. It's theirs—and quite likely for keeps.

The same as true for those whose identity is known for the good things they do, the high values they hold, their attitudes of caring and compassion, their acts of kindness and helpfulness.

These are excellent question for all of us to think about: What do I want to be known as—to be known for? When others sum up who I am, what are the features I want them to note—and the characteristics that I do not want to be known for?

It's very important to know who we are—and that who we are is who we really want to be—and that others know our real identity

WARINESS AND POLITICS

Most people the world over have a certain wariness about politics and politicians—and rightfully so. Politics involves the quest to govern and control, the quest for power and authority. It can and has led to all sorts of corrupting power plays in which people have been deprived of rights and even enslaved.

In our democratic system, all politicians bear watching by the electorate. The politicians have much to gain and the people have a great deal to lose. Wariness is definitely in order.

While purported misdeeds and various kinds of chicanery should be checked out through judicial means, you can be certain that most of those doing the checking have political motivations.

There are times when the people must call for a halt to obvious political gamesmanship that will have a destructive impact on our nation. Monetarily, these investigations and special committees are costly. But when it comes to rationality and common sense they could cripple our nation.

Ever since George Washington and Thomas Jefferson, most people with the moxie, wisdom and wherewithal to govern have a skeleton or two in their closet. Let's face it—those elected to govern are sinners, not saints—human beings, not robots or puppets.

There is a need to be wary—but not irrational or willfully blind.

COMMUNION OF THE SAINTS I

Susan and I spent part of Holy Week, 1998, in Wales. Palm Sunday we worshiped in St. Teilo's Church in Swansea, where I was privileged to deliver the sermon. We truly experienced Christian fellowship, shared beliefs and aspirations.

Just before we had visited the Brecon Cathedral—where we stood, as it were, with saints who had worshiped on that spot since the Norman conquest of 1066.

The key word is "continuity." Surrounded by reminders of centuries of Christian presence and witness, we felt immersed in the values and high hopes to which they aspired. Standing in such a cathedral with its soaring arches and magnificent furnishings, can make one very thoughtful of the realities in that ancient creedal phrase, "communion of the saints."

On Good Friday we again experienced that communion as we worshiped in the Cathedral of St. Peter in Bremen, Germany. A church has been on this spot since the early 8th Century. Along with the city of Bremen, the great Cathedral suffered much destruction from the bombings of World War II. More than 62% of Bremen was demolished, and great loss of life and injuries were suffered by the populace.

That suffering, along with all the sufferings of humanity, impact the communion of the saints.

I hope that awesome communion is part of your life.

COMMUNION OF THE SAINTS—II

Life can yield some awesome experiences if we will only be on the lookout for them.

Several years ago I was interim pastor of the Ebenezer Presbyterian Church in George, Iowa. One of the joys of that time of service was getting to know Henry Oehmsen, a German immigrant to America, who had been imprisoned by the Russians for 32 long months following the end of World War II.

Henry and Annegret now live part of the year in George—and the rest in Bremen, Germany.

On this past Easter Sunday Susan and I worshiped in the 700 year old Kirche of St. Urbanus in Dorum, Germany. We sat with Henry Oehmsen and Annegret—and were very mindful that this was Henry's home church—where as a child he was baptized, and then confirmed as a young lad. Henry calls the confirmation of those days "a graduation to long pants."

The day before we had stood on the very spot where Henry crossed from the Russian Sector into the British zone. A British soldier assured him, "You're free now."

Less than half of the Germans captured by the Russians ever made it home. yes, indeed—we truly experienced the communion of saints in that Dorum church.

BATTERED EMOTIONS

Part of what makes and keeps a society healthy is the exercise of good taste. Bad taste involves matters and expressions that deeply offend others—that cut down, trivialize and brutally mangle their emotions and sensitivities. Often there is little difference between battering a person physically and battering their emotions.

A case in point is the recent work of a newspaper cartoonist who was out to make his point against capital punishment—and especially for Timothy McVeigh and his crimes in the bombing of the Oklahoma City Federal Building.

The cartoon did a takeoff on the picture of the fireman cradling a dead child in his arms. The cartoonist has the child saying, "No more killing." And the fireman answers, "O shut up!"

The parents of the child in the picture protested, along with many others, including fire fighters from across the country.

Ever so reluctantly the cartoonist and newspaper officials finally apologized—although the cartoonist stated that if he had it to do over again, he would—which gives us a measure of his sensitivity and intelligence.

Why is it that many of the folks who ardently protest against the execution of vicious criminals have no reluctance whatsoever in battering the emotions of the victims of these cruel killers?

HAPPINESS IS A CHOICE

As with most of us, I've done my share of listening to gripers and complainers—most of whom in reality had little to complain about.

Along life's way I've also found that persons who really have the most right to complain, have the least to say. And it isn't so much that they bear it all silently and stoically—they've chosen happiness.

Every person needs to learn that happiness is a choice, not an accident. And conversely, so is unhappiness. We choose.

I've said to many groups something like this: "Every person in this place has a tragedy in their lives. Everyone has experienced horrible loss, or some form of spectacular trouble they could not avoid. We have no choice in those matters. But in the matter of how we stand up in the face of life's calamities, how we meet them and rise above them, the choice is ours to make and live."

Happiness has certain key ingredients. One of them is gratitude to God for the gift of life, no matter how troublesome it has been. He who forgets the language of gratitude can never be on speaking terms with happiness.

Another key ingredient is contentment. The person who is always afflicted with "the wants," will have a difficult time creating happiness.

Take charge of your life—and choose happiness.

THE CHURCH'S DANCE WITH CULTURE

One day I got to wondering about dancing. In these days of women taking on leadership roles denied them for so long. who leads on the dance floor—the man or the woman?

Perhaps in the contemporary forms of dancing, nobody leads because everyone is doing their own thing.

Some time ago I was contacted by a pastor whose friendship I treasure, and he expressed his sorrow at discovering that, in effect, his church was dancing with the culture, and that apparently the culture was doing the leading!

When confronted with a certain issue with stark moral overtones, most of his church board waffled in the twinkling of an eye—and in effect sided with cultural immorality—wrongdoing painted with the colors of acceptance and congenial permissibility.

Many branches of the Christian faith are experiencing a wild dance with the culture that surrounds the church and would invade it. And guess who is dancing in the lead role?

Every church, every denomination, needs to recommit to a leadership role in the culture, in which at the very least bad morals and worse thinking are not allowed to intrude into the theology, worship and practices of the Church of Jesus Christ.

CONCEPTS OF HIGH VALUE

I think of a "concept" as an idea or gathering of thoughts that has greater complexity and more force than a mere word would suggest.

There are what we call conceptual expressions, and there are concrete expressions. The concrete is much easier to understand. Words such as chair, pencil, desk, piano, automobile, truck and water are concrete words, and usually have a minimum of variety and complexity.

But think of words such as hope, love, truth, sacrifice, encouragement, service, redemption, faith, caring and concern. These and many other words like them are healthy, positive concepts, with a high degree of complexity and depth of meaning.

There are positive and negative concepts—the negative expressed by words such as hate, spite, meanness, deviltry, violence, crime, bitterness, anguish and troublesome.

We need to fill our minds, hearts and actions with concepts of the highest value. The world has more than enough of negative, damaging concepts. Fill your life with all that builds up, encourages and blesses folks around you.

There is a Bible verse that declares a very solemn and perceptive truth: "As a man thinks in his heart, so he is." To me that means each one of us is a collection of reality concepts, negative and positive. It's our choice as to what dominates our thinking and living—the negative or the positive.

HOLY AND COMMON

In Leviticus 10:10 we read: "You must distinguish between the holy and the common, between the unclean and the clean."

Right there is one of the most important challenges of life—we need to be discerning about what is holy and what is common, what is sacred and what is secular.

I've known people who insist that there is no difference. They assert that everything is sacred—and in their zeal for their position, they miss the point that this means everything is common. It's all the same. No difference.

Well, there is a difference. Most things, most experiences and happenings in life are common and ordinary. And then there are the sacred—those happenings and events that draw us close to God. There are experiences of God at work in our lives. They are sacred.

There also are places that are sacred. They have been set apart for those great happenings in our living. The naves of our churches are considered sacred. They are not place to play or goof off. The most significant passages of life take place in our churches, as well as meaningful times of worship and the sharing of the sacraments.

We need to know when we are on holy ground, when we're dealing with the sacred.

CONDUCT DISORDERS

Burt Smith joined three other young men from Kirksville, Missouri, in brutally murdering Rebecca Hauser of Marshall County, Iowa on October 4, 1994. He confessed to the crime. His companions are already serving time in prison.

But Burt appealed his sentence of life imprisonment, blaming his attorney for being ineffective throughout the trial and appeal—such as not pushing his youth hard enough. Burt was just a month short of 16 years when he joined in the savage killing of Mrs. Hauser.

The crowning criticism was that his lawyer should have offered more evidence about his "ailment." Burt Smith claims he suffered from "conduct disorder."

I'm bemused by this defense of a "conduct disorder." In my estimation, to a degree everyone suffers from that affliction.

Anyone who breaks one or more of the Ten Commandments suffers from a conduct disorder. Gossip mongers have a conduct disorder. But now and ultimately they are accountable for their destructive actions. Liars, thieves, adulterers and abusers are all "victims" of conduct disorders.

Behavioral or conduct disorders are among the greatest afflictions of the human race. Not one person is free of them. But most folks come to terms with societal demands for self-control and resistance to evil impulses—and they abandon their rationalizations and excuses of "conduct disorders."

TRULY MEMORABLE

Some years ago the world experienced a much needed lesson in expressing respect and grief for two persons whose influence was and is massive: Princess Diana of Wales and Mother Teresa of Calcutta, India.

The occasions of their deaths are memorable first of all because the common people of the world recognized and paid tribute to goodness.

The awesome reverence and stark grief accorded Diana and Mother Teresa were unprecedented in their focus on self-sacrifice, devotion to the poor and downtrodden—in effect, the plain, unvarnished goodness advocated by the Word of God.

We live in a time of dreadful cynicism, when the expected and normal reactions to the good a person has done are more apt to be disbelieving sneers, putdowns and criticism—rather than applause and praise.

So many in society salivate at opportunities for destructive criticism and harsh nit-picking directed at anyone who may display some considerable virtue. For far too many there seems to be a kind of dark satisfaction in scorning and deriding goodness, and concentrating on the flaws, failures and shortcomings of anyone who comes into the limelight.

The recent experiences taught us that it is far more blessed to find and praise good, rather than obliterate it with lurid tales of misdeeds and faults.

CULTIVATING SYMPATHY

To a certain extent the whole complex of a person's mind, emotions and attitudes is developed and cultivated. We may be born with the potential to love, care, sympathize and be considerate—but until and unless we work at these character traits, they will not blossom, let alone bear fruit.

One's capability for sympathy is a case in point. People have a range from unfeelingly coldhearted to highly sympathetic, in which they actually feel with a person's needs and discomforts, joys and sorrows.

You can be sure that from a Biblical point of view, coldheartedness is no virtue. But the quality or trait of sympathy is considered not only a virtue, but a necessary one for God's people.

In I Peter 3:8 we read: "Finally, all of you, live in harmony with one another; be sympathetic, love as brothers, be compassionate and humble."

Sympathy just "goes with" the other virtues we are to cultivate—love, compassion, harmony and humility.

There are some concept words and phrases that we may use to describe sympathy: a tender heart, an affectionate spirit, the ability to feel with the troubles and triumphs of others, and a caring heart.

Think now, on a scale of 1 through 10—1 being cold hearted and unfeeling, and 10 being highly, intensely sympathetic—how would you rate yourself on sympathy?

EDUCATION IN THE HOME

One of the most persistent myths of our society is that school is where children learn and home is where children do everything but learn.

There is a mythical corollary held by some who earnestly believe that school should be all fun. How many parents have you heard expressing the worry that their child is claiming that school is "boring"—"not any fun"—"too hard"—and that "their teacher just expects too much"? In most cases those are reasons to applaud the school! Education is not all fun and games, and the mission of the school is education.

And so with the home. One of the very first principles of home life is this: *Home is where the best and most important learning takes place.* Willy-nilly, parents are educators, teachers, models and examples—full time!

Home is where values are learned—where language and vocabulary are shaped—where children learn the true meaning of love and sacrifice—where faith is shaped and practiced—where the greatest issues and truths of life are imparted, explained and lived out.

Manners, or the lack of them are learned in the home. Attitudes are shaped there, as are prejudices, or the lack of them.

The greatest educational institution in the world is not some great university—but the home!

HEALTHY HUMOR

Probably most of us have known one or more persons whose sense of humor was abrasive and destructive. Such people use it to cut down, to diminish others, and to detract from whatever good there might be.

I believe that a sense of humor is one of the healthiest attributes a man or woman can have. But only if it is a healthy sense of humor, injecting wholesomeness and humorous clarity into a situation. If one's humor is destructive toward others, change is needed.

The comedian Red Skelton died recently. I remember his saying: "If I can't be funny and clean, I'll just be funny." He scorned the filth, the destructive putdowns and the socially harmful humor indulged in by many actors and humorists.

Healthy humor helps us laugh at the foibles of life, makes burdens lighter, and builds relationships. I marvel at how every good comedian has experienced deep sorrow and adversity in their lives.

Good humorists build on that deep knowledge of the trials and tribulations of the human spirit. They may even poke fun at human troubles out of the conviction they then are more easily overcome.

While good, healthy humor is intense in its clarity about the realities of life, it helps us rise above the forces that would pull us down.

KNOWING WHAT'S RIGHT

I occasionally hear someone ask, "How does one know what *is* right or wrong these days?"

I believe we determine right and wrong by following Jesus Christ and by heeding His Word, the Bible.

If you decide right and wrong by taking a poll from time to time—you will have great difficulties—and your notions will change almost weekly if not daily.

Or if for you right and wrong are a matter of personal feelings, that will also give you a lot of trouble. Feelings are not always reliable—they often deceive and mislead us.

When Jesus lays down matters of rightness and wrongness about life it is not always pleasing to us. Sometimes we may feel like arguing with Him.

But there is a quiet assurance that if anyone knows what he is talking about when it comes to right and wrong, it is Jesus.

Jesus is the Creator. He has fulfilled all the law and the prophets. He is absolutely devoted to truth. And He came to redeem us from the mess we have made of life—because we did not know how to decide right from wrong.

And one more thing about Jesus—He gives us wisdom and power not only to choose, but to follow the right and reject the wrong.

HURT OR HELP?

In most of our relating, casual or intense, we make frequent choices about whether we will hurt or help the other person.

Sometimes these are subtle matters. Sometimes they are overt and as plain as day.

When we listen to a bit of juicy gossip, and even moreso when we pass it on to someone else, we put ourselves in the hurting category. We are doing damage—tearing down instead of building up.

When we keep quiet in the face of the obvious accomplishments and successes of someone we know, we are not being just discreet—we inflict hurt by our silence.

It's good to examine our vocabulary to assess our stock of helpful words and expressions—and at the same time place some destructive, hurtful ones in a file marked "Discontinued."

Also, we need a keen awareness of how some words and expressions may be interpreted one way or the other by the tone of our voice.

For example, the word "really." When used with a certain intonation it can express doubt and even scorn—or it can be an expression of delight and joy, offering affirmation to the other person.

Before opening our mouths it's a good practice to ask ourselves the question, "Will this hurt—or help?"

IDENTITY BASIS

Everybody has a base on which to build their personal identity. Whatever might be out of character with our base should be examined carefully, and perhaps discarded—or it could be that the base itself needs changing!

Along with many others, I have found my value base in a Person. I am convinced that Jesus the Messiah of God sets before us the proper responses to the most important concerns of life. His ways are not always easy, and demand agonizing choices.

Jesus said little about self-satisfaction, human "happiness" and "rights"—but He said and modeled much about self-giving, being a dispenser of redemptive and reconciling grace, and the virtues of humility, love, faith, freedom and vision.

Nicodemus was a leader of Israel. His visit with Jesus is recorded in chapter 3 of John's Gospel. It's obvious that Nicodemus was seeking a value base greater than opinion and tradition. He wanted lucid answers to the darker aspects of life—and assurances about the life to come.

That learned man was in hot pursuit of the path to meaningful and eternal life—in other words, a sense of lasting, unfading, dynamic, and eminently worthy *identity.* He wanted an identity base—and he was wondering if Jesus just might be it.

Nicodemus changed his identity base, beginning life anew.

WILLFUL IGNORANCE

I came across some comments about ignorance: "The recipe for perpetual ignorance is to be satisfied with your opinions and content with your knowledge." Another: "There is nothing more terrifying than ignorance in action." And this: "Ignorance is not the real problem. It's not knowing we're ignorant that causes the difficulty."

There are times when ignorance may be an adequate excuse. But the more we delve into life's urgent matters, including the marvels of the Christian faith, the less tolerance we find for ignorance.

The Apostle Peter proclaims an end to the excuse of ignorance. He wrote: "As obedient children, do not conform to the evil desires you had when you lived in ignorance. But just as He Who called you is holy, so be holy in all you do." (I Peter 1:14,15)

In Ephesians Paul deals with the sins of willful ignorance:

> **You must no longer live as the Gentiles do, in the futility of their thinking. They are darkened in their understanding and separated from the life of God because of the ignorance that is in them due to the hardening of their hearts. Having lost all sensitivity, they have given themselves over to sensuality so as to indulge in every kind of impurity, with a continual lust for more.** (Ephesians 4:17-19)

Yes, indeed—there is a deliberate and knowing ignorance that God simply will not excuse.

JOYS OF AUTUMN

One of the best things about living in our part of the country is the change of seasons. We're experiencing fall or autumn, and we meet each new day with anticipation of change, color and blessing.

One fall morning I drove to a church up north, and the journey was sheer pleasure. It was harvest time, and the fields have yielded their produce. The colors of harvest were all around me as I made my way over back roads. Beans had been harvested earlier, and now the corn was almost done.

I slowed to appreciate the sight of loaded wagons of corn in recently harvested fields. These sights under a beautiful sky testified to an abundant harvest.

One farm home along the way had hundreds of pumpkins out in the yard, beckoning families to come and buy for Halloween—or better yet, to make pumpkin pies! The green and yellow of squash and colorful Indian corn peeked out from among the harvest display.

A harvest time such as this evokes thanks and praise in the minds of folks who appreciate the handiwork of God in league with the hard work of farmers—men and women who planted in the conviction that God would be faithful, and the earth would once again produce.

LIFE'S MEASURE

Think now—against what or whom do you measure your life, your standards, your sense of success, your worth?

If you measure your life against other people, you're making a big mistake. That can be so misleading, and ultimately frustrating and disappointing.

Some measure their lives against some inner standards they themselves have developed. They remind me of the little boy who came running to his mother, saying excitedly, "I've measured myself, and I'm 20 feet tall!" Of course, he had fashioned a measuring stick by guesswork—with no relationship to accepted standards used in measuring things, matter and people.

I would not want to buy from a store that created its own weight system. The owner might define a pound as 12 ounces, instead of the standard 16 ounces. His opinion really does not concern me—I want things measured and weighed by acceptable standards.

For our lives, there is only one acceptable measuring device as we try to assess worth, values and success, and that is Jesus Christ—the peerless Word of God Who is found in the Bible, the Word of God.

Over and over again the Bible assures us that He is the One by Whom we measure life with all its complexities and variables. Only He can be the standard, guide and measure for our living.

MAINTAIN THAT SENSE OF HUMOR!

If you don't have a healthy sense of humor, work to develop it. If you do have one, then maintain that sense of humor with all your heart and strength!

Humor makes life much more fascinating and worthwhile—and, of course, healthy.

All the evidence points to the fact that people with a healthy sense of humor live longer and with more contentment.

I hope you've picked up on a phrase that I have used twice: *a healthy sense of humor.* There is a difference. Good humor is not just the ability to laugh—but to laugh and enjoy in ways that build up, not tear down.

Healthy humor is constructive humor that includes others in the enjoyment. It never hurts another for the sake of a laugh or a lark. It is highly empathetic, sensitive and always hopeful and helpful.

Some think of themselves as having a good sense of humor, when the laughter they induce is at the expense of others. The truth is, they are mean and spiteful persons who have learned to use humor as a weapon for both offensive and defensive purposes.

Sarcasm, derision, ridicule, criticism, judgmentalism, spite and prejudice are all characteristic of destructive attitudes and have no place in the expression of healthy humor.

Good counsel: maintain that *healthy* sense of humor!

MAKE IT A FUN TIME

I believe that fun times are great for children—and for adults, too. But as we approach Halloween let's think with clarity and common sense.

A fun time does not need to scare the living bejabbers out of children—which, by the way, happens because adults with a tinge of sadism enjoy doing the scaring.

A fun time does not need to flirt with demons and devils, witchcraft and satanism. Again, adults and older kids think it's hilarious to deck out the small fry with paraphanalia offering more than a hint of evil and destructive mischief.

Costumes do not have to symbolize and express the worst of humankind and the most evil of fallen spirits. Steer clear of allusions and illusions of the satanic and demonic.

A fun time does not have to be destructive of the property, peace of mind and emotional wellbeing of neighbors, friends or total strangers.

Halloween fun time certainly does not need to include even one of the raunchy, bloody, violent, murderous movies that are intended to give viewers the fright of their lives. Enactments of the gruesome and inexpressibly cruel are simply not fit fare for adults, not to mention children.

Keep Halloween safe and sane—and make it a healthy fun time for the children.

MATTERS OF OPINION

There is a sense in which we all are opinionated—which means, among other things, that some have the truth and have it right, and others have just their own opinions.

We've come a long way when we understand that while our personal opinions may have the ring of truth, more often than not we are anywhere from half right to totally wrong.

Recently I came across some interesting comments about opinions:

- People generally have too many opinions and not enough convictions.
- Most people, when they come to you for advice, want their opinions strengthened—not corrected.
- Every man has a right to his opinion, but no man has a right to be wrong about the facts.
- There are two kinds of fools: those who cannot change their opinions and those who will not.
- It is a sign of mediocrity to have settled opinions on unsettled subjects.
- A foolish opinion shared by thousands is still a foolish opinion.

Living by faith is much more than living by opinions. Faith has foundations—including the centuries of experiences and testimony of people who have held that faith—lived by it, suffered for it and even died for it.

It is a wise person indeed who knows the difference between mere opinion and faith's convictions.

MEDIOCRITY

Here's a good question to ask yourself: "How easily satisfied are you?" There are people who are tied forever to mediocrity precisely because they are easily satisfied to the point where nothing they do comes even close to the assessment of "Excellent."

A person who strives for the best does so within the limits of his or her capacities and resources, including intelligence, education and opportunities. But the mediocre person is quickly and easily satisfied with a minimum of effort and investment no matter how great the capacities and resources. We are mediocre when we refuse to strive to the limits of our potential.

W. Somerset Maugham wrote: "Only a mediocre person is always at his best."

We're not sure who wrote the following, but it's good counsel: "The characteristic trait of the mediocre man is his deference to current opinion. He never speaks; he repeats. He judges a man according to social and economic position, his success, his wealth." Probably we've all known such persons.

A person stuck in mediocrity is always a follower, never a leader. He sticks with the tried and familiar, and is never an innovator. The new is too frightening, too challenging.

Mediocrity is a sad condition. The call of God to every man and woman is to flee mediocrity and give our best to every situation of life.

MERCY

Here's a good question for all of us: "Do you remember the last time you showed mercy to someone else?" Try to remember, because mercy is one of the most important character traits of anyone who desires goodness for their lives. Believe it! There is no goodness without mercy.

My *American Heritage Dictionary* defines mercy as "compassionate treatment, especially of those under one's power. . . a disposition to be kind and forgiving."

When others think of your disposition, do they even think of terms such as "kind" and "forgiving"?

There is an ancient legal maxim which states: "In case of doubt it is best to lean to the side of mercy."

But in terms of seeking to live life as a Christian, the demand is that even when all doubt is removed, mercy must be part of the human disposition.

The writer Alexander Pope wrote a prayer with these lines:

> Teach me to feel another's woe,
> To hide the fault I see;
> That mercy I to others show,
> That mercy show to me.

Ask yourself: What do I need from God more than anything else?

It's not money; not looks; not health. What you and I and every human being need the most from God is mercy. And the same is true of persons with whom we relate.

MIND AND FEELINGS

There seems to be a lot of deep concern these days about feelings—mainly one's own feelings, not necessarily those of others.

A philosopher once said, "I think—therefore I am." Today it's more like "I feel, therefore I am."

But feelings are only one facet of the human dimension—and not always the most important. The mind must be the main controller and guide for life. Acting and living by feelings most often leads to disaster. Feelings are assessed and given weight by the mind—not vice versa.

A notion that seems to have taken hold of many in our society is that if one's feelings are appropriate and in harmony with the situation, that's the end of the matter. Be happy. Feel happy. You're OK. Nothing further is required. Walk away with a glow in your heart.

That is a faulty outlook. Our mind and feelings working well together should generate action, behavioral responses that do something about the matter at hand—injecting us into it in good and healthy ways.

It's interesting that the Bible makes it very clear that true faith is not measured by the intellect or by feelings—but by our actions in response to the challenges of life.

In other words, it should be "I act—therefore I am."

NO TIME TO BE PICKY

There is such a thing as being too picky. Sometimes we call this unhealthy pickiness "perfectionism." That sounds a lot better than "picky."

But if we're talking about an unreasonably demanding personality—someone who tears everything apart looking for weaknesses and flaws—that is pickiness!

There are people for whom everything and everybody has a flaw. Things are either too sweet or too sour, too tall or too short, too big or too small—and never the right color!

And when it comes to people, everybody's faults and shortcomings are known and described by these picky souls. And if their flaws are not quickly evident, the picky will use their imaginations and cook up a few!

The opposite of being picky is to have a generous, tolerant spirit—an attitude that readily gives others the benefit of a doubt—and then some. There is understanding, compassion, forgiveness and acceptance.

In all truth, "picky" sounds unchristian in its determination to see only faults and flaws. The call of Christ to each of us is to develop a spirit of tolerance, understanding and acceptance.

After all, that is the way most of us want to be treated by others.

Life is too short for pickiness!

NOT A LAZY BONE

We definitely would like to think otherwise—but there actually are people in this world who love to plan and work at mischief. And they are hard workers—with not a lazy bone in their bodies.

In Proverbs 16 we read: "A scoundrel plots evil, and his speech is like a scorching fire. A perverse man stirs up dissension, and a gossip separates close friends."

One of the things I love about God's Word is its frankness and bluntness. The Bible tells it like it is. Probably we are more apt to say, "There is good and bad in everybody"—which is true. But it's also true that in persons who are riddled with perverse and destructive tendencies, whatever good there is never outweighs the evil they concoct and set in motion.

The destructiveness of such persons focuses mainly on relationships: "A perverse man stirs up dissension, and a gossip separates close friends." Perhaps some who are reading have experienced significant losses in their lives caused by scoundrels who plot evil, and gossipers who manage to separate us from others who previously formed our support group.

It's a sad observation, but I have known very few with those tendencies who ever realize the magnitude of their evil doings. They just never say "I'm sorry"—because they simply cannot see it.

OUR PERSONAL PANDORA'S BOX

Remember the old fable about Pandora's Box? The story goes that the first woman, Pandora, brought the box to earth with her—and finally opened it, releasing into the world every human ill and folly that we now experience on Planet Earth.

There is a sense in which we all have our personal Pandora's Box. It sits there within, tempting us to open it and release all kinds of troubles. Being human, we sometimes yield to the temptation to open our personal Pandora's Box—out of simple curiosity, a sense of boredom, or just plain orneriness!

The point is that most of our troubles are of our own making! *We* open Pandora's Box. We trigger folly and sin, we set forces in motion that should have been left at rest.

We open our personal Pandora's Box whenever we act destructively, whenever we nurse grudges—and allow jealousy, greed, envy and hate to fester in our minds and hearts, and sin to rule and determine our thoughts and behaviors.

The story of Pandora's Box is a lesson on consequences. The Bible puts it this way:

> **Do not be deceived. God is not mocked. What a man sows, that he will also reap.**
>
> (Galatians 6:7)

In other words, keep the lid on your personal Pandora's Box!

OVERSIMPLIFICATION

In spite of the complexities of all human relating there are those obtuse souls who insist that for God to be God, He must be simple. How dare He be otherwise? And for that matter, everyone else should be simple, too!

I wish I could regain some of the hours spent with persons whose "faith" has been shattered by complexity. I have become a bit jaded by the egotistical questions of "over simplifiers" who ask: "Why does God allow this to happen to me?" "Why doesn't God just put a stop to evil doing?" "What have I done to deserve this kind of treatment from God?"

Then there are those theological summations of simplicity, such as, "The Bible says that God is love—and that means He is wonderfully simple." This from folks who hold some mighty skimpy notions of the nature and demands of genuine love.

The one that earns the biggest hoot from yours truly is the offhand remark, "I want my faith and religion to be simple—like the Sermon on the Mount."

To get the full thrust of the amazing and naive hilarity of that comment, get out your Bible and read chapters 5, 6 and 7 of the Gospel of Matthew.

In effect, all the truly important matters of life should carry a big warning label: "Don't Oversimplify!"

PAGANS AMONG US

We don't hear the word "pagan" as much as we used to. "Pagan" refers to persons whose lives are devoid of any of the beliefs that characterize people who fear and love God. Pagans are godless—or have made gods out of things that make for their own convenience and self-protection.

Could it be that the word has lost its usefulness because so many people in our culture have become pagans in their attitudes and living? Whereas we used to think of godless people in other lands as pagan—now we're surrounded by them in our own nation.

Pagans are ungrateful clods, because they don't know Whom to thank. Pagans revile God with their profanity, and abuse their minds and bodies in orgies of drinking, drugs and sexual perversity.

Contemporary pagans scorn compassion, understand and practice only self fulfilling interpretations of love, ridicule prayer, reject all restraints on their sexual drives, abhor commitment in marriage, make truth and morals matters of personal opinion, and will resort to almost any means to get what they want.

Intelligent and somewhat sophisticated pagans attack the Bible and God's commands with care and subtlety, seeking to induce doubts and disobedience among the faithful. The more overt pagans are always ready to express their scorn.

"Pagan" may no longer be a familiar word—but genuine pagans continue to be all around us.

PERFECTIONISM

Recently someone gave a marvelous insight into people who are reputed to be perfectionists and thrive on it—asking everyone around them to be understanding and accepting, because after all, striving to be perfect is a virtue.

"Nonsense!" this woman said. "They really are not perfectionists. They're just plain self-centered, wanting everything done their way."

To be honest, I had never thought of perfectionism quite that way—but she has a point. Probably 99 times out of a hundred, it isn't so much that perfectionistic personalities want things done "right"—but that they want things done their way—which, in their view, is the only "right way." A faulty perception, if there ever was one.

There's a song of yesteryear that could be the theme song for perfectionists: "I Did It My Way." Just add the words, "And you should, too!"

Perfectionists are very trying, mostly because they tend to be so disdainful about what they view as the carelessness of persons who don't kowtow to them.

Perfectionists I've known are complainers and whiners. They don't get enough credit or enough applause for their achievements. This adds to their being a pain in the neck.

By all means strive for excellence—but in the process make sure you are following objective and established standards, not just your own ideas.

PLAYING FAST AND LOOSE WITH TRUTH

It seems that in today's culture there is a lot of what I call "playing fast and loose with truth and reality." There are deliberate lies, all kinds of misrepresentations and obfuscations—and a constant sell job on fantasy and other ways to dodge the hassles and responsibilities of the real world.

Such deliberate obfuscations also bedevil all churches—probably some worse than others.

In a recent issue of a magazine of my denomination an advertisement seeks a pastor who will interpret the Bible from "a critical historical perspective."

This means interpreting the faith on the basis of certain crass and purportedly "scholarly" assumptions—such as: "Dispose of all thoughts of the miraculous. Scorn the supernatural. Eliminate all of Jesus' claims to be more than merely human—that He is the very essence and being of Deity. Make psychology and superstition explain away eye witness accounts of angels, wondrous healings, storms calmed by our Lord's command, the dead raised, literal revelations from God, and a crucifixion and resurrection that are saving and redemptive." And for sure "historically critical" approaches will put the avid moralizing of the Apostle Paul "in proper perspective."

All pastors and laity would do well to remember that Jesus claimed to be "the Truth"—as well as "the way" and "the Life."

BEFORE SUNDOWN

The Bible has a lot of good advice for practical, successful and healthy every day living.

In Ephesians 4:26 and 27 we are given this good advice: "Do not let the sun go down while you are still angry, and do not give the devil a foothold. " (Ephesians 4:26, 27)

The counsel is clear: deal with your anger before sundown. We should not take it to bed with us, where it will compound and multiply in the depths of our psyche. Anger should be settled before bedtime, making whatever reconciliation and peace is necessary.

Many of us know folks who seem to enjoy their anger. They look for reasons to be ticked off. Many claim that their anger is always righteous, always above reproach. The thought that they might be sinning with their anger never crosses their minds. How could anything so right and so justified ever be called "sin?"

Anger is sin because 99 times out of a hundred it aims to take revenge on other persons. Anger is riddled with destructive feelings—along with a desire to put that destructiveness into action.

Anger might be a natural reaction—but it can be terribly destructive. So deal with it before sundown. Don't take it to bed with you, and certainly not into the next day.

POWER—GOOD AND BAD USES

Power is one of the greatest goods of life—and paradoxically it also can be a source of the greatest evils. It's a fascinating and at times depressing sight to watch how people use whatever powers they have.

We all know the old adage that power corrupts—and that absolute power corrupts absolutely. Probably there are many more bad than good things about people's uses of power.

But think about this: We all have power of one kind or another. Every person has power to wield, and must make distinct choices about using their power for good, bad—or for nothing at all.

We all have power to influence the environment in which we live. Have you ever noticed that when certain persons enter a room or a conversation, the place or situation livens up? They exert the power of joy and pleasure.

Then there are those bleak souls who walk in and spread gloom, doom, and doubt. One wishes they would have a permanent power outage on that kind of influence.

The best uses of power are for the good. There is power, mighty power, in grace, in love, in compassion, in friendliness, in forgiveness. And we all have access to those powers. Use your power to make an impact for good.

PRESCRIBING HUMOR

Don't be surprised if some day your physician hands you a prescription with one word on it: "Humor." That's right! *Bona fide* scientific research has demonstrated the therapeutic affects of humor.

According to the June 1, 1997 *USA Weekend* of the *Des Moines Sunday Register* there is an American Association for Therapeutic Humor to which 600 doctors and health care professionals belong—and evidently they take humor very seriously as a health producing force in life.

According to the *USA Weekend* article, the research findings "have shown laughter causes an increase in the activity of natural cells that attack and kill tumor cells and viruses. Laughter also activates T-cells for the immune system. antibodies that fight against harmful microorganisms. . ."

All this is encouraging news—but it's really not all that new. Way back in King Solomon's time that man of wisdom penned these words: "A cheerful heart is good medicine, but a crushed spirit dries up the bones." (Proverbs 17:22)

So the message of both the Word of God and medical science is, "For healing, lighten up and laugh it up!"

For troubled and overly serious persons, finding something to laugh about may be a problem. one might start with the internet, where humor abounds. And by the way, The American Association for Therapeutic Humor has its own home page on the internet:

http://www.humormatters.com

RIGHTS

Many Americans seem obsessed by the idea of personal and group rights.

The August 4, 1997 issue of US News and World Report carries a column by John Leo bearing the title, "A man's got a right to rights." (page 15) Leo relates some current quests for rights, such as: Every writer's right to get published—The constitutional right to wear backpacks to schools that prohibit them—Prisoners' right to procreate before being executed—The right to steal or burn bundles of newspapers so others cannot read them—the rights of trees and rocks—Women's rights to use men's restrooms—the fundamental right to proportional representation on television—and the right to a satisfying career.

I'm sure there are dozens more—rights claimed by individuals or groups whether or not they are deserved, and regardless of how they might impinge on the basic rights of others.

It seems rather obvious to me that any right automatically carries with it certain responsibilities and even accountability. Not for one moment do I believe that the writers of our Constitution and Bill of Rights envisioned rights without responsibilities. The implication is that lack of responsibility might be sufficient cause for curtailing and even removing rights.

When I hear someone spouting about their perceived rights, I just have to ask about his or her perceptions of the responsibilities that accompany those rights.

SCHOOLING YOUR CHILD

School days consume a lot of the lifetime of our children, and I'd like to offer some counsel to parents and grandparents who are listening—especially about your attitudes, and the attitudes you try to instill in the heads and hearts of children as they attend school.

First of all, schooling is a stark necessity of life—and I'm referring to the solid academics, not just the extra-curricular stuff. Hold a hard line with your offspring that signals there are no compromises and precious little tolerance for goofing off on the important matters.

Second—get to know the teachers and others who impact your child during the school day. Avoid all urges to pickiness and criticism. Encourage them—and applaud their efforts to impart knowledge, coping and research skills—the raw materials that will mark your children as "educated," and thus better equipped to meet the real world.

Third—don't back away from getting your child into cultural stuff: music, chorus, art, drama, speech. For sure, sports activities are important, but participation in the arts is absolutely essential for the whole person.

Fourth—insist on a debriefing every day of school—and never allow the child to shrug off anything or to clam up. Be caring, sympathetic and empathetic to beat the band—but don't permit pity parties, easy excuses and cop outs.

MALEFIC PERSONALITIES

Have you ever thought about the adjectives that may be rightly used to describe your personality? I could write a long list of adjectives I would not want used as descriptors of who I am and what I mean to others.

One such adjective is the word "malefic." Whenever a word includes the prefix "mal" it carries a bad and even evil meaning. "Malefic" describes a person with malicious and evil tendencies and intentions. It's used to describe a malignant personality.

I am convinced that nearly all persons who perpetrate evil do so not because they are crazy or mentally disturbed. Rather they are in the grip of evil. They have made all kinds of choices along the way that add up to their minds and hearts being dominated by malevolence. They gradually became malefic personalities.

Such persons may also have some mental and sociopathic problems that exacerbate their evil tendencies—but it is that malefic orientation that makes them such a danger to others.

Serial killers are malefic personalities. Anyone who plots harmful mischief against others is malefic.

I've known persons who have merited the adjective "malefic" because they are so bent on malice-filled gossip about others. Anyone who works destructively toward other persons is earning his or her malefic badge—and that is no badge of honor.

SEASONED CONVERSATION

For some folks, it seems that the limit of conversational responses are a few grunts now and then. Apparently they are incapable of stringing words together into a sentence.

And there are those personalities, who when they *do* have something to say it comes across as graceless, crude, bitter and rude.

There is a real sense in which what we say is what we are—our conversation presents our character and values. The minute we open our mouths, we show what we are.

There is a verse in the book of Colossians that advises us:

> **Let your conversation be always full of grace, seasoned with salt, so that you may know how to answer everyone.**
> (Colossians 4:7

"Seasoned Conversation" is a worthy aim for us all—words and phrases spilling forth from our mouths in ways that make the surroundings pleasant, communicate truthfully and bless persons with whom we speak. Usually a grunt or two just won't even come close to that.

Seasoned, graceful conversation is considerate of the feelings and comfort of others. And the seasoning, as in any good meal, is added deliberately, with forethought and wisdom.

I guess we could call some conversations "plain delicious."

SHINE

Some time ago, Susan and I watched a powerful film production: *Shine,* the story of Australian pianist David Helfgott.

After the viewing I searched the internet for information about this gifted and eccentric pianist, who at the time was on a world tour. Indeed, Helfgott is a musical genius.

The movie's main theme was recovery from a condition which had its beginnings in a home ruled by a ruthless father who thought he knew the meaning of love and family, but didn't. The father broke with his son as David pursued his music career against Papa's wishes.

The film reminds us that great potential and creative genius need caring family support, not suppression. One of my recurrent themes is the surrogacy syndrome, in which parents coerce their offspring to be and do and become *for them.* Children who experience this become sacrificial lambs to the tainted and overblown egos of parents. Their hopes and aspirations are mangled and their emotional stability shattered by a terrible lack of love and support for their ambitions.

As I think about these matters, an old joke comes to mind about the wife who snaps at her husband, "Shut up! When I want your opinion I'll give it to you!" That's surrogacy!

Thankfully for him, his many friends, and the music loving public, David Helfgott broke free of his chains—and "got a life."

SLOW DOWN—SPEED UP!

A little girl was excitedly telling a story to her grandfather—who finally stopped her, saying, "Slow down! You're talking too fast!" The girl drew back, looked her grandpa straight in the eye, and exclaimed, "No, Grandpa! You're listening too slow!"

I suspect that each of us has things we ought to slow down on, and others are urging us to speed up. In my years in the pastorate, I was often struck by the need for Christ's people to speed up on the listening, to hurry up on the doing of good—and certainly to slow down on the activities that might be hurtful to others—such as gossip and harsh criticism.

We all ought to be hearing "Slow down—speed up!" as they apply at the same time to different areas of our living.

Just one of the awesome lessons we can learn from the untimely death of Princess Diana is that life can never be taken for granted. It will surprise us—and sometimes will close us down long before we expected.

Her life also tells us to speed up on the doing of good, the sharing in the lives of people in need, the giving of ourselves to worthy causes.

And Diana's life reminds us to slow down on anything carrying the potential of destruction.

SOCIAL GRACE

If ever there was a word we need in our Christian vocabulary it's the word "grace." It means undeserved, unearned mercy—and implies lavish forgiveness for a sin list longer than your arm. The meaningful old hymn, *Amazing Grace,* continues to be the best known hymn in America—most likely because of intuition on the part of multitudes that grace is what sustains us all. We cannot live without it.

Grace is not only a religious concept, it is a social one. There are social graces—which in the main are good manners and the avoidance of crudity. But we need to understand grace as a necessity in the family, friendship, business and the work place.

Have you ever known someone who is picky legalistic and eagle-eyed for any mistake, any infringement of laws? Such persons are long on punishment, but very short on grace.

I've known parents who expect and demand far too much of their children—who go ballistic when a child offends them in the slightest way—but who apparently have never heard of, much less understood, a child's need for grace as well as rules.

Grace is not just an essential for faith—it is needed in all our relating. We have come a long way when loving forgiveness is the first thing that comes to mind when someone errs—not punitive and unbending legalism.

SOCIAL THEOLOGY

The Christian Faith is best expressed and lived out in social situations, in our relating with family, friends, classmates, work colleagues, neighbors and even casual acquaintances.

I feel a kind of sorrow for folks who severely separate their theology from their every day lives. They confine their Christian beliefs and practices to one tiny room of the mansion of their lives. They never let it out to generate goodness and beauty in their whole life activities and relationships.

Good theology, with accurate descriptors of God and human beings, is an intensely social force—intended to be expressed and fulfilled in the common as well as the extraordinary events of our living.

My theology, which derives from the Word of God, tells me that God is loving, just, compassionate, forgiving, merciful and understanding—to name just a few of His attributes.

At the very least this means that I must be the same in every situation—and not only because I am a Christian. Every person is created by God in His image—which includes compassion, mercy, love, truth, justice and forgiveness.

Every sociological system I have read about excludes theology as being a sideline and not important.

But the best sociology is based on theology—the revelations we have from God about His nature and being—and ours.

SPECIAL PREPARATIONS

As we think about preparing our children for all kinds of wonderful educational experiences, we need a keen awareness that increasingly our children move in multicultural situations—and there are some needed caveats and cautions.

Be alert for signs of prejudice and bigotry, and make time for discussion and correction. Zero tolerance is the rule for words and attitudes that debase persons of other colors and ethnic backgrounds. The same goes for looks, tics, habits, dress, capacities and other differences. Deal up front with a youngster's natural tendencies toward cliquishness. Encourage not only tolerance for contrasts and diversity, but wholehearted and enthusiastic acceptance, fostering a desire to learn from others.

Along this line, there is a need for frequent talks with our youngsters about personal standards—always keeping in the forefront the virtues that divert them from destructive acts and behaviors and point the way to health and stability.

Schedule two way discussions about guidelines for choosing friends, dealing with various crises, making choices about mind and body commitments—and the handling of all kinds of emotional challenges, from simple disappointment to what seem to be catastrophic failures.

It's a solemn but often ignored truth: Our children will get about as much value out of school and other learning experiences as their attitudes, standards and expectations enable them to take in.

TALK TO YOUR CHILDREN

A few Sundays ago I preached in a church bearing the name "Immanuel." That's a wonderful name for a church, and during the special time for the children I asked them the meaning of the name—even offering a quarter for anyone who got it right.

Not one child could tell me that "Immanuel" means "God with us." I shared that with them, and hope they will remember. But you know, if their parents don't pick up on it and remind them, reinforcing what they learned that Sunday, they probably will forget.

That Sunday I also talked to them about a symbol carved in the altar—a *chi rho* symbol, like an X with a big P rising out of it. They all agreed that it did not mean a railroad crossing. I explained to them that what looks like X and P are really *chi* and *rho*—the first two letters in *Christos,* the Greek word for Christ.

We need to talk to our children about the most important symbols of their surroundings. Some, such as stop signs and caution warnings are critical to their wellbeing. Others, such as symbolic words and figures carry rich and essential lessons for the spiritual dimension of their living—that which is eternal.

Please—talk to your children about great matters and their symbols!

TEN THINGS TO REMEMBER

The other day I came across a list of ten things for which no one ever has been sorry. They are worth noting and remembering.

No one has ever been sorry for doing good to all; for speaking evil of none; for listening carefully before judging; for thinking before speaking; for holding on to an angry tongue; for being kind to distressed persons; for asking pardon and forgiveness for all wrongs toward others; for being patient toward all; for stopping one's ears to a gossip; for the inclination to disbelieve bad reports about others.

I have some things to add to that list. I'll never be sorry for the Bible verses I've learned; for speaking to children with care and politeness; for appreciating and sharing good humor; for letting hurt persons know I care.

I'll never regret meeting Jesus Christ and accepting Him as my Savior and Lord; I'm not sorry for anything I have given for good causes; I'm not sorry for trying the new, discarding the outworn, for staying loyal to timeless truths.

I'll never regret standing by a friend in need; weeping with persons in their grief; encouraging someone who needs a friend; believing in the ultimate triumph of good.

I'm sure every listener can add to my list.

THE ART OF TACT

Do you know the identity of the virtue often referred to as "The saving virtue"? It is tact. My trusty *American Heritage Dictionary* defines tact as "acute sensitivity to what is proper and appropriate in dealing with others, including the ability to speak or act without offending." A tactless person is not only a bore, but can be very destructive.

Many of us have known people who take delight in their lack of tact. Just recently someone remarked to me how he tells it like it is, pulling no punches. In other words he enjoys playing the role of an insensitive, inconsiderate clod.

I consider tact a virtue, for it is more considerate of the feelings of others than one's own feelings—determined to be healing, constructive and solution-oriented toward others.

Solomon's proverbs say some helpful things in relation to tact and the tongue. From Proverbs 11:12—"A man who lacks judgment derides his neighbor, but a man of understanding holds his tongue."

In Proverbs 12:18 we read: "Reckless words pierce like a sword, but the tongue of the wise brings healing."

And Proverbs 21:23 tells us, "He who guards his mouth and his tongue keeps himself from calamity."

The message is clear: Control the tongue—and learn the fine art of tact.

THE BEAUTY OF FRIENDSHIP

One of the many interesting facts about the Bible is the value and high standards it places on friendship.

Jesus told His disciples, "I have not called you servants. . . I have called you friends." (John 15:15)

He even used the word friend toward the disciple who betrayed Him. Jesus greeted Judas Iscariot in Gethsemane with the words, "Friend, why are you here?" (Matthew 26:50 RSV) Jesus knew full well why Judas was there—but it was as though the Lord was reminding Judas of a relationship that Judas was sacrificing for gain and fame. He got neither.

Judas Iscariot will always be a reminder of dark betrayal—and also of the fact that we can kill off even the best of friendships.

Someone wrote: "People make enemies by complaining too much to their friends." And along that line, another quote: "A good friend is one who can tell you all his problems—but doesn't."

A friend certainly is one who knows more about us than others do, and yet sticks with us. A true friend is someone who stands by you even when he or she gets to know you real well.

I like this description of a friend: "A friend is one who walks in when the rest of the world walks out."

One final word: To *have* friends, we must *be* friends.

THE BREADTH OF EDUCATION

As summer rolls toward its end children and young people start heading back to school. For sure their attitudes will play the major role in how much they gain from their educational experiences.

One of the main educational attitudes we need to foster in our own minds as well as the minds of our children, is the broad scope of education. As the youngsters get back into school days, there should be planned involvement in other educational agencies in our community. Our schools are not the only institutions offering significant and whole life educational and extra-curricular activities.

Churches offer weekly Sunday School and Worship, special youth activities and other opportunities in which the entire family participates. The fact sometimes eludes folks: our churches and other religious institutions are the only cross-cultural and trans-generational entities in our society.

Many youngsters spend some of their quality time engaged in piano or voice lessons, dance training, art classes, participation in church and community projects and programs—and the pursuit of personal hobbies and recreational activities.

There also are 4-H clubs, Scouts, YMCA and other groups that are able to add significant and needed dimensions to the life experiences and training of your child.

As you help your children plan their involvements, for the sake of educational breadth, work for balance and variety.

THE COMPLEXITY OF AFFLICTIONS

Within a few minutes I heard the good news from my former college room mate that his cancer has been arrested by treatment—and the bad news that another friend had died of cancer.

The complexity of all this brought a lot of things to mind, including the advice of the Apostle Paul: "Rejoice with those who rejoice; mourn with those who mourn.." (Romans 12:15)

That verse often describes the typical "mix" of our daily living. There is good news and there is bad news. Sorrow is the lot of some, and joy the lot of others. And we must be ready to share in both!

One of the most common questions asked when afflictions strike is "Why?" Please, please—understand this once and for all: Disease and accidents are nearly always irrational events—happenings concerning which there are no cogent, easily explained reasons.

When we try to boil that complexity down to simplicity we do injustice to ourselves, to God and even to others.

I remember so well a family who came to join our church in Minneapolis because the folks in her church insisted she must have sinned terribly to be afflicted with raging cancer.

When it comes to the afflictions of life, bear in mind that there is a complexity that defies oversimplification or easy explanations.

DISCERNING SPIRITUALITY

Spirituality is a characteristic of every human being. Our spirituality gives us the possibilities of sharing in a larger reality than the five senses allow. Because of spirituality we can pray, we can call on God's help, we can discern His activities and become aware of His purposes.

Our spirituality permits us to develop the finer, better qualities of being a human being—raising us far above the animal world, with its primitive calls to survive even at the expense of others. Our spiritual nature keeps us from becoming predators and scavengers.

We discern our spiritual attributes in our calls to service and every good thing we are motivated to do.

Our spirituality can become stunted, weakened and even dead. Its very survival is dependent on our nurturing this indispensable attribute of our being—through prayer, worship, meditation and the intentional doing of good.

Ultimately our spirituality is resourced by the Spirit of God. Paul wrote in I Corinthians 2: "We have not received the spirit of the world but the Spirit Who is from God—The man without the Spirit does not accept the things that come from the Spirit of God, for they are foolishness to him, and he cannot understand them, because they are spiritually discerned."

A good question: How spiritually discerning are you?

THE COST OF SUCCESS

"Success" is a strange word to a lot of folks—perhaps because they have never aimed for anything of significance. They are content with small achievements, minimal growth, limited knowledge and associates and friends who are as simple as they.

But success is what we humans are made for.

It's also true that the higher one's aim and the greater one's aspirations, the more the nit pickers, enemies and critics one encounters—and the more intense the battles with the jealous, envious and weak-minded.

Mother Teresa was more than a doer of enormous good. She had a powerful belief system which made her an ardent enemy of abortion—and that stirred no small opposition to her. "How dare she!" was the indignant response of many. As though the abortion issue is a settled matter in favor of the destroyers of life. With all her good, this marvelous woman stirred opposition.

Someone wrote: "You can't make real success without making real enemies. You can't hold a strong position without strong and continued opposition. You can't seem right to many if you don't seem wrong to many. A useful life can't be entirely peaceful and carefree. . . The greater you are, the greater the penalty of your progress. . . . So long as you aspire, others will conspire." (Anonymous)

THE CYNICS AMONG US

Among the many detractors are folks we call "cynics." They are spoilers because they refuse to attribute good to any one. They claim that nobody has worthy motives. Everybody is in it for the money, or for their own personal pleasure.

Most cynics I've known are all too willing to attribute nothing but good to their own actions, but not a smidgen of good to what anyone else does.

It's true that anyone who does a good deed may have mixed motives—but there are more than enough incidents of unselfish acts of good and even heroism to confound the bleak outlook of all cynics.

Cynics among us offer no example to follow, no good news for the human family. Theirs is a philosophy and message of gloom and doom—with no redeeming features.

The best attitude is to celebrate and commend all the good that people do—and leave the judging to God. The words of Jesus are aimed at the cynics among us:

> **Do not judge, or you too will be judged. For in the same way you judge others, you will be judged, and with the measure you use, it will be measured to you.** (Matthew 7:1,2

Now that's food for thought for any of the cynics among us!

THE GATHERING

Someone told me of visiting a home of well educated persons, The meal was served buffet style, and then all were expected to sit down in front of the television set and watch the family's favorite sitcoms. No conversation. No discussion. No sharing.

This phrase should be an urgent part of family life: "The gathering." Every family needs a daily gathering that is unencumbered by television drivel or the reading of the morning paper. You gather to talk, to eat, to laugh, to share. "The gathering" is indispensable to healthy family living. When you sacrifice it to work or schedules or other activities, you simply are paying too great a price.

We also need "The gathering" of the church—when the family of God comes together to learn and share, to comfort and encourage.

In Hebrews 10:24 and 25 we read: "Let us consider how we may spur one another on toward love and good deeds. Let us not give up meeting together, as some are in the habit of doing, but let us encourage one another—and all the more as you see the Day approaching."

There we have the rationale for "The Gathering" in our homes and churches: that we may "spur one another on toward love and good deeds."

How long has it been since you've shared good conversation and rich and meaningful fellowship in "The Gathering?"

THE GOLDEN THREAD

There are 66 books in the Bible—39 in the Old Testament and 27 in the new. They are diverse in subject matter, settings and authorship. They speak of God—and they speak not only of the good of humanity, but also the evil. The 66 books tell of betrayal and failure, of sin and perversity.

But with all that, there is a golden thread that runs through every book from Genesis through Revelation. The Golden Thread is the Messiah, the Christ—the One we know as Jesus.

The Old Testament points to His coming, leading God's people and the nations toward the simple yet awesome birth in Bethlehem. The New Testament tells of His life among us, His teachings and prophecies—His imperatives and judgments.

This means whenever you read the Bible, in whatever book, look for the Golden Thread.

There is a parallel and a lesson for our own living, and the most serious question of our entire lives is this: "What is the Golden Thread that runs through the whole of your living, every nook and cranny of your life?" In other words, what is the major theme of your life—that to which everything else relates?

Hopefully, it is the same Golden Thread that runs through the Bible, the Word of God: the Golden Thread of Jesus and all He means.

DISCERNING GOD

Ordinarily when we speak of grace we're referring to the nature of God. His grace is awesome and perfect—and is the very ground of His being. The Bible tells us that "God is love"—which is another way of saying God is grace.

John tells us in his gospel, chapter 1:

> **The Word became flesh and made His dwelling among us.**
> **We have seen His glory, the glory of the One and Only,**
> **Who came from the Father, full of grace and truth.**

Any expression of God, and certainly the incarnation of God in Jesus Christ, is discernible by the overwhelming presence of grace.

We simply cannot think of God, or His full revealing in Jesus of Nazareth, without thinking of grace.

Grace is also to be our highest virtue—and we strive for it with the help of God's Spirit Who dwells within us.

As with God, our grace is marked by selflessness, sacrifice, humility, love, caring and compassion. Grace in us is when we do good without expectation of a return or payoff.

When we reach for those conditions, divesting ourselves of self-interest and shabby motives as much as we can, then we become persons of grace—and by so doing we brush close to God.

GRACE IN OUR LIVES—GOD'S PRESENCE

"Grace" is a key word in human affairs as well as in theology. If we are to create and sustain great works and powerful institutions for good in our communities, a great many people must think and act by grace.

We need a strong consciousness of the vagaries of human acts of grace. We also need an awareness of the differences in the grace of God and the grace of human beings.

The grace of God is characterized by the purity of self-giving, uncluttered by the considerations and hangups associated with human expressions of grace.

Unlike God, every thought of our mind and every act of our being is tainted and carries the potential of devilish corruption. There is nothing so obscene as the acts of persons who claim and tout grace, but actually are hypocritical and horrendously self-serving.

Consider the matters of giving and gifting—which at their best are exercises of grace.

Too often we humans are cheated out of the divine thrills and spiritual rewards of self-expending grace by the encroachments of crass self preservation, sordid self concerns and starkly conflicting motivations.

The Scriptural teachings are clear: We are at our best when we rise above the taint, and brush close to God in our quest for the highest and purest grace.

THE PERSONAL CHALLENGES OF GRACE

Grace operating in our lives is absolutely essential if we humans are to accomplish any lasting good in this world.

We must aspire to attitudes and actions of grace so self sacrificing that by and through them we brush close to God, and with His help do great things.

In John 14:12 Jesus makes this awesome prediction:

> **I tell you the truth, anyone who has faith in Me will do what I have been doing. He will do even greater things than these.**

What did He mean that we would do greater things?

I believe Jesus was taking into account the difficulties we must overcome when we seek to think and act by the highest, purest grace. The greater things happen when we manage to create hospitals, churches and educational institutions that bless and heal and help the multitudes.

These are some of the greater works to which Jesus referred, greater because it is tougher for us to overcome the horrible taint of sin in all we do.

It is difficult—but we best express the grace of God as we overcome the taint, as we set aside self-interest and poor motivations. On a human level the accomplishments of grace are awesome—but in like manner, our failures of grace are horrendous. God's grace in us offers the greatest challenges of our living. And His grace helps us meet those challenges.

THE QUALITY OF LEADERSHIP

We individualistic Americans tend to develop a scorn for leadership. We're all equal, we say, so why should anyone be over us. Think again. In any organized group devoted to any kind of program of effort, we need good leaders.

We need leaders in business, in education, in science, in the Church—and literally in every area of human endeavor.

Bishop Fulton J. Sheen once said, "Civilization is always in danger when those who never have learned to obey are given the right to command."

Poor followers rarely if ever make good leaders. A great deal of the training of our leaders is in their learning to follow.

And this is another maxim of leadership: A good leader inspires others with confidence in him or her. A great leader inspires others with confidence in themselves.

All leadership is trained leadership. Officers of our churches do their church a terrible injustice when they lead by impulse and prejudice, by vague feelings and a distorted sense of their own importance.

Some years ago I wrote a training manual for church officers that is used in many churches. The title is one of the most significant things about the work: *Redeemed to Serve—Ordained to Lead.*

No one should be placed in a position of leadership without training. That is unfair, and certainly unwise.

"THEY" AND "ANY NUMBER"

A church officer in a former parish was prone to bolster his position with a comment to the effect that "Any number" of people have called or spoken or complained to him. His tone of voice implied that his phone was ringing off the wall.

But I soon tumbled to his not-so-subtle deception, and every time he started to say "Any number," I would remind him that zero is a number. as are one or two.

He enjoyed his gamesmanship, and I'm sure it helped him win—too often.

Equally culpable and annoying are those folks who refer to "They," as in "They say"—or "They have found that"—and unwittingly we could be led right down the proverbial garden path.

If we're not careful our lives can be bedeviled by the mysterious and invisible "theys." We may become slaves to a faceless expression of public opinion that really has never been expressed. And in 99 cases out of a hundred, who cares what "they" think?

Most often "they" are persons of little consequence who really should have no say in our lives because they have no stake in our lives.

So avoid the phony, faceless judges who mainly derive from our imaginations. Give them no place—and no say in your life.

A CHRISTIAN MARRIAGE SERVICE

Is there such a thing as a Christian marriage service—a wedding that is distinctively Christian?

I certainly believe there is. I have officiated at many such weddings—one of them just a short time ago.

The question faces the bride and groom from the very start of their planning: "Do we want this to be a Christian wedding service as the beginning of what we intend to be a Christian marriage and family?"

The first guideline is that it is a worship service, to be planned in consultation with their pastor. The second guideline is that it should express their personalities, not those of friends or parents.

Some might assume that such a service is stuffy and pious, the very air dripping with moralistic platitudes.

God has a sharp and delightful sense of humor, so humor is not only appropriate—it is essential.

At such a service recently, the best man reached into his pocket for the bride's ring, then frantically began searching all his pockets. He turned in panic to another attendant, and they both searched—pulling from their pockets socks, handkerchieves, napkins and all sorts of paraphanalia. By this time the congregation was in stitches. Finally the ring was found—firmly planted on the little finger of the best man. And the service continued to completion. Memorable!

AN UNBLEMISHED RULER

It's interesting that the people of Old Testament times were waiting for a ruler without flaws. With all the goings on in Washington, DC and other places where flawed human beings hold forth as presidents, prime ministers and kings, the whole world longs for an unblemished, incorruptible ruler.

The predictive prophecies of just such a mighty ruler are found in the Old Testament forthtellings of the coming of the Messiah. He would be King Jesus—a ruler such as the world has never known.

In Isaiah 9:6 and 7 the prophet gives us these promises of God:

> **For to us a Child is born, to us a Son is given, and the government will be on His shoulders. And He will be called Wonderful Counselor, Mighty God, Everlasting Father, Prince of Peace. Of the increase of His government and peace there will be no end. He will reign on David's throne and over His kingdom, establishing and upholding it with justice and righteousness from that time on and forever. The zeal of the Lord Almighty will accomplish this.**

Historically, all the world's rulers have been corrupt and oppressive. But now we have a new King—Whose yoke is easy, and Whose burden is light. All hail to King Jesus—the world's only unblemished ruler.

ANSWERED PRAYERS

When it comes to answered prayers, we need to be prepared for surprises. Many mistakenly believe that prayers are either answered exactly as we want, or not at all. As the old song says, "It ain't necessarily so!"

Another guideline is that God's answers are in keeping with His will and His glory. If two prayers conflict, you can be sure that the Lord will answer the one which is closest to His will and purposes.

Many times I have received God's help from this anonymous writing:

> I asked for strength that I might achieve;
> He made me weak that I might obey.
> I asked for health that I might do great things
> He gave me grace that I might do better things.
> I asked for riches that I might be happy;
> He gave me poverty that I might be wise.
> I asked for power that I might have the praise of men;
> He gave me weakness that I might feel a need of God.
> I asked for all things that I might enjoy life;
> He gave me life that I might enjoy all things.
> I received nothing I had asked for;
> He gave me all that I had hoped for.

God is very thoughtful and creative about how He answers our prayers—and we should be on the lookout for those kinds of answers, *His kinds of answers.*

ANTHROPOMORPHIZING

My daughter once showed me a book for children, asking what I thought of it. After perusing its text and illustrations I told her it was ghastly,

It carried a theme of cruel violence to animals who were anthropomorphized—that is, they were humanized via thoughts and conversations, fears and anxieties.

When we anthropomorphize we attribute human minds, emotions and ambitions to animals. In so doing we transfer certain matters to our human relating. If we put a big "OK" on cruelty and violence to humanized animals, we put that OK on the same treatment for human beings.

Anthropomorphizing may come off as cute and even wholesome. Or we may unwittingly set children up for unhealthy and untrue thinking about life, creating unnecessary fears and saddling them with needless problems.

There are a lot of things about animals, birds and reptiles that we do not know. But one thing we do know and should keep in the forefront of our mind: they are not human. They do not exercise the complex thought processes we do. And also remember that we are not animals.

Recently I came across this little gem written by Imogene Fey: "The difference between man and the animals is that man is, or should be, aware that there is more to life than begin, beget and be gone."

APPEARANCES

The source of a lot of lying and deceit is in our attempts to keep up appearances. Appearances are not the reality, but often are intended to disguise and hide reality. We work on appearances so that the reality will not be known.

While some attempts to improve appearances may be fairly innocent, when we intend to hide the truth and keep people from knowing it we have joined forces with evil.

In the letter Jesus dictated for the church at Sardis in Revelation 3, He chided them for appearances that do not match reality. "I know your deeds; you have a reputation of being alive, but you are dead." When it came to appearances, that church was highly regarded. But it was like perky makeup on the face of a corpse. As a church they were lifeless.

We know that political campaigns, jury trials, job promotions, and various forms of popularity often turn on the matter of appearances. If someone has truth and righteousness on his or her side, but fails in appearances, success, rights and justice go right down the drain.

The logical answer to all this is to refuse to be deceived by appearances, and to carefully look beneath the surface. That's the location of reality. We read in Galatians 2:6: "God does not judge by external appearance."

God does not judge by appearances, and neither should we.

BAD FOR THE HEART AND SOUL

A man named Bernard Gimbel wrote: "Two things are bad for the heart: running uphill and running down people."

Trashing other persons may be a form of amusement that some love to get into. But it is one of the most destructive forces in human well being and relating. It produces not a scintilla of good.

Some do it because it bolsters their own ego to put others down. That makes for a dirty, unwholesome way to live—nurturing our own self-esteem off the battering and destroying of reputations. To put it mildly, it's a rotten way to live.

Running down people always goes public—even if you tell only one person at a time. The net result is destructiveness for the lives of others, and a treacherous weakening of community. It nurtures mistrust and wariness of the very people we need for our own wellbeing.

I am very wary of persons who always have a story about the misdeeds and failures of others. From experience I know that they are painting themselves white while they paint others black.

And I always wonder what they might be saying about me in private conferences with others. In short, I don't trust them and I won't trust them—because they have earned mistrust—and little else.

BENEATH DEPRESSION

When a person tells me he or she is depressed, I always take it seriously. For one thing, depression can produce awful physical pain, along with feelings of alienation and worthlessness.

It just doesn't work to tell a depressed person to "snap out of it." It's also unfair and unwise to accuse a depressed person of engaging in a pity party, or of being a self-centered clod.

Depression always has bigger issues and concerns beneath it—such as frustration, disappointment and anger. And more often than not, the three work together to build a case of mild to severe depression.

Depression all by itself will rarely yield to treatment, except on a very short term basis. What needs to be dealt with are the underneath factors: the disappointment, frustration and anger over something in the past or present.

Some folks have a volcano percolating underneath the surface. Occasionally it may bubble a bit, and they feel the blues or a mild case of depression. When it erupts, depression goes big time. Rage is underneath—deep anger that continues to hurt long after the incidents that caused it are history.

It may take therapy to uncover that anger and deal with it. For sure it will require wisdom, grace, love and forgiveness to root it out once and for all, and declare it an unwelcome and unwholesome visitor to the stage of the here and now.

BIBLE POUNDERS

I'm torn between pity and scorn when I hear somebody call a person a "Bible pounder." The term is one of contempt—a putdown.

Because I know what the Bible has to say, and understand and appreciate its core message of the revelation of God, I can also understand the unbridled enthusiasm that stirs people's hearts and minds when they come to grips with the realities of the Word of God.

While the football or basketball game may be very important and generate some wild enthusiasm, the game does finish up, and it's all over until the next game. But not so with the Bible. Its impact rolls on throughout one's life in an unceasing and unrelenting fashion.

When someone attacks another for being a Bible pounder, my quick question is, "Well, what are you pounding? Where are you getting accurate information about God and life? Or are you even trying." Critics of Bible pounders can get excited about what amount to the silliest and most trivial matters—and expect everyone to look with kindness on their fanaticism.

Getting excited about the Word of God and trying to communicate its teachings to others are very worthy and worthwhile things to get excited about.

Tell me. What are you pounding these days?

BRINGING BEAUTY TO THE WORLD

I want to pay tribute, as should we all, to those men and women who bring beauty to the world.

Artists and poets, photographers and song writers, sculptors and fabric weavers—and more. They pull us away from all that is destructive and lacking in hope, and show us the greatness of which human beings can be capable.

John Keats wrote in his *Endymion:*

> A thing of beauty is a joy forever;
> Its loveliness increases; it will never
> Pass into nothingness; but still will keep
> A bower quiet for us, and a sleep
> Full of sweet dreams, and health
> And quiet breathing.

Keats is one of those who brings beauty to the world—and to one's personal being. Somehow poets such as Keats connect earth to heaven, and stir the best in humankind.

The workers who bring great bridges into being, the makers of stained glass windows, the architects and engineers and artisans—we owe them much, for they bring beauty to our world.

And those who sacrifice and love and lay down their lives for the good of others—theirs is an offering of beauty, and they help to make our world beautiful.

Would that all of us would so live and work that we leave a legacy of beauty.

CONSPIRACIES

Psalm 64:2 expresses what constitutes a much-needed prayer for some: "Hide me from the conspiracy of the wicked, from that noisy crowd of evildoers."

I once saw a sign which read: "Just because you're not paranoid doesn't mean they're not out to get you."

Here's more of Psalm 64:

> **Hide me from the conspiracy of the wicked, from that noisy crowd of evildoers. They sharpen their tongues like swords and aim their words like deadly arrows. They shoot from ambush at the innocent man; they shoot at him suddenly, without fear. They encourage each other in evil plans, they talk about hiding their snares; they say, "Who will see them?" They plot injustice and say, "We have devised a perfect plan!" Surely the mind and heart of man are cunning. But God will shoot them with arrows; suddenly they will be struck down. He will turn their own tongues against them and bring them to ruin; all who see them will shake their heads in scorn.**

At least ninety-nine times out of a hundred, being involved in a conspiracy is collusion for mischief-making—for the doing of evil against someone who has not harmed them, and who seems to be an easy mark.

Conspiracies are *not* the makings of heroes or models—much less Christians.

COMING TO TERMS

The expression "coming to terms" usually refers to making reconciliation and finding ways to get along with others—often after a period of alienation, followed by approaches and negotiations.

But have you ever thought of the need to come to terms with yourself?

Everybody has regrets they need to come to terms with. Others have shame, guilt and failure. We may have to come to terms with unfulfilled ambitions and lost opportunities.

Pity the person whose life has been so ordered and humdrum, there is nothing they would go back and change—if they only could.

Coming to terms with ourselves most often involves deliberate acts of self forgiveness. Ron Palmer wrote that in these matters "Forgiveness or regret are the only choices we have." How true.

We deliver ourselves from a lot of useless baggage of shame, guilt, regret and sorrow when we come to terms with ourselves—when we accept that as with all members of the human race, there is much to regret—and the only sensible and healthy alternative is reconciliation with our personal histories, and forgiveness of ourselves.

I also believe it's true that only when we have come to terms with ourselves can we really come to terms with others, and exercise the healing grace of forgiveness and reconciliation.

CONSPIRATORS

To conspire is to plan with others to commit a wrongful act against someone. A conspiracy takes place when two or more people get together to plan and carry out a harmful, evil and illegal act against someone.

The persons who get involved in such evil doings are conspirators. They always see themselves as lily white—even noble. What they are plotting is for the overall good—or so they tell themselves. Their ideas are rotten to the core, supporting the devilish notion that human beings can perform evil acts in order to accomplish good.

Their real reasons for conspiring center in hate, not love, in destructiveness, not building up, in massaging their own twisted egos, not really trying to benefit anyone else.

There is something sadistic about conspirators. They get to the point where they actually enjoy hurting their victim. It gives them genuine pleasure. But, of course, they would deny that. They consider their motives as pure as the driven snow.

Whenever the words "conspire," "conspiracy" or "conspirator" are used in God's Word they denote evil plotting. To do evil against others is always to do evil against God.

In Psalm 83 we read: "O God. . . See how Your enemies are astir. . . With cunning they conspire against Your people; they plot against those You cherish." Steer clear of persons who conspire.

CONSPIRING IN THE CHURCH

An article by Clark Morphew of the *St. Paul Pioneer Press* appeared in the October 12, 1996 issue of the *Omaha World Herald.* Morphew wrote about church conflicts that result in the abrupt firing of a pastor without any severance considerations and with no appeal.

His article tells us: "The result is a fractured congregation, a demoralized member of the clergy and a power group within the church that believes it can run over anybody without a reason."

Morphew continues:

> These mean-spirited church conflicts usually begin with a small group within the congregation complaining among themselves about the pastor and then moving the discussion into ever-widening circles. They begin with small complaints. . . and then escalate the conflict by raising dozens of complaints. The Pastor is helpless in this kind of maelstrom. . . . By the time the conflict arrives at the pastor's doorstep, the power group is usually stirred into a righteous frenzy and acting like crusaders advancing on a holy task. (Page 57)

Whoa! Wait just a minute! Surely he does not mean the church—*the Church of Jesus Christ!* Can it be that *Christians* would do such evil? Would people who call themselves "Christians" gossip and conspire a minister right out of his or her job and calling? Don't you find that hard to believe?

THE COSTLY EASE OF PROCRASTINATION

This topic is something with which I am especially familiar and in which I am well experienced: procrastination.

Procrastination is almost always a result of poor decisions, planning and work habits on our part. We may blame other factors, and occasionally the work does not get done because of unexpected intrusions on our time. But if that really is the case, it's not authentic procrastination.

I remember as a college student jokingly having as my occasional motto: "Never do today what you can put off until tomorrow." I took courses in Spanish so *manana* rolled off my tongue with ease.

Speaking of ease—procrastination does provide it, along with a sweet release from immediate and pressing demands.

But every time I yield to the siren calls of procrastination, no matter what release I may feel, I pay a terrible price. The work still has to be done. There is less time to do it. The work may suffer because I don't have the time to research and refine.

In short, procrastination is a dumb and costly habit to indulge. The only way to fight it is self-discipline and an intense determination to follow a sane and sensible approach to work and other responsibilities. But the end results are well worth it.

DEFINING FRIENDSHIP

One quickly learns that in the literature available to us, friendship is approached with both admiration and caution.

Mark Twain wrote in *Pudd'nhead Wilson*: "The holy passion of Friendship is of so sweet and steady and loyal and enduring a nature that it will last through a whole lifetime, if not asked to lend money."

Jeremy Taylor was more idealistic: "By friendship you mean the greatest love, the greatest usefulness, the most open communication, the noblest sufferings, the severest truth, the heartiest counsel and the greatest union of minds of which brave men and women are capable."

An old English proverb advises, "Sudden friendship, sure repentance." The winner of a contest on defining a friend stated: "A friend is the one who comes in when the whole world has gone out."

High quality, long lasting and intimate friendships are rare—but also enhance life enormously. Jesus described His relation with His disciples as friendship. That's the best friendship we ever could know.

And James the Apostle cautions us in James 4:4:

> **You adulterous people, don't you know that friendship with the world is hatred toward God? Anyone who chooses to be a friend of the world becomes an enemy of God.**

DEITY AND GENDER

In an article in the June 17, 1996, issue of *Newsweek,* writer Kenneth L. Woodward comments:

> Most Christians and Jews still pray to God as Father. But not for long if feminist theologians have their way. In the nation's elite divinity schools, students are taught to mind their metaphors: God the Father is out, unless coupled with God the Mother. . . . Few theologians these days seem to want a God who takes charge, assumes responsibility, fights for his children, makes demands, risks rebuffs, punishes as well as forgives. In a word, a Father. (pg. 75)

Theologically speaking—and not simply as metaphor—it is perfectly correct and frankly preferable to address God as "Father." That is what He proclaimed Himself to be, that is what Jesus called Him, and throughout the Old and New Testaments He is referred to as Father—as well as Son and Holy Spirit. At no point is God called "Mother."

It's politically correct in certain "churchy" circles to offer public prayers which address God as "Mother" or as "Mother/Father." Use "Father" and you're fair game for criticism and out and out condemnation.

I must confess that whenever I hear someone utilize female ascriptions in referring to deity the question pops to the forefront of my mind: "To whom on earth is this person praying?"

DELIVERANCE

A great deal of our praying should concern our need for deliverance from habits and attitudes that harm, enslave and ultimately will defeat us. It is a fact that there are forces arrayed against our wellbeing—some of them operating from within our psyche, others coming at us from outside. We need deliverance from these unwholesome assailants.

Count on it—every human being needs to pray for deliverance from some preoccupation, obsession, faulty attitude or vile sin.

Some years ago I came across this African prayer:

> From the cowardice that dares not face new truths,
> From the laziness that is content with half truths,
> From the arrogance that thinks it knows all truths,
> Good Lord, deliver me.

What would be the content and thrust of your prayer for deliverance?

In that model Jesus offered for our praying, there is a cry for deliverance. "Lead us not into temptation, but deliver us from evil." Maybe that would make a good beginning—and then go on to name the evils that seem to be at your door.

I love this encouragement from Psalm 32:7: "You are my hiding place; You will protect me from trouble and surround me with songs of deliverance." Make that confident assertion part of your own prayer for deliverance.

DEVOUT PAGANS

When what we rightfully and sensibly *need* becomes an obsession, a new god enters our consciousness. From that moment we are in opposition to the true God, Who alone is to be loved and worshiped.

Have you ever wondered where ancient cultures found all their gods? They sprang from their own distorted values and viewpoints. Normal human needs were elevated and emphasized all out of proportion. They became obsessed with them, and in turn were consumed by them.

I saw a recent cartoon in which one poor soul was prostrated before a huge dollar sign. Two figures were in the background, one saying to the other, "He is very devout in his religion." Pagans usually are—because their gods are grounded in their expanded psyche, their neurotic obsessions with what should be ordinary matters.

At any time of history it would be difficult to find a bunch of pagans as devoted to sexual urges as are many Americans. The adulation of sex is all encompassing.

Sexual obsession and devotion have all the characteristics of a fervent religious pursuit. Sex has all the attributes of a deity. False and ultimately destructive, yes. But a god who demands and consumes its followers.

To be truly free is to be liberated from those pagan urges and creations. Jesus demands—and sets in motion—our liberation.

DISPLAY OF FEELINGS

Probably we all know individuals who wear their feelings on their faces. One old expression calls it "wearing your heart on your sleeve." Such persons are not too sharp about hiding their true feeling. They show the way they really feel, no matter what their words they say.

Feelings of pleasure or displeasure; feelings of caring and feelings of indifference; feelings of love or feelings of hate—they are all right out there on display for everybody to see.

There are some folks who think it virtuous to let it all hang out. Don't hide what you feel, they say—communicate it!

We do well to remember that we sometimes pay a high price for putting our feelings on display—for letting it all hang out. Most other folks are more apt to take offense and consider it rude than to admire someone for being so open and easy to read.

Others may be hurt by our emotional display. While we intend honest candor they read us as disrespectful and even hateful.

Rather than hurt others, replace the scowl on your face with a smile. Instead of that sneer, make your face signal acceptance and understanding—whether or not you agree.

Ruthless honesty is often just that—ruthless, and destructive.

DUPLICITY

Proverbs 11:3 tells us: "The integrity of the upright guides them, but the unfaithful are destroyed by their duplicity."

Duplicity. Now that's a word we ought to know—and a practice we ought to avoid like the proverbial plague.

My trusty *American Heritage Dictionary* defines duplicity as "deliberate deceptiveness in behavior or speech." Duplicity is being two-faced—saying one thing but really intending another. Or it is the covering over or disguising of one's real, and frankly *dark* motives—while professing other, more noble and socially acceptable motives.

In Luke 20:23, when Jesus was asked a tricky question, the Word tells us: "He saw through their duplicity."

All but the most naive and trusting see through duplicity very quickly. But normally the persons who perpetrate duplicity somehow convince themselves that their prey or victim does not catch on. In other words, they are getting away with it. Usually they are dead wrong.

One of the things we learn about such sins as duplicity, is that they always travel in company with other sins. Paul wrote in the first chapter of Romans: "They have become filled with every kind of wickedness, evil, greed and depravity. They are full of envy, murder, strife, deceit and malice." Deceit and duplicity are twins—and they are always joined by other sins. They never stand alone in their evil doings.

ENCOURAGERS AND DISCOURAGERS

Do you see yourself as more of an encourager toward others—or more of a discourager—or completely indifferent to others. Those are three awesome choices, and we are driven to make them time after time, day after day in our personal lives.

George Bernard Shaw wrote in reference to indifference toward others: "The worst sin towards our fellow creatures is not to hate them, but to be indifferent to them: that's the essence of inhumanity." Well put.

Even when we can do little to alleviate the misery of others, we do them honor by our concern and compassion, our feelings of caring sympathy for their plight, and shame for the human perversity that caused it.

And what of discouragers? Have you met any of them along life's way? They beckon others to mediocrity and failure. They are the purveyors of a dismal outlook on anything others undertake. Steer clear of those peddlers of misery and heartbreak.

But to be an encourager—now there's a work that pleases God! To instill faith and hope in others' hearts and minds is surely one of the noblest works of mankind. Genuine encouragers do not press us toward the foolhardy, but often toward the difficult and challenging.

If you would move on to better and more noble accomplishments. surround yourself with encouragers. And better yet—become one yourself!

ERSATZ SUCCESS

There are many facets and aspects to any dependency syndrome—and one of the most common is to depend on others to be successful for us, in our place.

Some get very coercive about this, demanding sacrifices and hard work from their children or even close friends to the end that the manipulators feel the glory and enjoy the victories *as theirs.*

In a kind of wild frenzy of surrogacy, a child's successes become those of the parents, so the parents step way out of bounds in forcing their child into grueling hours of disciplined practice. *They* (the children) must have a great performance—so *they* (the parents) will feel successful!

Dependencies always manipulate and use others to one's own ends, and surrogacy is one of the worst. I sometimes call it "ersatz success." because such surrogacy is phony, a pretense, a sham, not the real thing.

Surrogate success, in which we drive, manipulate and coerce others to do what we wish we could have done and to do it on our behalf, can never really be *our* success—precisely because it is surrogacy. When we have finished with the matter we may be wise enough to understand that all we have done is to enslave another to our own rather questionable ends.

Reflected glory and success have scant reality, and in the end yield little if any satisfaction. That should come as no surprise.

FACES OF EVIL

To keep our lives from going destructive we must be able to recognize the faces of evil—as well as those of goodness.

One face of evil is in the approach that claims: "This is for your own good." That should ring alarm bells whenever someone says it. Each of us should make the decision about what's for our own good—and not turn those choices over to someone else, no matter how close or friendly they might be.

Another face of evil is in any approach that tries to lay blame and induce shame. When someone wants to make you a scapegoat or shame you into following their lead, run, not walk to the nearest exit!

Another approach that should ring warning bells is any appeal to long time precedent or to a higher power to bolster the virtue of the person trying to control you. When someone says, "God told me to persuade you to do this"—make a fast exit, and there's no need to explain.

There are many other examples, but just one more: An overt appeal to our greed or pride or lust. Evil comes on strong when signals of self-interest jump start a person. Our tendencies toward greed, selfishness, pride and lust are easy targets for evil forces.

FAMILY VALUES

A young delegate from Milwaukee was being interviewed about his impressions of the Democratic Convention, and the topic of family values came up. The delegate nervously asked if his interviewer meant the family values espoused by the "far right, like the Christian coalition." These days the utterance of certain words and phrases automatically puts one in the camp of the extreme right: "Morality," "values," "family values," and even "patriotism."

The views of many non-Christians on family values are very close to mine as a Christian—and in some areas they are identical. For example:

• Value: A cohesive, two parent family is the best arrangement for the wellbeing and whole-life nurture of children. Does the Christian coalition really have a monopoly on that viewpoint?

• Value: Homes are the best and most logical place for the basic and continuing education of children, with schools and religious institutions offering support and resources. This makes wondrous sense. And it not an exclusive point of view of any religion.

• Value: Families should discipline themselves to work for a living, and not develop a lifestyle characterized by dependence on welfare handouts. To identify that common sense, socially benefiting value as a product solely of the Christian Coalition is to play very fast and loose with truth.

FANATICISM

It hurts to be accused of being a fanatic when in actuality one is enthusiastic, fervent and excited about one's faith. In our culture it's perfectly acceptable for one to get all excited about sports, the kind of beer one drinks, hunting and fishing trips and gambling. No one's enthusiasm for those areas names him or her a nut or worse.

But get excited about your faith, your thrill at being a Christian, your gratitude for the grace and love of God that give you redemption—and you'll irritate folks around you who will be quick to call you a fanatic, nut, Bible Thumper and worse. You automatically are classified as narrow, condemning, intolerant and fanatical.

But that kind of fervor for one's enormously precious faith is not necessarily fanaticism at all. I've always known more closed minds in the liberal camp than among enthusiasts for Christ. I've found among so-called "Christian fanatics" more understanding, more compassion, more tolerance and more love than I ever have found in liberal, "believe anything you want" circles.

Fanatics lose touch with reality. Genuine Christians are prime realists—with a devotion to truth and whole reality.

I think Ralph Waldo Emerson hit it right: "There is no strong performance without a little fanaticism in the performer."

And that goes for the one who is intent on doing his or her best as a Christian.

FEARLESSNESS

One of the most important concepts of the Bible is that of a remnant. Not everyone who claims loyalty to God is part of that remnant. They are too unstable, too weak, too lacking in faith and resolve.

But there always has been a remnant, a select few, who can manage the faith and commitment that mark them as God's true believers. They also are characterized as fearless.

In Zephaniah 3:13 we read: "The remnant of Israel will do no wrong; they will speak no lies, nor will deceit be found in their mouths. They will eat and lie down and no one will make them afraid."

There is a fearlessness in the remnant because they are straight and honest with each other and with God. They tell no lies, they practice no deceit, they try to do no wrong.

When you find someone who lies and deceives with ease, you can be sure they are not at ease—but full of fears.

If anyone finds themselves growing comfortable with deceitful practices, they should recognize that their very souls are in danger, their salvation suspect, their faith questionable, their fears dominant.

Ultimately deceitfulness is a dead end. God sees through it as do others. In the longest Psalm in the Bible, Psalm 119, verse 118, we read: "You reject all who stray from Your decrees, for their deceitfulness is in vain."

FINDING HAPPINESS

I will be the first to criticize the title above: "Finding Happiness." Ordinarily one does not stumble on happiness, but creates it. A better title would be "Creating Happiness," or "Making Life Joyful."

Others cannot do it for us, either. I cringe when I hear someone saying to another: "You *make me* so unhappy!" No one can make us either happy or unhappy. Their presence, words and actions meet with the happiness and joy we have deliberately chosen and fashioned within the depths of our souls.

Normally and most often happiness and unhappiness are of our intentional and deliberate creation.

Long ago in her work *Dominion,* Jean Ingelow wrote: "It is a comely fashion to be glad—Joy is the grace we say to God." And Joseph Marmion wrote in his work, *Orthodoxy:* "Joy is the echo of God's life within us."

You see—in the makings of joy and happiness there are some essential ingredients. Without them, we'll not be able to create joy and happiness. And the one absolutely essential ingredient is faith and confidence in the God Who loves us, forgives us, reconciles and redeems us in Jesus Christ.

Within the context of that awesome knowledge, sorrow and grief are strangers, ouchy spirits are unthinkable, and joy and happiness are inevitable and unescapable.

FIRST LOVE

Jesus didn't write any letters, but He dictated some—and they are found in the first few chapters of the Book of Revelation. They were written down and sent on by the Apostle John, as part of that wondrous vision of the Christ and what was to come. He wrote it all down in the Book of Revelation.

In one letter Jesus gave the church at Ephesus some deserved words of commendation, and then issued a declaration of criticism. He told them they had lost their first love. (See Revelation 2:1-8)

All people come to the Christian faith from a life of sin and disbelief—and they celebrate the love of God, the forgiveness of their sin, and the security of knowing they are heaven bound. They are overwhelmed with love for the One Who has redeemed them from sin and hell, and are willing to do whatever He asks.

But with time, that first love tends to grow cold. Compare it with courtship, marriage—and then the diminishment of enthusiasm and excitement. That first love is terribly difficult to sustain.

But work on your relationship with Jesus and all it means. Nothing has changed except that *within us* the fires have died down. Work to regain your first love—the time spent with Jesus in prayer and devotions, the excitement of deepening your faith, the satisfaction and joy in serving Him.

FOSTERING RESENTMENT

Speaking figuratively, most of us have "foster children" that we may not be aware of. By this I mean adjuncts to our lives that are not really meant to be ours, but by our own choice we care and nurture them.

A foster child in a home is a commendable act. But keeping "foster children" in our psyche is neither wise nor healthy.

One such "foster child" is resentment. When resentment knocks on our door—as it will, and often—many throw open the door and invite resentment into their lives, urging that it feel right at home. And it does! But not to their benefit.

Resentment makes a victim out of us, whether or not the facts support it. Our self esteem is lowered by resentment. Our happiness is chased away by resentment. Our drives for creativity and accomplishment are short circuited by resentment.

We have a "right" to resent people and circumstances—just as we have a "right" to a headache or a broken arm. Who wants it?

Someone wrote: "To harbor resentment is to harbor an enemy." Believe it! Resentment is no friend to spiritual and emotional health, and no friend to our powers to achieve and relate.

So when resentment knocks—don't answer the door!

FRIENDSHIP'S VALUE

We infer from such Biblical reference as 3rd John 1:14 that in the early church the word "friends" was the way Christians designated and greeted each other. John wrote: "I hope to see you soon, and we will talk face to face. Peace to you. The friends here send their greetings. Greet the friends there by name."

I have not heard that term used in churches of today. Maybe that's because it cannot be used. Perhaps the relationships among typical persons in a typical church are so shallow they could never be called "friendships."

While it's terribly hard to put a value on friends—that value most certainly is there.

Thomas Hughes wrote: "Blessed are they who have the gift of making friends, for it is one of God's best gifts. It involves many things, but above all the power of going out of one's self, and appreciating whatever is noble and loving in another."

Jesus taught: "Greater love has no one than this, that he lay down his life for his friends." (John 15:3

Probably in reference to that verse, one man commented: "Dying for a friend is not so difficult. Finding a friend worth dying for is the big challenge."

You know—I'm glad our Lord did not think that way.

GARBAGE CHURCHES

Recently it came to my attention that a certain church in a nearby community has been dubbed "The Garbage Church" by the contented folks in other churches.

It seems that this church has the audacity and poor taste to welcome confessing sinners, people with failed lives, folks with problems, moral cripples and various seekers of redemption and wholeness.

They not only welcome them, they provide for their nurture, offering counseling, supportive fellowship and relevant programs that will help them sort out their lives and reach for Christ's best. Are these approaches even a bit Biblical?

Jesus told a story about a man who invited neighbors and friends to a banquet—and not one of them showed up. Then the owner of the house became angry and ordered his servant, "Go out quickly into the streets and alleys of the town and bring in the poor, the crippled, the blind and the lame." (See Luke 14:15 ff)

Get that? "The poor, the crippled, the blind and the lame"—euphemisms for the refuse of humanity. It turned out that in spite of the absence of all those "worthy" and "righteous" folks, the banquet was a huge success.

Congratulations to all churches deserving the title "The Garbage Church." They have caught the themes of the cross—Redemption, Reconciliation and Regeneration.

GATEKEEPING

I often think of that basic computer principle: "Garbage in—garbage out."

That's true of our lives, too—and especially of our mind and spirit. What we allow into our heads and hearts will determine what we will produce. Allow in mainly garbage and our lives will produce mainly garbage.

We all need a gatekeeper of sorts, whose task it is to filter the input to our minds and emotions—who prevents the entry of things that are unwholesome and unworthy of our beings and identities.

Gatekeeping for our minds and emotions is accomplished by certain decisions and determinations we have made, principles and values we have chosen, standards of worth and excellence to which we are loyal. By all these assignments and empowerments for gatekeeping, we measure the worth of whatever tries to get into our heads and hearts at the entry points. Such choices constitute a gatekeeper for our total psyche—via the ears, eyes, feelings and thought patterns.

When we have not made such critical determinations, just about anything is allowed in. We can get very confused about the bad and the good—and things tend to settle down and feel right at home in our lives, when really they do not belong.

Take some time to think about what does the gatekeeping for your mind and heart.

WHEN WE'VE BEEN BURNED

When we've been burned—physically or psychologically—it tends to make us wary, careful and cautious. Only someone who enjoys suffering—a masochist—keeps going back for more hurt, more pain.

Many run from life after being burned. Their reaction is understandable, but it is not the wise thing to do. Burns can heal, if we will let them. Attitudes of fear, anger and indignation can be tempered by time, humor and wisdom.

However others may have burned us, there comes a time when we must go back and try again—wiser and perhaps more cautious—but reenter we must. Otherwise we trash the best of life.

Burning most often occurs in the most sensitive areas of human interaction, where we expected to find joy and acceptance—and perhaps love and recognition. But the tables were turned on us, and we experienced the very opposite of what we needed and wanted.

To learn lessons from our burnings is wise. To let such harsh experiences at the hands of others turn us into bitter cynics is to give them the victory.

Yes, risk is perilous. Letting others get close is risky. Venturing into the unknown could lead us over a cliff.

But it is only through such risk taking and challenging adventures that we find the exhilarations of life.

GENUINE SPIRITUALITY

We live in a time when notions of being "spiritual" are popular. In just about every corner of society you'll find folks touting their version of "spirituality."

The Scriptures make it clear that spirituality has some defining characteristics if it is genuine and authentic. It is not something we can develop all by ourselves, apart from God.

In I Corinthians 2 we read:

> **The Spirit searches all things, even the deep things of God. . . This is what we speak, not in words taught us by human wisdom but in words taught by the Spirit, expressing spiritual truths in spiritual words. The man without the Spirit does not accept the things that come from the Spirit of God, for they are foolishness to him, and he cannot understand them, because they are spiritually discerned.**

Worldly wisdom claims that to be spiritual is to be in touch with yourself—with your feelings, with who you are, with your ideals and destiny.

According to God's Holy Word, the essence of spirituality is to be in touch with the Spirit of God—to be taught by Him, nurtured by Him and led by Him.

One cannot be genuinely spiritual apart from God's Spirit within—and that condition is a gift of God, wrapped up in the salvation granted us by Jesus Christ.

HOPE

Hope is an extremely important concept for our living. Someone wrote:

> Age is a quality of mind;
> If you've left your Dreams behind,
> If hope is cold, If you no longer look ahead,
> If your ambition fires Are dead, Then, you are old!

Apparently you also are hopeless—a terrible condition for anyone. Charles L. Allen wrote: "When you say a situation or a person is hopeless, you are slamming the door in the face of God."

Christianity is exquisite hope based on the promises of God. Abraham is surely one of the best examples of this stance of hope. Paul wrote: "Against all hope, Abraham in hope believed and so became the father of many nations, just as it had been said to him, 'So shall your offspring be.'" (Romans 4:19)

God promised, and Abraham based all his hopes on those promises. And he was not disappointed.

The best of hope is tied to the faith given us by Jesus Christ. Matthew wrote of Jesus: "In His Name the nations will put their hope." (Matthew 12:21) And Paul prays in Ephesians 1:18: "I pray also that the eyes of your heart may be enlightened in order that you may know the hope to which He has called you, the riches of His glorious inheritance in the saints."

HATRED'S AWESOME POWER

The philosopher Jose′ Ortega y Gasset wrote: "Hatred is a feeling which leads to the extinction of values."

Some have learned the hard way that hate is an insatiable god who demands the sacrifice of the best of one's life. It simply cannot be a neutral force—quiet and undemanding. Hate destroys not only relationships, but truth, hope, love, integrity and every other value.

Hate and love have nothing in common—except the power of metamorphosis. Hate and love both tend to transform us, creating a new person. Hate develops the ugly and destructive. Love results in the beautiful and all that builds up.

There is nothing commendable in hate, nothing worthy of admiration. It is one of the blackest, most despicable of all human forces—and it is powerful precisely because so much time and energy are spent in keeping it alive and active.

The person who hates is usually obsessed with it. He or she is hooked on hate, and just will not let it go.

I've known some folks who claim to be Christian and yet hate with great intentionality and constancy. Instead of "Amazing Grace, how sweet the sound that saved a wretch like me," their song could well be "Amazing Hate, how sweet it feels, while it destroys a wretch like me."

HOLD THAT THOUGHT

Let's be honest: Most of our thoughts are not worth much. But we all have occasional thoughts that are worth keeping.

I mean worthwhile, uplifting, soul-enriching, character building thoughts—and certainly not thoughts of hatred and revenge, not lustful thoughts, not even lazy thoughts.

I'm a doting grandfather, and thoughts about my grandchildren's personalities and love of life give me a real charge. Those thoughts are worth holding on to.

There are special times and seasons when I am almost swamped by good thoughts—heartwarming, grateful, immensely comforting thoughts.

Whenever I enter a church, good thoughts crowd my mind. I avoid thinking about the length of the sermon or the quality of the singing. God is among the people who gather there, and that is a thought worth keeping.

It takes work and concentration, but I often succeed in banishing dark thoughts *by deliberately turning to good thoughts.* Lofty music helps me do that. Great and timeless music can induce some pretty nifty thoughts in one's head and heart.

Paul shared keen insights when he wrote in Philippians 4: 8: "Finally, brothers, whatever is true, whatever is noble, whatever is right, whatever is pure, whatever is lovely, whatever is admirable—if anything is excellent or praiseworthy—think about such things."

HOME TO ROOST

Human beings have a tendency to neglect a very important principle of life—which I call "the law of coming home to roost."

Often it seems that evildoers rarely if ever get their comeuppance. But God is patient, and we can be sure that eventually their chickens will come home to roost.

The Bible has some interesting references to this life principle. One of them is found in Proverbs 21:13: "If a man shuts his ears to the cry of the poor, he too will cry out and not be answered."

You see—God has an intense concern for the poor, and expects us to feel the same way. I did not say the slackers, the lazy people who refuse to work, the indolent who want everything handed to them on a silver platter.

The real poor are those who have run into circumstances that stripped them of opportunities to make a decent living. When they cry out for help, the godly pay close attention—and then do something that is in their power to do.

In his first letter, chapter 3, verse 17, the Apostle John asks this enormously relevant question: "If anyone has material possessions and sees his brother in need but has no pity on him, how can the love of God be in him?"

A pertinent question for us all.

HUMAN NATURE?

I wonder how many people excuse their daily perversity, evil doings and other mischief by attributing their awful conduct to "human nature."

How should we describe human nature? What are its boundaries? When does it become inhuman or less than human, or totally lacking in what humans should be and do?

When a father locks his children in barrels—is that an expression of human nature?

When a mother sets her automobile rolling into a lake to deliberately drown her children, or a father slits the throats of his children, or a mother kills her baby by leaving him in a locked car in hundred degree weather—are those acts of human nature?

Does human nature sometimes go demonic—and just when is that, and how do we recognize it?

The Bible makes no bones about the potentials of human nature apart from divine guidance and help. It is not enough to act as a human being. We are to think and act as God's people, recognizing and freeing ourselves from the evils into which human beings fall all too easily.

What God tells us in His Word is that human nature simply cannot be our excuse or rationale for murder, mayhem or worse. His call is to be transformed children of God, whose abhorrence of evil and passion for righteousness mirror His.

ILLUSIONS OF HONESTY

Make no mistake about it, honesty is a virtue. Honest persons most often deserve accolades. But as with any other virtue, honesty cannot stand alone. It has to be tempered with other virtues, such as knowing when to be silent, the capacity for compassion, and a sensitivity to others' feelings and fears.

Dr. Rose Franzblau wrote: "Honesty, without compassion and understanding, is not honesty, but subtle hostility." Now, that's something to think about!

We probably know a few who use their honesty as a weapon. They swing it at others in a manner that says, "I'm being honest, that's all. If it hurts or harms you, that's your problem. I must be honest."

There are alternatives honest people can select to keep their honesty helpful. At appropriate times they could shut up, keep silent, say nothing. But there's not much of a kick in that!

Relationships have been driven on the rocks because someone thought honesty was more important than kindness or love. Someone unloaded in what may have amounted to a delectable frenzy of telling truths that are better left unsaid, of truthfully reminding someone of their jaded past, of pointing out faults and failures that should remain buried and forgotten.

Be honest. But be careful in your honesty that it not become a weapon that does far more harm than good.

ANTIDOTE TO DESPAIR

Acute depression brings us to the very brink of despair. It's a paralyzing force, sometimes defeating our ability to work, our sense of self-esteem, and even our will to live.

Dr. Alfred Adler once said that we can be cured of depression in only fourteen days if every day we will try to think of how we can be helpful to others.

Of course, one of the problems that characterizes many depressed persons is that they can't possibly think of the pain and problems of others, because they are so wrapped up in their own.

One of the best things churches do is to help us get outside ourselves—to start thinking of others, even people we don't know.

When you really think about it, it is absolutely amazing that Jesus *commanded* us to love one another. He didn't suggest it—He ordered it! The popular notion is that love is a matter of uncontrollable feelings. But our Lord made it clear that in the main love is a product of the mind, of willful intentionality.

When the norm for our living is to reach out to help others in the context of the love taught by Jesus—depression and despair simply cannot maintain a hold of our minds and hearts.

HANDLING THE DARK SIDE

All human beings have to handle what I call "the dark side of life." By that I mean the truly troublesome and even horrific that comes into play when evil intrudes big time, and life begins to fall apart.

Most human responses to the dark side are simply ways and means of repression and avoidance.

Stoicism yields small and fleeting satisfaction. Hedonism and materialism create only temporary diversions. Cynicism is one of the big time spoilers of life, and ends up making matters worse. Determined agnosticism or atheism lead into deeper shadows and beg all the questions.

Many find at least a bit of relief in religious exercises and contemplations. But glorified navel gazing and religious tripping only skim the surface. Indeed, they tend to compound misery and despair simply because they keep the focus on one's massive and insatiable ego.

Dealing with the full reality of life requires a dive into the mystical and mysterious—the authentically spiritual.

That "dive" can only be made when we recognize that in essence we are spiritual beings with physical, emotional and psychological attributes. Unless and until we accept that, and treat the big questions of life as matters of spirituality, we will be very alone, disoriented and perhaps at our wits' end whenever life becomes too much to handle, too dark, too hurtful.

JUDGING

God's Word is very specific about the fact that God alone is qualified to pronounce judgment on human beings—we are not.

A lady in an airport bought a book to read and a package of cookies to eat while she waited for her plane. After she had taken her seat in the terminal and gotten engrossed in her book, she noticed that the man one seat away from her was fumbling to open the package of cookies on the seat between them.

She was so shocked that a stranger would eat her cookies that she didn't really know what to do, so she just reached over and took one of the cookies and ate it. The man didn't say anything but soon reached over and took another. Well, the woman wasn't going to let him eat them all, so she took another, too.

When they were down to one cookie, the man reached over, broke the cookie in half, handed half to her—then got up and left. The lady couldn't believe the man's nerve, but soon the announcement came to board the plane.

Once the woman was aboard, still angry at the man's audacity and puzzling over the incident, she reached into her purse for a tissue.

It suddenly dawned on her that she really should not judge people too harshly—for there in her purse lay her still-unopened package of cookies she had bought.

CUT IT DOWN

To the best of my knowledge there is no place in the Guiness World Book of Records for prolonged anger and grudges. But for sure to keep such ill will alive and kicking takes some thought and work.

What should one do with pent up, long-term grudges, with their accompanying desire for revenge?

In his book, *Lee: The Last Years,* Charles Bracelen Flood reports that after the Civil War, Robert E. Lee visited a Kentucky lady who showed him the ugly remains of a grand old tree in front of her house.

She bitterly cried that its limbs and trunk had been destroyed by Federal artillery fire. She looked to Lee for a word condemning the North or at least sympathizing with her loss.

After a brief silence, Lee said, "Cut it down, my dear Madam, and forget it."

Protracted and nurtured anger in our lives is like the ugly remains of that old tree in front of the woman's house. Its presence spoils our days and years, impacts our lives in destructive ways and turns us into sour and bitter persons.

My advice to all who nurture anger and thoughts of recrimination and revenge is the same advice Robert E. Lee gave to the Kentucky woman: "Cut it down—and forget it."

YET YOU ARE RICH!

One of the most fascinating portions of the Bible is found in the 2nd and 3rd chapters of the Book of Revelation, where the risen, reigning, cosmic Christ dictates some letters to the seven churches of Asia Minor.

His second letter, Revelation 2:8-11, is to the Church at Smyrna. Today the city is called Izmir, and is in Turkey. The Lord tells those Christians: "I know your afflictions and your poverty—yet you are rich!"

How in the world can that be?

It seems almost heartless to confront someone in the deepest poverty and troubles and tell them: "Yet you are rich!" Presumptuous? Cheeky? Or stark truth?

I believe that our Lord would not say this to just any poor person—probably not to most. There are the poor who have nothing to lean on or look to.

But these poverty riddled Christians in the Church at Smyrna had a lot more than their afflictions and poverty. They had Christ, His salvation, His forgiveness, His comforting Presence and His promise of life eternal.

So while poor in worldly terms, they were rich. The wealth of life is simply not measured in terms of financial wealth and possessions.

You see—there is more than one way to figure your net worth. How do you figure yours?

WHEN YOU CAN' T SLEEP

The other night I watched Larry King interviewing Billy Graham. In response to the host's question about best times to pray, Dr. Graham mentioned that he often has trouble sleeping at night, and that's when he does some of his best praying.

I can identify with that. My sleeplessness is often caused by nagging thoughts that mostly have to do with myself. When I turn my mind and heart to God, and start praying for others, it's remarkable how quickly sleep comes.

Because I am convinced that prayer has an impact on the people for whom we're praying, I've done a lot more good through my praying than just tossing and turning, preoccupied with thoughts that won't go away—without the help of prayer.

Psalm 63 tells us of the value of our prayers in the night: "On my bed I remember You; I think of You through the watches of the night. Because You are my help, I sing in the shadow of Your wings."

And then we have these comforting words from Psalm 4:8: "I will lie down and sleep in peace, for You alone, O Lord, make me dwell in safety."

Faith in Christ is a wonderful force. At times it keeps us awake—and there are times when it enables peaceful slumber.

WORTH KNOWING

In your opinion, what are the qualities that make a person worth knowing?

I've known folks who looked at others only for what they might get out of them. Such persons are out and out users—and most of us have fallen victim to the manipulations of such characters at one time or another.

There's an old saying: "It isn't what you know, but who you know that counts." That is a very jaded outlook on the forming of relationships. "Relate if it will get you something." That is not a noble approach to relationships.

In a sense, everybody is worth knowing. All have something to offer in terms of life experiences and outlook. But inevitably, some are more worth knowing than others.

Persons who in one way or another have stood firm against the forces of evil are worth knowing. They did not cower, run or hide. They stood firm. I have been blessed by such persons.

Persons who have gone through travail and pain, heavy battles of the soul and torment of spirit are worth knowing. They have seen more of the darker side of life, and so they have much more appreciation of what is good and worthwhile.

Good questions for all of us: Am I—are you—worth knowing? And why?

WHY WORRY?

Worry is the process by which we use up energy and waste our resources on matters that may never happen, on troubles that may never come. It is one of the devil's greatest victories when he persuades us to take leave of the important matters of spirituality and the Kingdom of God, and waste our energies on pointless, fruitless worries.

Someone wrote: "The devil would have us continually crossing streams that do not exist." And another anonymous writer advises: "Leave tomorrow's trouble to tomorrow's strength; tomorrow's work to tomorrow's time; tomorrow's trial to tomorrow's grace and to tomorrow's God." That is excellent counsel.

Jesus had some choices comments about worry—such as His words in Matthew 6:31-34:

> **So do not worry, saying, "What shall we eat?" or "What shall we drink?" or "What shall we wear?" For the pagans run after all these things, and your heavenly Father knows that you need them. But seek first His kingdom and His righteousness, and all these things will be given to you as well. Therefore do not worry about tomorrow, for tomorrow will worry about itself. Each day has enough trouble of its own.**

I interpret His words as telling us that worry is mainly a result of mixed up and misdirected priorities. Get those priorities straight, and worries tend to disappear.

WHEN ALL ELSE FAILS

I suspect that I am among a great number of persons when I own up to not being a "Read the Directions" person.

Occasionally a new computer program arrives. one I've ordered with great care and anticipation because the cost of software is not friendly to my budget. I rip open the package with keen anticipation, and find that with all the wisdom of Solomon, and apparently fully cognizant of whom they are dealing with, the software manufacturers have included a little card of basic directions for the likes of me—buyers who just can't be bothered with the 240 page manual they also have so thoughtfully enclosed.

But the adage still holds—"When all else fails, read the directions." Eventually one is crowded to the manual. So with my back against the wall, I bring the manual down from the shelf or call it up from a computer disk, and research. That happened just last week with a software program I bought months ago!

And truthfully, I regretted that I had not done the research earlier, for the program's possibilities are immense—when you read the directions!

That's also true of life. Many hate to read the directions found in that weighty Book given by God, the Holy Bible. When we finally get around to reading His directions, we wish we had done the research earlier, for the possibilities are truly and eternally immense.

THE GIRL IN THE YELLOW DRESS

Recently I heard of a play that is touring certain parts of the nation. It's called, *The Girl in the Yellow Dress.*

The play depicts a high school girl who came back to life to tell the story of her murder at the hands of her high school sweetheart—the boy she thought loved her. But violence entered the picture very early.

She thought she needed him desperately, and became willing to put up with conduct that no person needs or should allow from another human being.

And so there came the night when in a rage, the boy whom she loved beat her to death without a smidgen of compassion or mercy.

The play is a warning to teenagers and their parents. With some youngsters safe dating is a dangerous illusion—and their number is increasing.

With the diminishment of respect for others and the growing intensity of selfishness and even self-worship in our society—with the violence youth see modeled on television and in their sports heroes—there is no mystery about where this teen dating violence comes from or why it is growing in frequency and brutality.
Young people need to be very discerning about the persons they take up with—and should make up their minds that some costs for companionship are way too high—and often dangerous.

CAVEAT EMPTOR

The old Latin expression, *Caveat Emptor,* "Let the Buyer Beware," is as relevant today as it was when the warning was first coined.

Rip off artists are on the loose all over the place. Misrepresentation is rampant. The purchase of any kind of goods and services is definitely an area where a little suspicion is very good for the soul—and your bank account.

If the knock at the door reveals a representative from some out of town outfit who has a terrific deal for you on any kind of house repair—quickly close the door, without so much as a "by your leave," and immediately call the police.

Watch for scams in the mail. You might be getting some small return on your money, but often you're paying dearly for the promotion, not the merchandise.

When it comes to those enticements to believe you have a good chance to win millions—well, *Caveat Emptor*—let the buyer beware. In nearly every case the deal isn't worth the postage, let alone the purchase of magazine subscriptions.

If some stranger suggests that with a little financial help, he or she could put hundreds or even thousands of dollars in your bank account, laugh uproariously and scurry away.

Respecting everyone, including strangers is a virtue. Trusting them is not.

WHEN THE MAJORITY RULES

In our nation and society, we profess great respect for the principle of "the majority rules." Some of us are naive enough to think that is always a good thing. We have a perception of the masses as having a collective wisdom that is unerring and benevolent. If you believe that, I have a bridge I'd like to sell to you.

That seemingly sacred majority more often than not plays the fool. The majority engineers lynchings, clamors for entitlements, scorns the highest truths, dotes on televised violence, and yells "Jump" to a man standing on a roof contemplating suicide.

Many of the great injustices of history have been committed in the name of the unchecked and unbridled "majority rule."

The late Senator James A. Reed of Missouri, said the following in one of the most forceful speeches ever delivered to the Senate:

> The majority crucified Jesus Christ; the majority burned the Christians at the stake; the majority established slavery; the majority jeered when Columbus said the world was round; the majority threw him into a dungeon for having discovered a new world; the majority cut off the ears of John Pym because he dared advocate the liberty of the press.

More often than not in history it is the voice of a minority that rings with truth and righteousness, that calls for nobility of conduct and points us to the high road.

WHEN AND WHAT TO OVERLOOK

Everybody thinks that grandparents really have it easy. The grandchildren come for a visit, they enjoy them and spoil them rotten, and then send them back to their parents for readjustment.

But that is not always the case. It really depends on the qualities of the grandparents.

Susan and I are committed to mirroring the homes of our grandchildren in terms of expectations, discipline, affection and love.

But at the same time we want their visits to be joyful and memorable, and that means developing a lot of wisdom about what to overlook and when.

Our oldest grandson likes to load his bread with at least a half inch of strawberry jam. Do I make an issue of it? The little darlings slurp in their spaghetti by sheer suction power. Do I overlook, or do I offer a lecture? One of the youngest insists on doing everything for herself, sometimes making a mess of it. Do I step in and do it for her, or do I overlook?

Come to think of it, all our lives we seek the wisdom of knowing what and when to overlook—so that remembrances will be of tolerance and laughter, joy and good will—instead of memories of rebukes over a lot of stuff that ought to be overlooked.

TRINITARIANS

Whenever we confess Jesus Christ as Savior and Lord, we are laying claim to being Trinitarians—that we believe that God is Triune, three-in-one, three distinct Persons within one Godhead. This stance is in comparison with folks who are Unitarians, thereby rejecting the Biblical teaching of a God Who is Father, Son and Holy Spirit. One wonders what on earth such folks are doing in any Christian Church, for Christianity is based solidly on Trinitarian beliefs.

The Trinity is not intended to be a mathematical formula, but an expression of complex truth and complicated reality.

One of the oldest ploys of unbelieving scoffers is pointing out that the words "Trinity" and "triune" are not found in the Bible. And they are right. But they also are wrong in setting forth the idea that therefore the Bible teaches nothing about God's Triuneness.

Take a look at just one verse among many that testifies to God's nature as three-in-one—Matthew 28:19:

> **Therefore go and make disciples of all nations, baptizing them in the name of the Father and of the Son and of the Holy Spirit.**

We need to understand that the concept of the Trinity is immensely important to our Christian belief system. Without it we find no grounding for God's incarnation and saving work in Jesus Christ, along with His coming again in power and glory.

LIVING FORWARDS

The Danish philosopher, Soren Kierkegaard, gave us a pretty nifty insight when he said: "Life can only be understood backwards, but must be lived forwards."

We ought to ponder that statement—especially those of us who have a tendency to scorn the past and become overly preoccupied with change and the future.

The past matters a great deal. We can learn from the mistakes, build on the successes and gain enormous wisdom for living in the present and towards the future. The present tells us little unless we know how we got to where we are.

It was Hodding Carter, Jr., who commented: "There are two lasting bequests we can give our children: One is roots. The other is wings." When we think about it, we soon realize that without the collective wisdom and attachments of roots, there can be no wings.

Roots assure us of the past and all that was and is meaningful in it. Wings make the past a springboard for venturesome flights into a future. The more we know of what lies behind and below us, the more exciting the venture.

This is one reason why historical revisionism is so deadly. Not only does it pollute and destroy the truth, it fails to give us our rightful and enormously helpful roots and heritage.

ON BEING SUPER SENSITIVE

Izaak Walton was a wise person, and one of his pithy sayings goes like this: "There are offenses given and offenses not given but taken." He was referring to super sensitive people who imagine slights and offensive thoughts and actions directed toward them when there are none!

If you often feel slighted by others—put down, maligned, ignored and ill-used—it could be that it's mainly in your own head. Your psyche may be perceiving slights when there just aren't any. None was intended. None was given. But you took something the wrong way, filled it with your imaginings, and then grew resentful and angry that anyone would treat you in such a manner.

To some extent what I am describing is paranoia—fearful imaginings without foundation.

And I'm also referring to persons who have problems with their feelings of self-worth, so they project what amounts to their own misconceptions about their worth into the innocent approaches of others.

And there is the element of plain and simple fairness. If someone really is not giving offense, I do him or her an injustice by taking offense.

I've heard comments that being super sensitive is a minor defect, hardly worth the trouble of correction. Wrong. Being super sensitive is a major defect—harmful to one's self and to others. Get it under control!

LOVE—OR DEPENDENCE?

A young woman told her story in a therapy group, and ended with the comment: "I thought I was in love—but I was just dependent." She had learned a hard lesson—to differentiate between love and dependency. And while there might be beguiling and deceiving similarities, there is a great deal of difference.

The similarity is in the fact that love does learn to trust and to rely on certain qualities and character traits. Love does depend on the other person—but never as a substitute for personal responsibility, action and accomplishment.

Dependency, as one writer describes it, is "acting out an addiction"—which always means the loss of freedom, choice and ultimately one's dignity and self-respect. Dependency is demeaning and degrading. Authentic love could never lead to that kind of crushing of the spirit and will.

Dependency goes ballistic at the thought of losing the relationship, and comes to the point where the dependent person will do anything to hang on to a relationship that is just plain no good.

It's wondrously refreshing to see a person discovering the awful truth of dependency, and then shucking if off. And it's even more delightful when that same person finds real love.

Good advice for all of us: "Learn to recognize the signs of dependence—and do whatever is needed to neutralize, depart from it and avoid it."

OUR TRAIN OF THOUGHT

One of my grandchildren knows more about trains than I ever hope to. He's fascinated by them, collects them, plays with them and reads about them.

But next time I am with him, I'll have to ask him if he knows about the most important train in his life: His train of thought. Have you ever heard someone say, "Oh, I've lost my train of thought"?

Joseph Fort Newton wrote about the train of thought: "Every man has a train of thought on which he rides when he is alone. The dignity and nobility of his life, as well as his happiness, depend upon the direction in which that train is going, the baggage it carries, and the scenery through which it travels."

A lot of trains of thought travel light. Not a weighty thought or heavy consideration on board. Ask them where their train is headed and they haven't the faintest notion. One has the feeling that the scenery is totally ignored. For the most part the whole adventure must be dreadfully unimpressive.

But then I've known a lot of people whose trains of thought are always loaded for the fullest of life. They move through magnificent vistas of scenery—and they seem to be headed in the direction of the Creator's ways and His eternal dwelling place.

How about your train of thought?

NON-PHARMACEUTICAL NARCOTICS

I'm indebted to John Gardner for the phrase "Non-pharmaceutical narcotics." Gardner wrote: "Self-pity is easily the most destructive of the non-pharmaceutical narcotics: it is addictive, gives momentary pleasure, and separates the victim from reality."

Have you ever thought of self-pity as a home-brewed narcotic? Persons who indulge themselves in what some call "a pity party" are really on a trip—into their inner being and away from the stark reality they hate to face. Pity-popping is a lot like pill-popping. It can become mindless, heedless and very destructive.

Another non-pharmaceutical narcotic is laziness or indolence. I cringe when I hear a young person whine about how difficult it is to learn this or that. They want life to be easy, just a snap! So they develop lazy minds and lazy bodies—addictive attitudes offering momentary pleasure and removing one from the hassles of the real world. Or so they think.

Every narcotic, pharmaceutical or non-pharmaceutical, eventually exacts an accounting—and an awful price in terms of the penalties of attitudes and behaviors such as self-pity and laziness.

Anything we take up and use as a diversion from facing the truth and doing what needs to be done is a non-pharmaceutical narcotic. It may dull the senses, mute the pain and give us a phony sense of exhilaration. But in the end we pay a terrible price.

MORAL CLARITY

"Obfuscation" is an interesting word. It is used to describe matters that are confusing, unclear, murky and dark.

Some are experts at obfuscation. They muddy the waters so it becomes difficult for their opponents to see with clarity. Politicians and anyone who is trying to gain an advantage over someone else often obfuscate to beat the band.

In the times of Jesus, obfuscation was a popular means of dialoguing and debating. Make the issues murky, and perhaps you'll gain the victory.

Probably this motivated one of Jesus' commands in His Sermon on the Mount, Matthew 5:37: "Simply let your 'Yes' be 'Yes,' and your 'No,' 'No'; anything beyond this comes from the evil one." In other words, don't obfuscate.

In matters involving ethics and morality, obfuscationists really go to work. They think up case scenarios that may rarely or perhaps never happen. They protest perceived rights violations of minuscule minorities. They try to show how following the rules inevitably will work hardship and deprivation for perceived victims. They call forth anything that will obfuscate the real issues.

But for sure—with most situations involving moral issues there is clarity if we will let matters stand within the contexts of truth and reality. The issues are clear, the options are obvious—until someone steps in, and with malice and mischief in their hearts, begins to obfuscate.

OUTLOOKS ON LIFE

Most people give little thought to their outlooks on life.

As a whole, how do you view life? Does your outlook reflect purpose and meaning? How far is your life horizon? Does God and His eternal purposes and plans fit into your outlook on life?

William James wrote: "The great use of life is to spend it for something that outlasts it."

From the author Herman Melville: "Life is a voyage that is homeward bound." And Goethe the German philosopher wrote: "Life is the childhood of our immortality."

All those are fairly good, along with other outlooks, expressed by a great many persons. But if we really want an outlook on life that is firm, truthful, dependable and genuine, we have to turn to the One Who said: "I am the Way, and the Truth, and the Life." His Name is Jesus. (John 14:6)

In Jesus we find everything that is worth living for—along with everything that is worth dying for. He shows us God, He relates us to God, He handles the failures and sins of our lives, He is with us to empower us in our needs, He will meet us when we leave this life and cross over to His eternal domain.

Without Jesus the Christ, any outlook on life is sorely lacking—and may completely miss the meaning of it all.

PATIENCE

We were two churches joining together for worship a few Sundays ago, and I led most of the service and preached the sermon.

Because of the crowd there were twice as many children, and at least that number of babies—noisy babies—lots of them—and nearly all vying with me for attention.

Over the years I've learned to tune all that out, and go full steam ahead on what I have to say. Occasionally I may lean closer to the microphone, to make sure the members of the congregation don't miss any of my golden words.

As is my custom, I stood at the door and greeted the departing folks on that particular Sunday. One woman swept up to me—yes, I think it correct to call it "swept up"—and without a word of greeting she said through tight lips, "I admire your self-control"—and swept out. She was from the other church, for sure.

Self-control is the basis for patience—a wonderful skill to develop and use.

Someone wrote that patience is the ability to keep your motor idling when you feel like stripping the gears. Self-control.

Patience learns not to expect the absolutely impossible. As one wag put it, "Patience will do wonders—but it was not much help to the fellow who planted an orange grove in Maine."

PAYBACKS

Let's face it—a lot of people are ingrates. Such persons are obsessed with desires to pay back evil for the good done to them. I recommend this verse from Proverbs 17:13: "If a man pays back evil for good, evil will never leave his house."

When we pay back some good with evil, it's like inviting evil into our own home—and it will stick and stay.

A lot of our troubles come from hearts that devise evil toward others, while expecting only good to come to us. That's very convoluted thinking—and life just doesn't work that way.

The formula is more like this: Do good, and good will come and dwell with you. Do evil, and evil will come and dwell with you.

It's another one of those rules of life that assures us that "You can't have your cake and eat it, too".

We do evil when we scorn the good others do. We do evil when we reject others for their sins and failures, while being highly tolerant of our own. We also do evil when we refuse to help when help is needed and it is in our hand to do it.

And somehow the worst of evils are perpetrated when we withhold mercy and compassion, and demand harsh judgment and consequences for others.

Guard against the desire to give paybacks in the "currency" of evil. They always boomerang.

POWER KICKS

The desire for power is a subtle force in the lives of many people. In fact, if accused of wanting power they would deny it. Such an accusation would startle them, so convinced are they of their purity of motives and desire when it comes to the matter of power.

But even so, power hungry persons are not a joy to have around. They want control of the way things are done not only in their lives, but in their church or club or school or whatever. They are highly manipulative and have little restraint when it comes to takeovers in the lives of others. Before you know it they are directing things, making suggestions, giving orders and ridiculing whatever is not their idea.

Gossipers are power hungry folks. When someone comes to you with some juicy tidbit about this or that person, they are making a power grab—showing their superior knowledge and manipulating you into subservience through acquiescence.

When someone wants to be on every committee in your organization or church, they are quite likely revealing their lust for power.

I appreciate this bit of wisdom from William Hazlitt's writings: "The love of liberty is the love of others; the love of power is the love of ourselves."

Right on target!

PRAYERS THAT MAKE IT

Giving advice about authentic and results-oriented prayer to a person with cancer is a very tough thing to do.

Persons whose bodies are harboring cancer are in deep distress. They want healing. They are not interested in the fine points of theology. God has to be concerned and loving enough to heal them.

But it is so much more complex than that.

God has created a world in which He permits matters to take their course, and only for very good reasons of His own will and nature will He interfere—even with evil in the making. And that's what cancer and other calamities are: "Evil in the making."

These forces, along with storms and accidents of every kind, "go with" the freedom of choice with which we are endowed. We cannot live in a rigidly controlled universe without being ourselves rigidly controlled.

So in the midst of our most hellish experiences we pray something like this: "My Father, I hate what I am experiencing and cannot believe for a moment that this is Your doing. If in Your heart and will You see that it is to my best interests to endure and see it through, so be it. But if my healing and recovery will in any way bring honor and glory to You, then please, God—give me healing and release. I pray in Jesus' Name. Amen."

A WONDROUS MOUSETRAP

The Danish Philosopher and Theologian Soren Kierkegaard commented that most of us read the Bible like a mouse tries to get the cheese out of the mousetrap without getting trapped.

Most of us are careful in our dabblings in Bible study, lest the Word of God captivate us and make demands on us.

We hear a lot about "Evangelical Christians"—and they are to be found in all churches. To some, being dubbed an "Evangelical" is akin to being called a fanatic or a Bible pounder.

Those are terribly unfair judgments, and usually are expounded by persons whose Christianity is shallow to the point of questionable existence.

Evangelicals are persons who have been caught in the wondrous mousetrap of God's Holy Word. They went after that bit of cheese, maybe even hoping not to get caught—but they were enveloped by the gracious and all powerful God, Who called them into service of various kinds.

Evangelicals take the Bible seriously. Where the Word intends to be literal, they are literal in their acceptance and interpretation. Where the Word demands human interpretation, they stand before God as they seek understanding and application.

In my estimation, a person should feel very incomplete if he or she has not been caught in God's mousetrap.

READY FOR LIFE

The late Cardinal Bernardin of Chicago was a man I admired for many reasons. He was outspoken but conciliatory, compassionate and tender and yet he had a demeanor that was steely. He was not shy of the new, but also not quick to dump the old. He was a man for his church—and for the universal Church of Jesus Christ.

The final days of his life have confirmed my assessment. Cardinal Bernardin was dying of cancer. Typically, he was determined to be open about it, to counsel and comfort others who are in similar circumstances, and to say his "good-byes" with firmness, dignity and meaning. The best thing anyone can say about his approaches to death is that they are Christian, rather than pagan.

The fact that we all are approaching death is an obvious truth. None of us can be sure about our length of time on earth.

Preparation is essential—and by "preparation" I don't mean some last ditch effort to set things right in relation to God and our relatives. I do mean knowledge of the Christian faith, the development of our personal faith in Jesus Christ as Savior and Lord, and the doing of all the good we can.

Those matters testify to our citizenship in heaven, prepare our rightful place there—and indeed are the very currency of the life to come.

RECEPTIVITY

The word "receptivity" can apply to many things. It has to do with radio and television reception, the education of a child, the skills of listening and reading, and openness to others—and the willingness to learn on the part of adults.

All of us are involved in that last one. There always is the matter of our personal receptivity to new knowledge, to new ideas, to new ways of doing things.

People are non-receptive when they don't want to hear, much less adapt and take into their lives anything that will disturb the status quo.

The Bible assures us that God is open and receptive to us.

But that will not help us a great deal if we are not open and receptive toward Him. The communication flow between us and God has to operate in both directions. God has a great deal to tell us. How willing are we to learn?

In speaking of the people of his time, Paul wrote: "But their minds were made dull, for to this day the same veil remains when the old covenant is read. . . . Even to this day when Moses is read, a veil covers their hearts." (II Corinthians 3:14,15)

He was describing a spirit of non-receptivity to the things of God. And you know, that is a very dangerous heart condition.

THE PRISON OF CYNICISM

Do you know what it means to be a cynic? I suspect that a lot of people are beset with cynicism and don't even know it—because it has become so natural to their daily living.

The word actually comes from a Greek word meaning "dog like"—probably because the cynic philosophers barked at everything, and were highly critical in all matters.

The word "cynic" came to mean a faultfinder. Everything is under suspicion. Everything is defective and deceptive. The comments and assessments of cynics are harsh and bitter. They have kind words for no one.

Tell them it's a nice day, and they will counter with predictions of storms, floods and tornadoes. Tell them about something good that has happened to you, and they will predict some dire misfortune because of it.

Oscar Wilde once wrote: "What is a cynic? A man who knows the price of everything and the value of nothing."

A determined cynic becomes a stranger to laughter—except the mocking kind. He or she is so suspicious of love and goodness, they simply cease to exist.

And so cynicism becomes a self-made prison of the human soul. It locks us in from the best of life, and locks out the joys and accomplishments and sharings that really are intended for us.

Don't even think of entering the prison of cynicism!

RENEWAL

It is absolutely amazing how much of the Bible is devoted to personal renewal—the revival of the hearts and souls of persons.

In His Word God gives us wondrous promises of renewal of our strength, the restoration of lost hope and the recovery of muted powers. And there are times when we all need that message—for we all need the reality of God's renewal.

One of my favorite passages is Isaiah 40:29-31:

> **He gives strength to the weary and increases the power of the weak. Even youths grow tired and weary, and young men stumble and fall; but those who hope in the Lord will renew their strength. They will soar on wings like eagles; they will run and not grow weary, they will walk and not be faint.**

It truly gives us magnificent assurance. But as with all of God's promises it is *conditional.* This assurance is for "those who hope in the Lord." God delivers on His promise in direct response to our faith and hope in Him.

In some ways God's grace seems so free and easy. We are tantalized by an implication that God will deliver it on the cheap. But not so. Grace comes to us through the channel of genuine faith—a faith that throws itself on His mercy, and gives Him rightful love and service. Only then can there be renewal.

REPENTANCE

There is a word that expresses the key to new beginnings, to a complete turnaround in one's living—moving from darkness to light, from a destructive lifestyle to one that builds and blooms. That key word is "repentance."

Someone wrote: To repent is to alter one's way of looking at life; it is to take God's point of view instead of one's own.

The two main elements of repentance are remorse for one's wrong doing, and change—turning from the wrong to the right, from misbehaving to behaving.

Remorse alone is not enough. One may feel sorry for doing the wrong, and yet keep right on doing it. That is *not* repentance.

St. Ambrose wrote: "True repentance is to cease from sin." And Martin Luther wrote: "To do it no more is the truest repentance."

In Acts 3:19 we read this charge: "Repent, then, and turn to God, so that your sins may be wiped out, that times of refreshing may come from the Lord. . ."

Genuine repentance opens the door to cleansing from all sin, and the salvation and refreshing presence of God in our lives.

When is the time to repent? I like the way Thomas Fuller put it: "You cannot repent too soon, because you do not know how soon it may be too late."

SATAN'S DEFEAT

The coming of Jesus the Messiah had several purposes—one of which was to do battle as a human being with our arch enemy, Satan.

The human condition is deviled by evil. Every element of human existence has a shadow brooding over it, and we all have known occasions of sheer goodness, beauty and even ecstasy that were absolutely ruined by the intrusion of evil's work.

Peter minced no words about the intentions of the devil. He wrote in I Peter 5:8: "Be self-controlled and alert. Your enemy the devil prowls around like a roaring lion looking for someone to devour."

It's intriguing that the very first Old Testament prophecy of Christ's coming and work assures us of the defeat of Satan. In Genesis 3:15 we read God's denunciation of Satan and the prophecy of his defeat: "And I will put enmity between you and the woman, and between your offspring and hers; He will crush your head, and you will strike His heel."

The Word of God assures us that Jesus will deal with Satan, even though He gets wounded in the process. It is a prophecy of the devil's defeat, and is given to assure the human race of God's powerful and final work through the coming Messiah.

THE PERILS OF PRETENSE

Children love to pretend. Whether it's a tea party or an old fashioned Western shootout, pretending is enjoyable. They pretend to be scared of some imaginary monster, or they pretend to be an astronaut or Superman. The ways and days of children are often filled with pretend.

In many ways these are healthy experiences. A child's imagination must be fed so it will grow and eventually make their realities all the richer.

Wise parents know when to call a halt to pretense and call their offspring back to the real world. And healthy kids are able to dump the pretense quickly, and connect again with the real world.

But such pretense in adults is quite another matter. While a little daydreaming usually does no damage, a stubborn devotion to fantasy and pretense will trip up an adult, and often ends in disaster.

Pretending to be what we are not is fraught with psychological dangers. A determined devotion to pretense can be the forerunner of emotional and relational problems.

Such unhealthy pretense usually begins with what seems to be a mild stretching of the truth, so-called innocent exaggerations. From that point on it might balloon into enormous and even outrageous deceptions.

The healthiest approach to life is to be content with who you really are—and make friends with that person.

SAVING IT UP

The poet Robert Browning wrote about "A bitter heart that bides its time and bites."

There is a bitterness in some that seems to be biding its time, waiting for an opportunity for vengeance. What is even worse is the determination to hang on to that bitterness, to nurture it and keep it alive—saving it up for some fantasized opportunity to get even.

I've known several persons who actually grew alarmed when they felt their bitterness fading. They worked harder to stoke up the fires of bitterness and hate.

Do such bitter hearts sometimes boomerang and do horrible damage to persons who just will not let bitterness die? Absolutely.

And it is amazing that bitter people who have a streak of common sense and even goodness find little satisfaction when they finally can deliver the bite. It just did not give the kick they thought it would.

Deliberately sustained bitterness is like a wound that will not heal. It begins to affect the rest of the body, everything else in our lives, and we become the sad and wounded victims of our own bitterness.

There are some things that should never be saved—and one of them is bitterness, along with all its counterparts such as hate, jealousy, envy and spite.

THE NEW GREED

I am a dedicated *laissez faire* capitalist, believing that capitalism best serves the interests of the nation.

But I also am devoted to certain principles and practices, regulations and norms that work to curb and minimize out and out greed. Human nature requires such restraints. No economic system automatically produces saintly idealists who will handle their money for the well being of all concerned. They have to be encouraged to do that.

Money corrupts, and what the Bible says about the love of it is proven true time after time: "the love of money is the root of all evil." (I Timothy 6:10)

A current phenomenon in our nation represents what I call "the new greed." There have been times when corporations ran into difficulties making and selling their products for a reasonable profit. So they had to make adjustments, lay off workers and trim their budgets.

In the new greed era companies at the very height of their prosperity are so eager to please their stockholders and offer greater profits, they downsize, trim and lay off thousands of workers—even though those workers are essential to production, marketing and research. They force the remaining employees to assume greater responsibilities.

These questionable practices may produce enormous short term profits for a company and its stockholders, but they erode the ethics essential to enlightened *laissez faire* capitalism.

SCHOOL DAYS

Some time during the first week of school, parents ought to sit down with their children and explain what education is all about—and that school days form only part of education.

All summer long the children have been doing various things—but there has been ongoing education in them all. Hopefully all summer long children have been learning to think, learning to process information and act on it and learning to live.

There is a real sense in which school is never out, learning is never done, education is never complete. What the child does not learn in the home, he or she may learn on the street—from peers and older youth whose views of life already are jaded and jaundiced by the education they are acquiring.

The church is also an essential place for learning. Believe it, learning to worship and learning to process information on the basis of Christian teachings are among the most desperately needed lessons of life.

And don't forget self-education. What the child does alone is a great part of learning—and it can be an education for good or for ill.

The movies watched, the games played, the books read or not read—all these and more make up the education of self.

SEEING THE SURFACE

Sometimes we look at other people's lives, and are so impressed with their success and poise, we envy them. We wish we could be like them. We forget that we're only seeing the surface. For the most part we really do not know the troubles and trials of other people.

Most folks are pretty good at keeping their real hurts and failures from going public. They do not parade their woes. They are wise, putting on a good show of laughing on the outside while they're crying on the inside.

Usually we do them no favor by intruding—no matter how good we might think we are at "fixing" the problems of others.

In many ways it is unwise to take our cues from others—wanting our success, happiness, looks and even possessions to be "just like theirs."

Baron de La Brede commented: "If we wanted to be happy, it would be easy; but we want to be happier than other people, which is always difficult, since we think them happier than they are."

A good rule is to tend your own garden, and to be grateful for the produce that is the product of your labors. The yield may not look quite like what others have grown—but it is *yours.* So celebrate it!

SEIZING OPPORTUNITIES

The other day I came across this bit of verse:

When opportunity does knock,
By some uncanny quirk
It often goes unrecognized—
It so resembles work!

I'm sure we've all known certain persons who would not recognize an opportunity if it landed smack in their lap. The problem is, they define opportunities as beneficial happenings that come their way and fill their pockets without any effort on their part. Those are miracles—and rarely happen to anyone.

God is in the miracle business in a minor way—but He's big time into opportunities for us. Recognizing them is the first concern. Making wise use of them is the second.

An old Japanese saying states that there are two kinds of opportunities: those we chance upon and those we create.

One of the greatest factors that trips up people is that they spend too much of their time looking for negative opportunities—meaning chances to get even, to show off and show up others, to win and be the victor at any cost, to gain advantages over others.

The best opportunities God sends our way seem to hold something good not only for us—but for persons around us. That means that selfishness can block us from using the very best of life's opportunities.

SERIAL CHILDHOODS

Have you ever known someone who seems to have failed to grow up, but rather goes from one childhood to another? I call this phenomenon "Serial Childhoods."

The writer F. Scott Fitzgerald commented: "Grow up—that is a terribly hard thing to do. It is much easier to skip it and go from one childhood to another."

It is sometimes irritating and frustrating to handle normal childhood antics. It takes a lot of patience to deal with children who are selfish, are playground bullies, tell whopping lies to your face—not to mention the wild tantrums and socially embarrassing behaviors they seem capable of producing at the slightest intrusion on what they perceive to be their territory.

But dealing with such attitudes and behaviors in adults who simply have not grown up is a real drag. Who needs it? Just as with a child, they expect their behavior to be not only tolerated but rewarded!

It has taken awhile, but I think all our grandchildren except the very youngest have learned that we will not reward bad behavior. But I know adults who have not learned that—and possibly never will.

We do such childish adults no favor by pandering to their serial childhood, and rewarding them with consideration they have not earned.

STALLED IN INDECISION

A short time straddling the fence can be a good experience, especially if we are using that time exploring options and working toward a decision.

But there are situations in which fence straddling becomes a long and painful time. We are stalled in indecision. We can't make up our minds—or more accurately, we *don't want* to make up our minds.

We may imagine that fence straddling is good for us. We escape commitment, and we dodge responsibilities. But the truth is we are acting in a cowardly fashion, and our inner psyche knows it. Self-esteem plummets to the depths when we can't or won't make up our minds.

Decision-making is not always easy, but not to decide can be crippling and stifling.

There is something exhilarating about reaching a decision and beginning to act on it. It frees us. It confirms our courage and determination. It heightens our self-esteem.

There are some matter in which not to decide is really to decide—and most often for the negative side. That can only compound the pain of fence straddling, and lower our self-respect all the more.

In Ezra 10:4 we read: "Rise up; this matter is in your hands . . . Take courage and do it." That's a message we all need.

STRENGTH FOR LIVING

Where do you get your strength for living—for doing what needs to be done—for the kinds of service you render—for overcoming temptation and resisting the devil's calls to give up and throw in the towel?

The Apostle Paul had prayed fervently for certain problems to be removed from his life. Hear what he wrote about his search for strength:

> **But [God] said to me, "My grace is sufficient for you, for my power is made perfect in weakness." Therefore I will boast all the more gladly about my weaknesses, so that Christ's power may rest on me. That is why, for Christ's sake, I delight in weaknesses, in insults, in hardships, in persecutions, in difficulties. For when I am weak, then I am strong.** (II Corinthians 12:9,10)

Many of us have found in life that we can live on our own strength just so far—and then we need more, much more. And there is only one place to draw it—from God Himself.

But His strength doesn't come to us until we recognize and confess that we are at the end of our rope.

It really can be a joyful moment when we reach the end of our resources and then turn to God for His.

SO, YOU'VE MADE MISTAKES?

The playwright George Bernard Shaw was a person I wish I had known personally. He was a mild cynic, but also expressed some absolutely delightful insights about life.

He wrote: "A life spent in making mistakes is not only more honorable but more useful than a life spent doing nothing." I'll buy that!

How I pity those souls who spend their latter years of living bemoaning the mistakes they've made in life. As though there is anyone who has never made mistakes!

Or worse—we cover our mistakes by blaming others, or crediting them to lack of opportunity, or to a life of adversity.

Or another bad approach: we do not learn from our mistakes. And how can we if we insist they never happened or that they lack even a hint of helpfulness to our lives?

Some are strong enough to seek wisdom from their mistakes—even by telling them to others. In James 5:16 we read: "Confess your sins to each other and pray for each other so that you may be healed. The prayer of a righteous man is powerful and effective."

There's a funny thing about righteousness or being good. If we can't admit the wrongs of our lives, we remain strangers to authentic goodness.

A CLASHING ATTITUDE

Have you ever heard the phrase "cognitive dissonance?"

Dissonance is used to describe discord and a lack of harmony. There is cognitive dissonance when different things we believe simply clash. They are dissonant and disharmonious—they simply do not jibe, and are irreconcilable.

A lot of cognitive dissonance surrounds the concept and reality of forgiveness. Every Sunday in churches across the land all kinds of people solemnly pray to God: "And forgive us our debts, trespasses sins—as we forgive those who sin against us." It's something of a miracle that we don't have a lot of sudden deaths by choking on Sunday morning.

For sure there are many who pray that prayer who have not forgiven, and who will not forgive. They are very determined about it. And yet they pray—perhaps thoughtlessly—for what amounts to conditional forgiveness from God. "Forgive us *as we forgive.*" That is a dangerous prayer and a clashing attitude if we have no intentions of forgiving. It constitutes severe cognitive dissonance.

Have you ever heard someone who is a faithful churchgoer and Christian say something like, "I cannot forgive him (or her), and I will never forgive." Cognitive dissonance. A clashing attitude.

Think about it: The refusal to forgive anything can never characterize the life and attitudes of a genuine Christian.

THROUGH TRIBULATION

God has given no promise that says people who love and obey Him will escape trouble. But He repeatedly said that He would be with us through it all.

In Isaiah 43, the first three verses, we read God's words of assurance:

> **Fear not, for I have redeemed you; I have summoned you by name; you are Mine. When you pass through the waters, I will be with you; and when you pass through the rivers, they will not sweep over you. When you walk through the fire, you will not be burned; the flames will not set you ablaze. For I am the Lord, your God. . .**

There are some new words to an old song, and it's called "All Will Be Well." The words were written by Mary Peters, and the tune is an old Welsh melody.

It's a powerful hymn, but one stanza really says it all:

> Though we pass through tribulation, All Will Be Well;
> Ours is such a full salvation—All will be well.
> Happy when in God abiding, Fruitful if in Christ abiding,
> Holy through the Spirit's guiding—All will be well.

When we stand firm with Christ, no matter how troubles assail us, we are wondrously confident that all will be well.

HATE IS NOT A FAMILY VALUE

Our mail brings a lot of strange and sometimes interesting items. The other day I opened an envelope and found a small bumper sticker with the words: "Hate Is Not A Family Value."

Certainly I agree with that assertion. When I saw the name of the sending organization, I knew what they were fighting. It is not hate per se, but hefty opposition to their organization on a lot of critical issues. If you don't like their stand, it shows you have hate in your mind and heart—and "Hate Is Not A Family Value."

But apart from their motives, the saying is true. There are parents who instill hate-filled prejudice in their children. At first it all may seem so innocent—and even protective.

"Don't go near the children in that family because. . . . "

"Well that's what you would expect from that kind of people!"

"Don't even think of playing with people of that color, much less dating them!"

The examples above are pretty mild compared to what I've heard children tell about attitudes in their families.

For sure the terrible happenings in Kosovo, Palestine, Israel, Ireland and elsewhere are due to hateful prejudice instilled in generations of children. The world no longer can tolerate hate as a family value.

DEEP IN THE HEART

One of the starkest pronouncements about the human capacity for evil and all kinds of wrongdoing is found in Jeremiah 17:9: "The heart is deceitful above all things, and desperately corrupt; who can understand it?" (RSV)

This is meant to be a statement of fact about the potential and possibilities for human beings to do wrong, to make enormous mischief.

The Bible speaks bluntly of every person's capacity for evil if we do not stick very close to God. We could become what is described in Psalm 36: "Transgression speaks to the wicked deep in his heart; there is no fear of God before his eyes. For he flatters himself in his own eyes that his iniquity cannot be found out and hated. The words of his mouth are mischief and deceit; he has ceased to act wisely and do good." (RSV)

Each of us needs to ask the questions: "Who or what is in charge deep in my heart?"

During a recent interview with Sam Donaldson, porn publisher Larry Flynt declared, "My business is smut, my hobby is politics."

"Transgression speaks to the wicked deep in his heart; there is no fear of God before his eyes."

There is absolutely nothing there to admire, much less model.

WHEN IS DEAD?

Question: "When Is Dead?"

A gravestone in an old cemetery carries these words: "Died at 20—Buried at 60."

Well, when is dead? Could it be that among us there are the living dead—persons whose lives have been extinguished by drugs, crime, crass selfishness, humongous greed and a mind that with great determination has shut God out?

Is dead when we cut all ties with forces for good, music that inspires, worship that both humbles and exalts, loving friendships that encourage and nurture? I think so! That is dead!

The Bible speaks of spiritual death as a far greater concern than physical death. In Proverbs 21:16 we have this succinct comment: "A man who strays from the path of understanding comes to rest in the company of the dead." That's certainly an answer to the question, "When Is Dead?"

The second chapter of the Book of Ephesians is helpful in gaining a fuller picture of what it means to be dead and what it means to be alive: "But because of His great love for us, God, Who is rich in mercy, made us alive with Christ even when we were dead in our sins—it is by grace you have been saved."

Now that's a passage to ponder.

COMMUNICATING CONCERN

Some time ago I was disabled after surgery. During that time I received many calls, cards and E-mail messages from friends, colleagues and loved ones who want to communicate their concern, prayers and wishes for a speedy recovery.

Every such communication gave me loads of encouragement. I am grateful for all who took the time to communicate concern. It is one of the most blessed and helpful things we can do.

Some used a bit of humor, sending perky cards with a fun-filled message.

Missionary colleagues wrote of their concern and then expressed admiration for my being able to keep up my writings during such a difficult time. They commended us with a verse from Psalm 104:16, as rendered in the King James Version: "The trees of the Lord are full of sap."

I'm not quite sure if they intended that to bring a chuckle, but Susan and I have had many laughs over it.

Incidentally, during times of difficulty and challenge we have found that a sense of humor is a prize possession—and enormously helpful in fighting off discouragement.

When you know of anyone who needs communications of concern, caring and sympathy, sit right down and do it. It is one of the best gifts we can give.

A MATTER OF PERSEVERANCE

I'm always enthralled by the athletes with their skills and training. Whether attending such events or watching them on TV, their strength and agility are marvelous to behold.

One thing we know for sure: They did not reach those heights of skill and endurance by being lazy or by quitting when the training and discipline got too tough.

Such athletes are living demonstrations of the importance and fruits of perseverance.

It is a fact of every day life: Nothing good will be produced in our lives without perseverance. And this includes the race in which we are engaged as Christians.

In Hebrews 12 we read this marvelous tribute to perseverance:

> **Therefore, since we are surrounded by such a great cloud of witnesses, let us throw off everything that hinders and the sin that so easily entangles, and let us run with perseverance the race marked out for us. Let us fix our eyes on Jesus, the Author and Perfecter of our faith, Who for the joy set before Him endured the cross, scorning its shame, and sat down at the right hand of the throne of God. Consider Him Who endured such opposition from sinful men, so that you will not grow weary and lose heart.**

CALLS TO PERSEVERANCE

Have you ever stuck with something—or perhaps some person—and later wondered why?

You persevered in a matter you deemed important. While there are some situations in which it may be wisest to quit, there are many others that are more than worth the effort.

To persevere or not to persevere becomes an issue in nearly every area of life. In the main, the decision is made on the basis of our values—and on the perceived worth we see in the entire matter.

Perseverance comes into full play when we run into difficulties and conflicts—when all is not what we hoped it would be. But since that's the way it is in most matters of life, the call to persevere has the edge—the higher demand—rather than feelings that we'd just like to throw in the towel.

Every student of higher learning has been confronted with demands to persevere on the one hand, or go for something easier on the other.

Other areas in which many give up too easily include marriage and other commitments. Shabby values, laziness and desires for certain comforts cause folks to be quitters, when they ought to persevere.

For sure the Christian faith includes a call to persevere no matter what the devil throws at us.

COMMON COURTESY

Have you ever called someone's home, a youngster answers the phone and sounds as though he has never heard of common courtesy or civility.

It goes something like this: "Lo. What you want? Oh, yeah? I'll get him." And then, with the phone held about 4 inches from his mouth, the lad yells out: "Hey Dad, some guy wants you on the phone!" No finesse, no courtesy.

Common Courtesy is definitely lacking in the teaching program of many homes. And it isn't just the kids. A lot of adults are about as courteous to others as a pen of hogs, and they exhibit similar manners in public.

Courtesy is one of the main elements that keeps us out of the jungle, and helps us to act like human beings created in God's Image.

Civility or courtesy are always indicators that a person sees himself as well as others as worthy persons, deserving of respect.

Courtesy shows an essential savvy about the fact that we are social beings, and that the fabric and worth of the society in which we live are exactly as we make them by our words and actions.

One of the things that raises children and adults head and shoulders above the common herd of humanity is courtesy.

EXPRESSING LOVE

Many just don't get it. They imagine they are expressing love, when all they are showing and sharing is a selfish streak, plain self-adoration and even unseemly lust.

Children need to learn the difference between using others and loving others. Of course, if the parents don't know the difference they cannot teach their children.

So we must begin with adults in learning the nature and expressions of authentic love.

True love divests itself of self-interest as much as is possible in our sinful human nature—not insisting on pleasurable return, not demanding tit for tat or more for any expression of love.

Love reciprocated is beautiful and powerful. But to expect it, to demand it, to hold back unless one gets it are monstrous distortions of what love is all about.

It's hard to top the Apostle Paul's descriptors of love, found in I Corinthians 13: "Love is patient, love is kind. It does not envy, it does not boast, it is not proud. It is not rude, it is not self-seeking, it is not easily angered, it keeps no record of wrongs. Love does not delight in evil but rejoices with the truth. It always protects, always trusts, always hopes, always perseveres. Love never fails."

Apply those descriptors to your expressions of love.

FEELING FUTILE

If we're honest we'll 'fess up that sometimes we feel futile about nearly everything in life. That word "futile" means completely ineffective and serving no useful purpose. It is the empty feeling that comes over us when we suspect that we don't count, life doesn't really matter, and we're helpless in the face of the forces working against us.

Such feelings are always more destructive than helpful.

Perhaps feelings of futility are due to our being unrealistic in our expectations. If we have a tendency toward perfectionism, then feeling futile follows minor setbacks, small failures and successes that we view as too small.

Feeling futile is also the lot of persons who have not prepared for some of the well-known passages in life, such as when an only child heads for school for the first time, or when the children finally make their break with home and parents experience the empty nest syndrome.

Some people feel futile because of an excess of selfishness. They simply want too much for themselves. They are too demanding, and when they don't get it, their system luxuriates in those feelings of "nobody loves me—life is worthless and I'm worthless."

Feeling futile? Fight it! In Christ's spiritual economy it's just not meant to be. Feeling futile is really a futile feeling!

LASTING MATTERS

Life has taught me that the best thing in life is to get hold of lasting matters—anything that defies time and deterioration.

So much of this world is trite and passing. That observation motivated King Solomon to write in Ecclesiastes, chapter 1:

> "Meaningless! Meaningless!" says the Teacher. "Utterly meaningless! Everything is meaningless. What does man gain from all his labor at which he toils under the sun?. . . . What has been will be again, what has been done will be done again; there is nothing new under the sun."

These are the words of a pessimist and cynic—evidently a phase through which Solomon passed as he sought and found the very wisdom of God.

Solomon learned that there are matters that are lasting and full of meaning in all ages, at all times, and forever. So he wrote in Ecclesiastes 12: "Now all has been heard; here is the conclusion of the matter: Fear God and keep His commandments, for this is the whole duty of man. For God will bring every deed into judgment, including every hidden thing, whether it is good or evil."

In these wonder-filled years of ours cynicism and pessimism will be of little help. Confident faith in God and loyalty to His commandments will lead us to the truly lasting matters.

LEFT BEHIND

There is something very sad about being left behind in some sport, contest, expressions of talent, or other matters of health and happiness. Being left behind can be tragic—even catastrophic.

Christians face significant dilemmas as they work out their salvation convictions. One such dilemma is the certainty that willy-nilly they are leaving some loved ones and friends behind as they move forward in their faith. There are persons whose choices in life have removed them from the running of God's eternal life. They are the "left behind" ones.

Some years ago a new set of novels came out called *The Left Behind* series—written by Tim Lahay and Jerry Jenkins, and published by Tyndale House. These deal with the end days of Planet Earth. They focus on all who will be left behind when Jesus returns to earth to take His people home.

There is a certainty that we are in the last times, and have been ever since the days of Jesus on earth.

The Word of God is clear: persons who reject God and refuse to heed His calls will be left behind—left out of all the realities given to us in Jesus Christ.

Sage counsel this: Believe and live in a manner that will ensure that you will not be left behind.

MAKING YOUR OWN REALITY

One of the most important matters taught by Jesus is His simple statement: "You will know the truth, and the truth will set you free." (John 8:32) Jesus helps us to stay close to reality, and to avoid the tendency to make our own reality.

We make our own reality mainly in the area of feelings. And while it's true that feelings are real, and we have to deal with them—the feelings may have little or no grounding in reality. In short, feelings often are untruthful!

Feelings of fear may be totally unjustified, but we hang on to them, again making our own reality. Our anger may be all out of proportion to what has caused it, and we blow up like a miniature volcano. Again, we are making our own reality.

Uncontrolled and unrealistic feelings can make us sense rejection when there is none; a lack of caring when there is concern aplenty; criticism when none was expressed; and an overwhelming sense of inferiority that is not related to anything except sheer feelings.

Whatever our circumstances, whatever harsh experiences we have to endure, be assured of the realities of God's Word. Paul's confident statement in Romans 8:28 is intended for all believers: "And we know that in all things God works for the good of those who love Him, who have been called according to His purpose."

The area of our psyche that trips us up the most, and causes the loss of the truth which make us free, is our emotions. Go for the truth of Jesus Christ, and live in His full reality!

PARENTAL CURRICULUM

Society has changed a lot since Susan and I were young parents. But those changes do not lessen the need for careful and wise parenting. Rather they increase the need for what I call "The Parental Curriculum."

The complexities of our culture are more intense than in past years, along with the lures to self-destructive behaviors. Childhood preparations may make the difference between living out either rich and rewarding lives, or lives of mild to intense futility.

One of the most important requisites of wise and successful parenting is the focus on the preparation of the child to live meaningfully and effectively as an adult. Granted, the child is "in process" toward that reality, and along the way must enjoy being a child. That awareness of childhood's proper domain is part of the preparation. Forcing a child too early into adult norms and restrictions can be counter productive.

But wise parents are always aware of the nature and goals of the game of life. Their children are to become functioning adults, mature and contributing persons in society, not a drag on it—much less a menace.

Of course, some of the worst sins of parents are in the areas of rejection, emotional and psychological detachment, willful ignorance and sheer laziness. The notion of "parenting without effort or sacrifice" is patently ridiculous.

PARENTAL CURRICULUM—CONSEQUENCES

A missing element in much home teaching is the reality of consequences.

This focus of the parenting curriculum teaches that what we think, what we do, how we act toward others, how we keep or break God's laws as well as the laws of our government—all have inevitable consequences.

The main thrust of this area is the destructive impact of bad attitudes and conduct on one's self, our families and the whole of society.

Teach it—when one associates with bad characters, lazy peers, thieves, blamers and unholy rebels, it will rub off. Eventually a youngster will take on the attitudes that mark a person as a sociopath or worse.

Teach it—when one associates with persons of high values, diligent students, persons who play fair in sports, ambitious workers and devout followers of Christ, it will rub off. Eventually that youngster will take on the traits that mark a person as having high values and loads of integrity and honesty.

Teach it—failing to study may mean failure in school. Laziness in a job can get you fired. Lying marks one as untruthful and therefore untrustworthy. Indulging in criminal acts lands one in prison. Driving too fast and too carelessly could cause maiming or death.

Don't omit consequences from the parenting curriculum.

PARENTAL CURRICULUM—PATIENCE

One of the main elements in the parenting curriculum is the simple yet always needed element of patience—teaching our children to wait, to postpone their wants, to defer their desires.

We live in a culture that pressures us to satisfy our wants immediately—so charge it, borrow for it, build up debt, pay big money in interest—all for the thrill of immediate, rather then deferred satisfaction.

Impatience certainly is not a virtue—patience most assuredly is.

Patience is a character builder, enhancing and increasing all other virtues.

A lack of patience seems to magnify other undesirable character flaws, such as a short fuse, a penchant for blaming others, a seeming inability to finish what we have started.

Impatience causes children to want to skip needed but difficult steps in some essential process. So the final outcome is bound to be less rewarding and less satisfying in every way. Children need to learn that losing patience is costly, and often in the short as well as the long run.

Impatience prods us to give up—to surrender to the lure of the more immediate and apparently more interesting.

One of the most beautiful and useful virtues our children need is patience. It always serve them well—in all ways.

PARENTAL CURRICULUM—SELF-DISCIPLINE

I wonder how many parents have drawn up a list of what they must teach their children concerning essentials for life. In effect, this would be a curriculum for parenting—a listing of what amount to courses for life.

In other commentaries I've tried to lay out some of the "basic courses" of a vital and full reality home curriculum.

In addition to faith and patience, parents must add to their home curriculum an ongoing course in self-discipline—which means the ability of the child to buckle down and complete tough tasks with little if any prodding from others. Encouragement, yes—coercion, no.

Self-denial is indispensable to self-discipline—including the ability to "just say no" to temptations from our inner self and from others that will lead to destructive conditions and behaviors.

Parents can say "NO" until they are hoarse. But the real payoff is the youngster saying it—with conviction and determination. If self-discipline is missing from the parental curriculum, that is very unlikely to happen.

Self-discipline also means the sticktuitiveness needed to complete difficult and even unpleasant tasks. This area ranges from household chores and homework to the more challenging opportunities of music, the arts, sports and high achievement in critical matters.

Parents must practice and teach self-discipline.

PARENTAL CURRICULUM—MONEY

Another important segment of the parental curriculum has to do with money and possessions—their place and meaning, their proper uses, and the dangers of excesses in attitudes and practices.

God's Word teaches that one of the most powerful and effective enemies of God and godliness is money. When money and possessions become our master. we are in deep trouble.

Money abuse and misuse emphasize all other vices and bad character traits. And in like manner, other bad traits impact our attitudes toward money and possessions—ultimately persuading the weak minded to make them into gods.

Jesus stated it bluntly: "You cannot serve two masters: God and money. For you will hate one and love the other, or else the other way around." (Matthew 6:24 *The Living Bible*)

Money and things always clamor for more allegiance, loyalty and servility than are ever justified. Parents and children must learn that money is to be mastered, and not to become our master. At best it is to serve the highest of our values and aims.

Thrift is an important element in this segment of parental curriculum. Waste of money and other possessions is intolerable simply because it is wrong—and terribly foolish. The responsibilities for handling and using money wisely must be learned early.

PARENTAL CURRICULUM—CIVILITY

High on any parental curriculum list must be attitudes and practice of respect or civility—taught and practiced within the home setting. The intended result is courteous and polite behaviors both inside and outside of the home.

This means zero tolerance for smart mouth, rude and harmful behaviors. Note the simple truth that if parents are not exemplifying civility, they can hardly expect it from their offspring.

I've known parents who are adept and showy in derogatory terminology. Parents who use animal designations to denigrate the child don't see their own behaviors as obscene, uncivil and enormously destructive. Worse, they demonstrate that they view their children as animals, rather than persons with divine origins and traits.

Implicit in our understanding and teaching of respect is the high value of the personhood of others. So within the "course content" of civility there must be communications about the worth and dignity of all persons, regardless of race, color, ethnic background, religion or economic status.

Civility is at enmity with all forms of prejudice. Along with self-awareness of one's divine nature and the essential of unconditional love, civility is the great antidote for hatemongering of all stripes.

Trying to teach civility in the home and at the same time communicate hateful prejudice is an exercise in futility, sham and shame.

PARENTAL CURRICULUM—FAITH

Please consider the truth of this assessment: Parents who shrug off religious responsibilities are derelict in their parenting responsibilities and obligations.

Are you aware that the basic essence of any human being is soul? We do not "have" souls, we are souls. That term "soul" speaks to our nature as a person made in the image of God, with enormous potential and high destiny—and in those parameters we must come to understand our worth and the integrity of our personhood.

But when? Is this part of our arrival in the mystical realm of adulthood—that all of a sudden we become aware that we are souls, and that we have the breath of God's immortality within us? Or is this really part of the essential parental curriculum of childhood?

Deep convictions about divine origins, identity and destiny are foundational factors in relating to our children, and are essentials in helping them enjoy their childhood while at the same time preparing them to become effective adults.

It is in the dimension and content of revealed and revealing faith that we find the rationale and descriptors for matters of origin, existential being, worth and destiny to guide our children into truthful and full reality.

To teach these matters requires that we ourselves know and experience them.

PARENTAL CURRICULUM— AUTHENTIC LOVE

Wise parents are always aware of the nature and goals of the game of life. Their children are to become functioning adults, mature and contributing persons in society, not a drag on it—and much less a menace. Thus the need for a parental curriculum.

Of course, some of the worst sins of parents are in the areas of rejection, emotional and psychological detachment, willful ignorance and sheer laziness.

The notion of "parenting without effort or sacrifice" is patently ridiculous. The most significant missing factor is authentic, unconditional love.

Unconditional love is a must for effective parenting. I am chagrined by the speed and immediacy with which some parents turn from unbridled permissiveness (which most often is an indicator of a lack of love) to notions and practices of "tough love." Often I discover that such parents never gave unconditional love a try.

Anyone who has some savvy about the various qualities and stances of love knows that unconditional love, which is grounded in the "amazing grace" of God, is much more difficult to sustain, and frankly is less satisfying to the parents' ego, than the rigors of tough love.

This item in the parental curriculum, along with all the others, must be practiced by the parents if it is to be learned by the child.

PARENTAL CURRICULUM—GENUINE LOVE

By word, deed and actions parents must include in their parental education curriculum the nature of genuine love—what it is and what it is not.

Genuine love is not simply extended selfishness, projecting itself into the lives of others in order to get what one wants from them—using others for one's own benefit and gain.

The *Koine* Greek language of the New Testament has four words for love: *eros,* which means lust, the lowest form of love, intent on pleasure for one's self; *storge,* which is family love. full of obligations and responsibilities, but offering a great deal of security; *philio,* brotherly love, with lots of affection and interaction; and *agape,* which is love at its highest expression—self-giving, always concerned, always encouraging and helpful. *Agape* love seeks to give more than to take—to enhance and encourage the other, rather than aiming for one's own self-enhancement.

Parents could use those Greek words as a guide, teaching that lust holds little love; that family obligations are essential to an understanding of love; that brotherly and sisterly love must triumph over sibling rivalry; and that true love comes straight from the heart of God, and is full of self-giving and sacrifice—thinking and acting with more concern for the other than for one's self.

A handy "curriculum" outline can be found in that great love passage written by the Apostle Paul: I Corinthians 13.

Read it! Live it! Teach it!

PARENTAL CURRICULUM—LASTING MATTERS

"Lasting Matters" is the subject of this final commentary on an effective parental curriculum. Another commentary also dealt with this theme.

This is the area of ageless, "carry over" truth—of enduring principles—of objective morality and other matters that are timeless and changeless.

The writer of the Biblical Book of Hebrews tells us that "Jesus Christ is the same yesterday and today and forever." (Hebrews 13:8)

He is one of the most stable factors in the overall milieu of our existence. Then in Hebrews 6:17 the writer assures us that "God wanted to make the unchanging nature of His purpose very clear." God is not fickle, undependable or flighty. His will and purposes for humanity have not changed.

Parents must teach their offspring to discern between passing fads, changing opinions, emotional flings and the great truths and lasting realities of God's ways and purposes. There are matters that never end and never change. In our perversity we humans might like to think so, but we will be confounded when we ignore or play fast and loose with the lasting matters.

I love the words of Psalm 103:17: "But from everlasting to everlasting the Lord's love is with those who fear Him, and His righteousness with their children's children." Every child should know about such lasting matters!

RELATIONAL REALITIES

Like it or not, we are born into relationships—the very beginnings of our lives are firmly grounded in the foundations off a relationship. Furthermore, we spend our early years in absolute relational dependence.

Even in seeking freedom and going through the classic breaks with home, young people have to find other supportive relationships.

We date, we may or may not marry, we may or may not have children—but always there are friends, work colleagues and other relationships.

Relational realities teach us that life is primarily relating and relationships—and we need to know how to handle them wisely and in healthy ways.

The very first relational reality we need to grasp is that it is to our immense benefit that we develop and sustain nurturing and supportive relationships, and avoid destructive ones like the proverbial plague.

We also need to get hold of the fact that good relationships don't just happen. They must be built and nourished, cared for and encouraged.

The Bible contains the most profound and trustworthy commentaries on human relating. It has golden wisdom about how you and I are to relate to God, and to each other. The Psalms, the Book of Proverbs, the parables Jesus told all focus on the joys and perils of human relating.

RELATIONAL REALITIES— TRUST AND COMMITMENT

It is a stark fact of relating to which many hardly give a thought: Only as we develop trust and commitment can we relate meaningfully to anyone, including God and our fellow human beings.

A relationship remains null and void when there is no trust, no commitment.

Only as there is trust can respect grow. Only as there is commitment can one share from the depths of one's mind and soul.

While there is a sense in which trust and a worthiness to receive commitment must be demonstrated, it is folly to insist that such proof be offered on every occasion, and that doubts and apprehensions be resolved with completeness and clarity. Trust and commitment rest mainly on faith.

If a person in whom you are interested demonstrates that he or she cannot be trusted and is incapable of honoring commitments, then why on earth would anyone desire a relationship with such a person?

Commitment exists when one is willing to invest time, energy and more in the joys and benefits of relating to another. There is no valid faith in God without commitment. There is no satisfaction in any human relationship that makes no demand on our existence.

Trust and commitment are among the greatest essentials of relational realities.

RELATIONAL REALITIES— GRACE

Have you ever thought of grace as a relational reality? By that I mean that you understand grace to be an absolute essential for sustaining a meaningful relationship with another human being.

One of the most profound and informative incidents recorded in Scripture is when the disciple Simon Peter asks Jesus: "Lord, how often shall my brother sin against me, and I forgive him? As many as seven times?" And Jesus' response is staggering: "I do not say to you seven times, but seventy times seven." (Matthew 18:21, 22 RSV)

What Jesus advocated is limitless forgiveness, which is what is mainly meant by the word "grace."

If one cannot seek forgiveness, if one cannot grant forgiveness, then one cannot truly relate.

Tie in with any human being, and you'll immediately find demands for an understanding and forgiving spirit.

While we know that grace is exercised primarily on the part of God, there would be no human relating to the Divine Being without grace—meaning His limitless and complete forgiveness of our sins, including the Lord's willingness to suffer for our sins in our place.

And for sure there cannot be authentic love without the grace that cares, understands, overlooks, forgives and is always willing, eager and hopeful for new beginnings.

RELATIONAL REALITIES—ACCEPTANCE

When we relate, it is a given that we relate as whole persons to other whole persons.

I marvel when some seem to insist that they like a person and enjoy his or her company, but they cannot accept this or that and more about the other's being, character traits and personality. Acceptance is a relational reality, without which there can be no true relating.

To be sure, there are elements in anyone's personal traits that could use revisions and change. But most likely that won't happen.

So to enter into a relationship with deep reservations and a determination to bring about desired changes will end in disaster.

Of course, if the other person senses distress because of certain qualities or personal ticks, then love might motivate change. But most of us want to be accepted just as we are—warts, foibles, habits and all.

It should be understood that evil tendencies and sins are not what we're talking about. When it comes to those matters God joins forces with anyone who insists on change.

But if what troubles us in a relationship is the way he parts his hair, or her food preferences, or social gregariousness—to name just a few—then we must learn to accept—and with graciousness and even enthusiasm.

RELATIONAL REALITIES—CHANGE

Change is one of the most formidable of all relational matters. If relating persons do not keep pace with each other, adapting and resolving the changes each experiences, the relationship will begin to deteriorate and finally end.

Change is a constant of life. But even so, it often takes people by surprise. "I never knew you felt that way" is a common comment—along with "You used to enjoy going to those kinds of things!"

There is a dynamism in persons that transfers into relationships. No one stays exactly the same, and we must meet those changes—adapt, make compromises and continue to move into the future with the persons to whom we relate.

If we simply cannot deal with unwanted and destructive changes, then we must figure out what alternatives there are—including the possibility of just living with the change, like it or not—or perhaps modifying or ending the relationship.

A couple I knew ended their marriage when the husband "discovered" (put that in quotes!) that he was gay, and began a relationship with another male. No marriage can tolerate that magnitude of change. So they divorced.

Change is one of the most significant of all relational realities. We must deal with it in healthy and productive ways.

PERILOUS ATTITUDES—INDIFFERENCE

We are known and measured by our attitudes. Sometimes we might assess someone as having a "bad attitude" or a "good attitude" in reference to some situation or happening in his or her life.

Attitudes show through. We communicate them to others in subtle ways, and sometimes quite blatantly and openly.

One of the worst attitudes we can have is "indifference." It is passive, not caring and never helping. The troubles of others do not move us. Crime and evil of every kind are shrugged off as having nothing to do with us. We are absolutely cold to the sufferings and victimization of persons and of whole segments of humanity.

Sometimes we are indifferent to matters and concerns that otherwise would yield honor, health and prosperity

Esau, returning hungry from the hunt, sold his birthright to his conniving brother, Jacob. Genesis 25:34 tells us: "Then Jacob gave Esau bread, peas, and stew; so he ate and drank and went on about his business, indifferent to the loss of the rights he had thrown away."(The Living Bible)

Many are indifferent to God. In Luke 17:26 Jesus prophesies: "(When I return) the world will be (as indifferent to the things of God) as the people were in Noah's day." (The Living Bible) Beware the horrific attitude of indifference.

PERILOUS ATTITUDES—SCORN

Have you ever experienced the ravages and savagery of scorn—either on the giving or receiving end?

The *American Heritage Dictionary* defines scorn: "Contempt or derision felt for a person or object considered despicable or unworthy"; and "the expression of such an attitude in behavior or speech."

To scorn is no small matter. The very thought sets us up as judge and jury over another human being—and if we put our scorn into action we become executioner as well.

Psalm 69:20 reads: "Scorn has broken my heart and has left me helpless; I looked for sympathy, but there was none, for comforters, but I found none."

Being on the receiving end of scorn is heartbreaking. Being on the giving end of scorn is lowly and contemptible.

Over and over the Word of God tells how Israel became an object of scorn because of their rebellion against God, His ways and laws.

All too often in our time we witness the fruits of scorn: prejudice, violence, victimization, fraud, indecency, hate, lust, theft, torture, murder, genocide—and cruelty of every form inflicted on the innocent by persons who have lost all sense of shame and have given themselves over to evil.

Scorn is an unhealthy attitude that opens the way to the worst of inhuman and ungodly actions.

PERILOUS ATTITUDES—PRIDE

In one sense pride is an attitude that is essential to our self-respect and our sense of worth and dignity. We also need to take honest pride in our accomplishments and successes in life.

But on the other hand, one of the most dangerous attitudes we can develop in our attitudinal matrix is pride that leads to disdain for others—pride that is arrogant and haughty—pride fed by faulty assumptions and too high an opinion of one's self, especially in comparison to others.

There is a pride that leads us down the garden path of broken relationships and discarded friendships—a pride that makes us difficult to work with and very hard to like, much less love.

Wrongful pride keeps us from truth, and proves harmful to all our relationships. At its worst, pride crowds God, the source and sustenance of our being, right out of our lives.

Psalm 10 gives a good description of destructive pride:

> **In his arrogance the wicked man hunts down the weak, who are caught in the schemes he devises. He boasts of the cravings of his heart; he blesses the greedy and reviles the Lord. In his pride the wicked does not seek [the Lord]; in all his thoughts there is no room for God.**

PERSONAL RESOURCES

Have you ever felt at the end of your rope—as though all your personal resources were drained?

Most have felt that way one time or another—as though they just could not go on. They felt finished, with not one ounce of strength left.

And many have discovered that when they thought they had reached the end of their rope, somehow they still were able to go on, they drew on strengths they did not know they had.

The truth is, nearly everyone has more resources than we imagine. What is lacking may be faith, motivation or ambition. But the resources are there, even though we may have convinced ourselves they are not. We have them, but we just aren't using them—for reasons of sheer ignorance, laziness or unbelief.

In times of trouble, we ask God to bless us—to work a miracle to get us out of the mess we're in. But in effect God often says: "Don't trouble Me for something you already have." He tells us to get with it and draw on the resources He has placed within us, plus others we have gained through education and experience.

From intelligence to strength for trials, we normally have much more in the resource department than we thought possible. Count on it.

NO ISLANDS

The words "isolationism," "insular" and "provincial" are used to describe being cut off from others, narrow in outlook, and perhaps even ignorant of the larger world in which we live.

John Donne wrote that famous saying, "No man is an island." He meant that we cannot really be insular or island-like in life.

Willy-nilly we touch other persons and even large groups. Our every act is like a stone tossed into a pool. We create ripples that go out and away from us. We do make waves!

God calls persons to be salt and light—to affect the savorless areas of life and to illuminate the darkness about us. We may never realize how far the impact of our saltiness and illuminating reach out.

The point is that we are to get at it, to work for quality control in the impact we make and the ripples we cause, so that their influence will be helpful, healing and redemptive.

We are always making waves. We just can't help it. But what kind of waves? What are the influences for good or bad that our lives exert?

What do you leave behind as you move through life: a trail of brokenness, hurt and bitterness?

Or do you leave the beauty, peace and healing of a Christ-dedicated life?

QUALITIES OF WISDOM

Let's think about wisdom.

Proverbs 24:13 and 14 tells us: "When you enjoy becoming wise, there is hope for you! A bright future lies ahead!" *(The Living Bible)*

On a practical level, wisdom is the ability to know when you are right or wrong, and can celebrate the one and learn from the other. We are wise when we truly learn from our mistakes and do not repeat them.

One of the most important qualities of wisdom is discernment—which is skill is weighing matters for their true value and meaning. Psalm 119:125 has this prayer: "I am Your servant; give me discernment that I may understand Your statutes." Discernment leads to an understanding of lofty matters.

Wisdom is also knowing what and whom to accord respect and reverence. Wisdom is never a scoffer. Where there is wisdom, ridicule and scorn are viewed as neither assets nor weapons.

And finally, the true and ultimate source of wisdom is God. He gives wisdom to individuals as a gift. It is not of their own making. James 3:17 speaks of the nature of such wisdom: "But the wisdom that comes from heaven is first of all pure; then peace-loving, considerate, submissive, full of mercy and good fruit, impartial and sincere."

This is good counsel for a lifetime: Seek His wisdom!

A MOST RELEVANT PRAYER

Most of us are familiar with the 23rd Psalm, and it is a favorite of mine. There are other portions of Scripture that bless our living and relating.

One of my favorites among the Psalms of Prayer is found in Psalm 30. The whole passage is exquisite, but let me share a portion with you that speaks to every person who has experienced frustrating trouble and sorrow:

> **O Lord my God, I called to You for help and You healed me. O Lord, You brought me up from the grave; You spared me from going down into the pit. Sing to the Lord, you saints of His; praise His Holy Name. For His anger lasts only a moment, but His favor lasts a lifetime; weeping may remain for a night, but rejoicing comes in the morning.**

That is truly a Psalm with whole life, from here to eternity relevance and deep meaning for every person who has agonized and struggled through the dark nights of life, and then found His magnificent joy in the morning.

It is also a Psalm for those who mentally and spiritually have dealt with the uncertainties of death. It assures us that the grave is not our final abode. God has rescued us through the death and resurrection of Jesus.

CAPACITY FOR GOOD

Because of our origins in the mind and heart of God, each of us has an enormous capacity for good. We are predisposed to good precisely because we are spiritual beings, made in God's image.

When we begin to ignore or even forsake the implications of our origins, we fall easily into sin and disaster. We go rogue, and start steering our existence toward hurt and destruction.

Because of the intrusions of sin and evil into the world and into our personal lives, we are quick to see personal advantage, ego strokes and perverse titillation in the temptations to turn downward instead of upward in our quest for meaning and fulfillment.

We become blamers and rationalizers. If anyone points out the errors of our ways we are quick on the trigger to offer what we perceive as neat and cogent reasons for our maladaptive and harmful attitudes and behaviors. Blame is always part of such sappy rationales.

In large part the coming of Jesus Christ is to call us back to our origins and to God's intentions for our lives—to remind us of our capacity for good and to empower us for all the good we are intended to follow and create.

Reminders of Whose side we're supposed to be on are issued every Sunday in the worship services of our churches. That's reason enough for faithful attendance.

DOUBTING LACKS SOPHISTICATION

I am not impressed with persons who are quick to express doubts about the verities of the Christian faith and the worth of the Church. Most often such doubters are reacting to a smattering of religion, and are basking in abysmal ignorance of what the Christian Faith is all about. In plain language, they do not know enough about the Faith and the Church to have any honest, intelligent doubts.

Also, such doubters often are driven by other concerns—such as commitment avoidance. They do not want to become involved in the faith or the church because they are smart enough to realize that to get that close would place demands on them. So they credit sophisticated intellectual doubts with their self-centered disinclinations to believe and serve.

And what is the more pitiable, they expect others to "oooh" and "aaah" over such magnificent intellect and wisdom. They want plaudits for their ignorant doubting—for their artful dodging of commitment and God's calls to understand and serve the highest to which human beings may aspire.

Doubt is not admirable. Faith and commitment are. Those life forces are authentic signs of maturity, not doubt. Nor is doubt a sign of wisdom. Belief and commitment within the context of full reality are evidences of a wise mind.

Note that phrase "within the context of full reality." That means not only the immediate environment and the meager and negligible knowledge that goes with it—but reaching out to the universe and its Creator. Without that intentional effort full reality is missing.

CULT-PROOFING

There are hundreds of cults operating in the USA, and they are very determined to captivate the young with their mind-mesmerizing messages and techniques. Let's face it: Too many of our citizens, young and old, are fair game.

My ideas about cult-proofing children and adults offer no guarantees that people will not fall through the cracks and involve themselves in slavish devotion to some charismatic monster. But certainly we can minimize the risks.

The focal point for cult-proofing is the home. Consider this axiom: Weak families produce weak children who become weak adults. I mean weak in everything needed for cult-proofing, as well as being weak in the required moxie and know-how if they are to live meaningfully and successfully in a chaotic world.

Cults prey on youngsters and adults who evidence low self-esteem and a lack of family structure, nurture and support.

Strong family ties, involvement in programs and worship that nurture faith, wholesome togetherness, stable discipline, mutual respect for family members along with loads of affection and affirmation—all these are enormously helpful in cult-proofing.

When the family is weak or nil in any of these areas, serious deprivation and defects are apt to show up in the life of the child and the adult he or she is becoming.

NEW YEAR SURVIVAL

What will be the main theme of your celebration on New Year's Eve—the arrival of the new year, or your survival of the old year? In either case, it's quite amazing to have made it through the old year—and now to enter the new.

People talk about what the new year will bring them. But an even more important concern is what we bring to the new year.

Will it be the same old habits, attitudes and behaviors? Will we take anything fresh and vibrant into the new year—or will next year be, in the main, a repeat of last year?

Moving out of the Christmas celebration we ought to have at least a few attitude adjustments that will stand us in good stead for the new year.

Take the hope of Christmas with you—not the thin, brittle kind of hope so common in our human thinking, but the hope that is defined by the Scriptures as confident expectations based on God's realities and promises.

Take dignity and stature with you into the new year—the right to stand tall and to know your value as a child of God, created and redeemed by our Maker.

Be very determined that in the new year things and events will not manipulate you. Go proactive, and with God's gracious help, shape your future.

MY MIND IS MADE UP!

A small sign on someone's desk reads: "Don't confuse me with facts—my mind is made up!"

I think I have another suggestion for a sign that describes some people's attitudes: "Don't confuse me with truth and morality—I'm determined to live my life my way, not God's way."

Another appropriate sign for some might be: "Don't urge me to think—I'm determined to follow my emotions in this matter."

Truth, justice, rightness and wrongness may easily make their way through to the brain—if egotistical emotions are not guarding the gates. But try to bring sense and sanity to emotions, and it's often hopeless.

Some people get into deep trouble because their thinking has gone awry. They're just not thinking straight and right.

But more often, folks get into trouble because they tell their brain to shut up! They are determined to listen only to their feelings, their emotions, their ego centered wants.

Small children are feelings oriented. They concentrate on emotions, not knowledge and know how. Why is it that so many adults seem at ease in reverting to such childish ways? And even worse, they have the audacity to make claims like, "I'm free. I'm liberated! I'm mature!"

The proper response is a hearty "Balderdash!"

WORLD IN A HURRY

In case you have not noticed, the world around us is in a hurry as never before. Everything seems to be accelerating.

We have an information explosion that keeps accelerating. People get in contact quickly around the globe, and the world is at our fingertips.

What's the rush? On this planet that is racing around our solar system, the answers seems obvious. Time is fleeting. We want to get more done and faster. There is so much out there that we can yet experience. We're in a hurry because that's the way things are!

In some areas of life, we really ought to be in a hurry. Delay can be very costly.

Be in a hurry to know and serve Jesus Christ, to accept Him as Savior, and follow Him as Lord.

Be in a hurry to do good and to demonstrate love. Don't put it off—not for a moment.

Be in a hurry to ask and offer forgiveness—the unconditional "brand" of forgiveness which is the one and only authentic forgiveness in God's eternal economy.

Be in a hurry to know and live out your Christian Faith in front of all the world.

Yes, indeed, some things are worthy of the hurry.

SUPERSTITIOUS?

What goes through your mind when you wake up to Friday the 13th! Are you superstitious?

Be of good cheer. Any normal, sensible person—and especially one who has taken on the Christian Faith—knows that superstitions at their worst constitute harmful nonsense that has meaning and power in our lives only if we permit it. Superstitions are for the gullible and naive. They thrive on ignorance.

Good sense defines superstitions as irrational beliefs about the power of totally unrelated things to exert an influence on matters, and declares that such beliefs are maintained in the main by continuing and often fearful ignorance.

Superstitions often get in the way of the most important force for good in our lives: our Christian faith. Faith overcomes superstitions, making them both powerless and downright laughable. While superstitions enslave us, and keep us from our best, faith liberates and empowers us for the good.

One thing I have noted is that superstitions thrive the most in lives that have no grounding in genuine faith. Being a Christian drives us to seek for truth and the influence of God—and to scorn superstition and all other falsehood.

We all face many challenges in life that are legitimate and real. We don't need the crippling silliness of superstitions that work their non-productive crazymaking to our life's detriment.

REACHING FOR MATURITY

Maturity is an important asset for life. It is what we want our children to achieve, and what we hope we demonstrate to others.

Persons who fly off the handle demonstrate a lack of maturity. When we lack discipline about important concerns of life, we show our lack of maturity. And when we are impulsive, moody or unpredictable, we lack maturity.

Persons who use moodiness, their whining ways, and pretended weaknesses to manipulate others show a lack of maturity. And the same with those who refuse to bear responsibilities which are properly theirs!

Anne Nunemaker wrote:

> "If you can hear a man argue a point of view which is contrary to your own, and accept his right to his own opinion without a feeling of smugness—that is maturity. If you can listen to someone criticize you, even unkindly, and receive instruction from it without hard feelings—that is maturity. If you can see a person do an act which is against your Christian standards and react without self-righteousness, that is maturity."

I've heard people say with harshness to their children, "When are you ever going to grow up?" Or, "Why don't you grow up?" And the thought comes: That child is being a child! And it is the parent who is demonstrating a lack of maturity!

REST AND STRENGTH

The Old Testament is more than the historical background for Jesus the Messiah and the New Testament writings. It is God's Word to us *now,* as well as the New Testament.

In Isaiah 30:15 we were blessed with this powerful passage:

> **For thus said the Lord God, the Holy One of Israel, "In returning and rest you shall be saved; in quietness and in trust shall be your strength."** (RSV)

It was a plea from God to His people to turn from idols, from the gods of pleasure and things, and return to Him and find their rest. Faith in God is the source of true strength for our living.

There are so many psychological fads that claim to foster self-confidence as the answer to the weaknesses of our lives. It's good for us to have self-confidence.

But self-confidence and self-reliance can take us only so far, and then we run smack dab into the brick wall of reality, and we are overwhelmed by the world around us.

Quiet, trusting, confident faith in the God Who is more powerful than any of us is our real source of adequate, sufficient strength for every question of life, and every trial.

REFLECTION TIME

Currently I am experiencing some health concerns, and am requiring a lot of help from the medical personnel and staff of our local clinic and hospital. I am learning much and am receiving excellent care from these wonderful professionals.

I know that many will join me in expressions of genuine appreciation for health care facilities and all of the gracious staff and support persons.

During these days of the stress and strains of treatment and recovery, my mind often turns to thoughts about the fragility of life—and also of its beauty and glory. This includes the sheer privilege of being and living.

Willy nilly, one gets back to basics when confronted with serious illness and emphatic demands for changes in lifestyle. The option is to become a complaining sore head, directing epithets at heaven itself for perceived maltreatment by the Almighty.

So I've done a lot of thinking about life's basic essentials, and one of them is a deep and abiding sense of gratitude for life itself, and for all who contribute their skills and personalities to making our days full of meaning, peace and healing.

Grateful hearts do not just happen. They are constructed and trained to the gracious attitudes that respond with thanksgiving and praise to God—and to others.

GREAT IS THY FAITHFULNESS

The hymn *Great Is Thy Faithfulness* strikes a powerful chord in the human heart precisely because faithfulness is such a rare element in our lives.

Lately I have heard of so many divorces, of so many failing marriages, of so much of betrayal and disloyalty it makes my head spin with dark foreboding of where we are headed as a society. This concern is on personal levels and also national and international.

God is good and only good. Unlike us, there is no "dark side" to God. What we must reach for is all the good of God for our own lives. And that includes what the hymn is singing about: His faithfulness. Because He is faithful, so must we be faithful.

When will we ever grasp that we give and help because it is the right thing to do? We stick with our marriages, with their obligations, joys and hassles—and even their deprivations—because it is the right thing to do; we forgive persons who have hurt us deeply, even when forgiveness is not deserved because forgiveness is the right thing to do.

The moment we attach "riders" and "qualifications" on any of these matters, we close the door on grace and open the door to crass egotism and spiritual darkness.

HUMANIZING THE ENEMY

One of the interesting facts of eternal life was pointed out in an article in the October 23, 2000 issue of *Christianity Today.* The article, "Love Your Heavenly Enemy," asks the question: "How are we going to live eternally with those we can't stand now?"

Now that is a sane and sensible question.

The writer, Miroslav Volf, relates how Karl Barth, was once asked the question, "Is it true that one day in heaven we will see again our loved ones?"

"Barth responded with a chuckle, 'Not only the loved ones!'"

Volf wrote, "The sting of the great theologian's response—be ready to meet there even those whom you dislike here—was directed against our propensity to populate heaven only with people whom we like."

Of course, this is fallacious, and it leads us to put off one of the main tasks we have on earth, to make reconciliation with persons with whom we are "on the outs." Make peace, and give and receive forgiveness.

We spend too much time dehumanizing our enemies—to such an extent that we read them out of God's Grace and heavenly place.

Rather we must humanize them in the highest sense—seeing and treating them as rightful objects of God's grace and love—and therefore ours, right now.

UPHILL CLIMBING

Our daughter and son-in-law at one time were involved in mission work at Woodstock School high in the mountains of India. One of the most impressive things about their mountainous setting is how far they have to climb up the side of a mountain in order to reach their classrooms.

They estimate that every day they have to climb the equivalent of the stairs in a 36 story building—and sometimes several times a day. And it's dangerous!

Elizabeth wrote to us in one E-mail communication:

> "Lots of stairs—uneven killer stairs. Lots of ramps—straight up ramps with 500 foot drop-offs on the outside and no railings. In the US this place would be neither kid-approved nor handicapped-accessible, for sure! Kids do occasionally fall down the "khud" (deep, deep ravine—the hollow between hills—make that "mountains"—usually at night when they're getting goofy. It's serious. When I get to the School Quadrangle, I drop off McCleary and then go up another 3 or 4 stories to the High School."

My response to all these difficulties is that they are a kind of metaphor of the meaningful, productive life. If you're going to do any good in this world it's mostly uphill. You have to climb those mountains, and walk the winding, dangerous pathways. In all truth, we all are assigned mountains to climb.

MEMORIAL DAY

Memorial Day offers us an opportunity to remember. But remembering with any sense of meaning and propriety demands deep understanding and high intentionality on our part. We have to make an effort to remember, and to be sure the remembering is for the right reasons.

A certain principle is involved in our observance of Memorial Day, and we need to get hold of it. Simply stated it tells us: "We owe the past. We are debtors to the past. What we have now as the most precious things of life are because of sacrifices made by others for the future and security of us all."

Another principle is that of heritage, of being in a line of heritage—in touch with the past and debtors to it, and in touch with the future and debtors to it. A sense of participating in a heritage line is a neat thing to have, and it makes Memorial Day all the richer.

We must buy into the conviction that we owe the future because of our present benefits handed to us out of the past. Others made sacrifices to maintain our liberties and opportunities, and we must do the same for unknown persons of the future.

A Memorial Day truism is this: "It must not end with those who have given service to our nation, with those who have died for our country." We are in the line of heritage that calls on us to do our part, to make sacrifices for the benefit and wellbeing of future generations.

DETOURS

Whenever I come to a "detour" sign on the highway, I speculate about what might happen if I ignore the sign, and just keep going on my planned route. Of course, those thoughts are fleeting, and I do manage to stick with common sense reality.

I know there might be a bridge out, impassable highway construction or other obstacles that could mean disaster if I don't obey the detour sign. So dutifully I follow directions, lose some time, drive over a road much worse, travel a greater distance—but all very necessary.

Life itself is full of detour signs. Thing happen to change our plans, to delay departures, to keep us from doing what we want to do—and willy-nilly we are on a detour. We grumble and fret about the delay, the loss and the inconvenience. But in the long run it's best that we obey the signs and do what must be done. In so doing we could be avoiding real trouble.

Detours represent the unexpected happenings and circumstances of life. They call for patience—and they call for expectancy of the serendipitous—which means unplanned and unanticipated experiences that turn out to be beneficial and even joyful. This means we have to be on the lookout.

Nothing is wasted or stupid when God is in the picture. Put the detours of life into His care and you likely will be surprised at the wonderful surprises that come your way—all because of those seemingly pesky detours.

PARENTING PITFALLS

Have you ever thought about how many pitfalls there are in parenting? Parents have no training for the tasks to which they are called by the birth of a child. Unlike most animals human beings are not endowed with parenting instincts, a sort of computerized, built-in parenting program.

One of the worst pitfalls of parenting is what I call "the ownership syndrome." Parents begin to think they have bought their children. They own them. They confuse the meeting of financial obligations with the out and out purchase of their kids. And if they own them, then of course the kids should obey them all their lives, follow parental advice, enter the vocation the parents think best, and spend money the way the parents advise.

There are children who have reached their forties and fifties. Their parents just won't let go and let them live out their lives with dignity, responsibility and self-determination. Parents want a say, and many times *the say* in what their children do.

If the offspring are not assertive, they knuckle under and continue a lifetime of sheer misery, from which only death frees them—either their own or their parents' death.

The dominating parents thought they were showing love—when really they were only holding tight reins on what they viewed as their property.

THE PITFALL OF PERMISSIVENESS

Yesterday we talked about one of the pitfalls of parenting, when parents assume an ownership stance toward their children even into the later adult years.

Another parenting pitfall is that of permissiveness, in which parents imagine that their children are best raised by giving them their head, turning them loose, letting them make major decisions for which they really are not prepared.

Parents can be terribly naive when it comes to maturity, discretion and good sense in their offspring.

They also are naive about the whole matter of human propensities toward evil, fouling up, failing and destructive behaviors.

A lot of sociologists have what I call the *tabula rasa* attitude toward a child's mental and emotional propensities.

Tabula rasa is Latin for a clean slate, and refers to the belief that the mind is just that before impressions and experiences from outside begin to inscribe information on it.

But Christians are aware that built into the human soul is a propensity for doing the wrong and rebellious. Our *tabula rasa* is messed up from the very beginning. Parents are faced with the challenge of taking charge and helping us shape up.

Permissiveness in the face of such reality is really the height of foolishness.

THE PITFALL OF SURROGACY

This might be a new word for some: "Surrogacy." It means having a substitute, someone put in the place of another—perhaps to fulfill the responsibilities that properly belong to the first party. But the surrogate carries them out.

Surrogacy is one of the main pitfalls of parenting. One of the parents wanted so much to do certain things in life, but for various reasons could not accomplish them.

Children are often pressured to work toward a vocation that mom or dad wished they had pursued. So the child becomes a surrogate or substitute for parental dreams and wish fulfillments, for the carrying out of ambitions and goals never realized by the parent.

The child is not considered as a distinct and separate personality. His or her characteristics, capabilities and potential are not given much weight at all—except as they relate to the surrogacy intentions of the parent.

In the process the youngster is divested of a major portion of his or her personality.

And even more tragically he or she is denied the fulfillment of what ought to be the aim of every parent: that under God their children grow into self determining adults—and that they not simply mirror the dreams and hopes of others. And that includes parents.

A LITTLE KINDNESS

On a recent visit to the outpatient clinic of Floyd Valley Hospital I experienced an unusually long wait.

The young lady who finally came to get me was very apologetic—and my response was "Don't give it a thought! There certainly are other patients here who need help much more than I do."

There was a pause, and then the young lady looked at me and said softly, "Thank you for being so kind and patient."

That tipped me off that she had run into some real grouches that day—persons whose main enjoyment seems to lie in griping, complaining, blaming and criticizing.

Such folks are *not* in short supply. They seem to become a different personality when confronted with delays or any other kind of inconvenience. Like brooding, moody predators they spill their bad feelings on persons who cannot respond in kind.

A little kindness goes a long way. Kindness and its expressions feed on patience, understanding and big doses of empathy with persons who play helping roles in our lives.

We all have the capacity to infect the world around us with joy—or with gloom, doom, despair and misery. A good rule of life is to spread your joy, not your misery and ill will.

Work at kindness.

A COMMUNITY OF DEBTORS

On this Veterans' Day, it is good for us to understand that we are all debtors. We owe, and big time.

Owing money is one thing. But owing others for our freedom, our way of life and peace in the land is much more profound, and a far bigger debt.

We cannot measure our debt to America's veterans in terms of money. That would be crass as well as plain dumb.

It's always too bad when we enter a war. There is horrendous loss. Awesome sacrifices are made for the good of our nation—for our good. Young men and women die and are mutilated and savaged by the horrors of war.

Those who live through a war are emotionally and often physically scarred for life. They, too, have made a huge sacrifice, and not just in terms of time served and hardships endured.

It's always good to know whom we owe and for what reasons. We may owe a bank for our car or home purchase. We may owe some superb teachers for mentoring us along life's way.

But the debt you and I owe to the men and women who have served in our armed forces is awesome—and can never be repaid. We can only say a huge "thanks"—and honor their sacrifices in whatever ways we can.

VETERANS' DAY

Warm thanks to all veterans of our nation's conflicts—those men and women who put their lives on the line for the sake of their country. Their service and sacrifices touch every one of us in a very personal way.

Last week I watched the coverage of the homecoming of the crew of the USS Cole—the American warship that was so viciously attacked by terrorists in the port of Aden.

There were tears in my eyes as I watched the loving reunions of families who not long before had wondered and waited in dread and fear for news that their family member had escaped death or injury.

Then I thought of the men and women who had been killed by the terrorist explosion, and I uttered a prayer of thanks for their sacrifices.

That's what we all should be doing—and not only on Veterans' Day.

We are living in wonderful times—but also in times of pernicious evil that stalks the earth. I was shocked when I heard that some members of the clergy of Islam have demanded from their pulpits that followers of Muhammad stalk and kill all the Israelis and Americans they can.

One other thought for Veterans' Day: We have no choice but to keep America's armed forces strong and ready for anything.

VALENTINE NONSENSE

On Valentine's Day all kinds of expressions about love and loyalty zoom through the air. Arrows of love strike home, protestations of love and friendship overflow—sometimes *ad nauseum,* because in many cases they are fraudulent and nonsensical.

Oh, I can hear it now—someone saying with irritation, "There goes Grupp with his Scrooge act again!" No, not at all. What I advocate is that Valentine's Day be a time to ponder the characteristics and implications of genuine love—the kind of authentic and overwhelming love that God Himself shows, and wants us to do the same.

Authentic love is not self-seeking or selfish. Its concerns always are for the wellbeing, dignity, health and wholeness of the other person in the relationship.

Authentic love operates on the basis of high morals, the best of ethics and good manners.

Authentic love is forgiving and redeeming, just as is the love of God.

Authentic love is a total stranger to notions of revenge for hurts, remembering mistakes and wrongs, and the desire to conquer even at the cost of the other person's dignity and rights.

There is a lot of nonsense in the Valentine Season. We all need to fill those Valentine expressions with the truth, caring, actions and behaviors of genuine love.

CHURCH GAMES

There are many outside the church who seem to have a lot of fun with a game I call, "Let's knock the Church!"

It takes two or more players who have the talents of majoring on negatives, finding fault, and picking out flaws.

There are important rules, such as: "Always select the most unworthy, miserable and hypocritical church members when knocking the church. Don't ever choose one of the many spiritual giants!"

Another rule: "Don't ever acknowledge that church members know they are sinners and are trying to do something about it. Keep insisting that they all think they are better than others."

Another important rule: "Don't ever let it be known that the church is often the solitary voice in this world for truth, right and justice." Keep emphasizing the church's mistakes and its failures.

If you have found the church to be weak, its members hypocritical, and its message shallow—then perhaps you haven't really seen the Church of Jesus Christ at all! It may be that you have only been in contact with persons who are busy at that other game, "Let's Play Church."

There are churches whose people see themselves as servants of.Christ in His world. They behave as active partners in His work of redeeming and reconciling love. And when you find such a church, you just might want to be part of it.

JP

ALL SAINTS DAY

Christians celebrate the first day of November as All Saints Day.

It is good that we know just who are the saints. In recent centuries sainthood has been accorded only to some super special persons who were credited with at least a couple of miracles generated by their life and memory.

The Bible is more generous about the identity of the saints. Paul opens his Letter to the Church at Ephesus: "Paul, an apostle of Christ Jesus by the will of God, To the saints in Ephesus, the faithful in Christ Jesus. . ."

And to the wayward Corinthian Church Paul opens with these words: "To the church of God which is at Corinth, to those sanctified in Christ Jesus, called to be saints together with all those who in every place call on the name of our Lord Jesus Christ, both their Lord and ours: " (I Corinthians 2:1 RSV)

By Paul's implication, if one is a believer in Jesus Christ, and therefore has been sanctified by Him, that person is a saint—maybe not always saintly, but nonetheless a saint.

All Saints Day is when we remember with love and gratitude all the saints who have gone on to their heavenly home ahead of us.

Indeed, we believe in "the communion of the saints"—which means that here and "there," we are still bound together with the unbreakable bonds of Jesus Christ.

A NOT SO FUNNY HALLOWEEN

On Halloween night have fun. Treat the little beggars with humor and candy. Keep scariness to a sane and sensible level. Make sure the kids understand that a lot of the pretend is just that: Pretend.

But at the same time, be cautious about "pretend" that has bitter and ghastly roots in reality.

I heard of a store that sells costumes and equipment for a chain saw murderer. Not funny.

Depicting real life monsters should give kicks only to the most addle brained adult, those whose sensitivity and savvy register a cold and unfeeling zero.

Scaring small children so much that their heartbeat soars and their fears are terrifyingly with them for months to come does not make for a funny Halloween—except for the most coarse and unfeeling among us.

A concern I have is that we must not make the dead into fearsome ghouls who are out to do us harm. The group that plans Halloween kicks in a cemetery is off base in my book. Everyone has loved ones whose remains are buried in some cemetery. It is not cool to demean and disparage folks who when alive were so caring and loving.

Have a fun and funny Halloween—but know the boundaries beyond which celebrations turn ugly and plain mean.

ADVENT AND CHRISTMAS

JP

ADVENT ANTICIPATIONS

The Season of Advent is the magnificent prelude to Christmas, covering the four Sundays preceding Christmas Day.

That whole era of time prior to the New Testament was the real Advent season—as the people anticipated the coming of their Messiah, the promised One Who would bring new life and hope to individuals and to the nation.

In that original Advent some erroneous ideas were developed about Christ's coming. We do the same, even though we have access to all the facts of His coming.

We can excuse the ignorance of Old Testament people far easier than we can our own. We ought to know better! We are living after the event—they lived before it.

In this Advent time what should we be anticipating for Christmas?

For one thing, the birthday celebration of the Redeemer, Jesus, Who is the incarnate God and our Savior.

We also need to anticipate the impact of that first Christmas and all its implications for our lives. What does the Christmas event mean to us, our life attitudes and behaviors, the values by which we live, the ways in which we look at and relate to other persons?

Christmas means change—in a big way. Even King Herod sensed that. Do you?

A COMFORTER WITHOUT A PERSONAL AGENDA

In those times when we have been troubled and sorrowful, we may have turned to someone for comfort—and found not a whiff of it. We may have found false comforters, such as those so-called friends who gathered around Job. They ended up being accusers, not comforters, and only caused his miseries to increase.

Most of the time the world's comforters have an agenda of their own. Whether they be pastor or psychologist, mentor or counselor, quite often they are focusing not so much on others' comfort as their own. Some of them get their jollies by assuming the superior role of a comforter. Most of them are still working out their own problems and hangups, and they do practice runs with clients and patients. Others have money in mind, or they're writing a book—or just trying to escape from their own humdrum existence.

But there is a Comforter without any agenda but our wellbeing, our destiny, our life fulfillment. The Old Testament tells about Him.

Long before Jesus came, Isaiah wrote in chapter 40:

> **Comfort, comfort my people, says your God. Speak tenderly to Jerusalem, and proclaim to her that her hard service has been completed, that her sin has been paid for.**

And behold this wondrous marvel: Christmas has given us a Comforter without an agenda.

CELEBRATE THE GIFT

Probably the question asked most often on Christmas Day and after is, "What did you *get* for Christmas?" I'm bemused by the fact that no one ever asks, "What did you *give* for Christmas?"

And I'm amazed that so few seem to know why we give and receive gifts at Christmas.

Here is the reason in a nutshell: When giving and receiving are done in the right spirit it's one of the best ways to celebrate God's magnificent Gift to us in the Person of Jesus the Christ.

The Baby of Bethlehem was saved from Herod's terrible and murderous wrath, and grew up to fulfill His mission of revelation and salvation. The awesome fact is that Jesus was born to do this, as part of God's plan from the beginning of creation.

Whatever you might give or receive as gifts at Christmas, they cannot come even close to the majesty and power of God's Gift to us in Jesus. That does not detract from our giving one whit—because our giving and receiving, small or large, are at their best when we understand that in so doing we are remembering and celebrating the greatest Gift ever given!

So celebrate the Gift with rejoicing and generosity in these wonderful Seasons of Advent and Christmas.

INAPPROPRIATE GIFTS

God's gift to us at that first Christmas certainly was an appropriate one.

The Gift of Jesus was exquisite, costly, long lasting, practical and much needed. How can we beat that?

I got some shaving lotion five years ago that still sits on my shelf. I know the giver paid a bundle for it, but the fragrance of it is not exactly fragrant to my nostrils—more like flagrant.

People often buy gifts without a great deal of thought, and end up giving what amount to inappropriate gifts.

Chocolate covered almonds for a diabetic make an inappropriate gift. So is a picture album for your blind uncle, or an album of Mozart for your nephew who loves hard rock. Come to think of it, that might be a good idea!

Narrow neckties are not appropriate at this time in history, and you might think twice before wrapping up that brand new leisure suit for good old Freddie.

When I see how aggressive some children are, it seems to me that play guns and other toy weapons are not the most appropriate gift.

Let your gifts speak of your love, testify to the rich meaning of Christmas, and jibe with the character of the one whom you are gifting. The best gifts show thought and time behind them—just like the Gift God gave to us!

JP

CONNECTING

During the Christmas Season we connect with more people than at any other time of the year. We call, we write, we E-mail, we send and receive cards, we give gifts, we attend parties—and many attend church services more often during the Advent and Christmas Seasons.

Human beings are intended to connect. Some people try to be loners, and usually end up being a bit odd—or maybe just plain off the wall. We need to connect.

Basically Christmas is the story of God connecting with Planet Earth—with the very persons He has created. It isn't so much that He has a need to connect with us, as it is our need to connect with Him—to be knowledgeably in touch with the Holy God on Whom we depend for the very breath of life.

I really like that painting of Jesus knocking at the door—the door of the human heart. When I was a youngster someone pointed out that there is no latch on the outside. The door must be opened from within. He wants to connect with us, but will not force Himself on us.

One of the most important questions you can ask during this Holy Season concerns whether or not you have heard His knock, have opened the door—and connected with the living Christ.

Revelation 3:20: "Behold, I stand at the door and knock; if any one hears My voice and opens the door, I will come in to him and eat with him, and he with Me." (RSV)

ADULTS AND "DISCOVERING CHRISTMAS"

If adults don't come to grips with the truth and meaning of the Christmas Season, how can we ever expect our children to discover Christmas realities?

The fantasies being palmed off on children during the season express values that reek with the lies of materialism and hedonism, the gods of an ego maniacal culture and commerce gone berserk.

Adults must take the lead in helping our children find the truth and full reality of Christmas.

Children did not write the Old Testament prophecies relating our desperate need for a Messiah and God's promises of His coming.

The historical persons of Christmas are adults. Mary was chosen by God for a touchy assignment—that was traumatic for her and her fiance, Joseph. The shepherds in the hills near Bethlehem weren't kids. They were adults trying to eke out a living by raising sheep.

The wise men were adults, too. They were looking for something far more significant than toys. Neither they nor the star were the trappings of fantasy. In faith they began an arduous journey to pay homage to a Child over Whom was cast the tragic shadow of the cross.

Let's face it: Christmas is not kids' stuff. It is meant mainly for adults—who must comprehend the truth before our children can ever "get it."

A GOOD NEWS GOD

Perhaps with some humor, most us probably have concluded that persons are either good news persons or bad news persons.

There are those folks whose approach almost makes one wince with pain, because our whole being senses that bad news is on its way. So get ready to endure the disagreeable.

Bad news persons have a lot of resources and support behind them. One has the distinct impression that at any given moment the world has more bad news to offer than good. But that doesn't mean we have to major on it.

Then there are the good news persons. Their very approach brings joy and inspiration, for at their coming our whole being anticipates welcome news, good news.

We really have made progress when we understand that God is a Good News Person. Yes, He has some bad news for people who scorn and mock Him—promising exacting judgment and lasting consequences.

But for every seeker, for every person who does battle for the good, for every broken spirit and every broken heart God has good news.

God's good news is wrapped up in the Person and accomplishments of Jesus the Christ—the preeminent Good News Person! In His company every new year can only offer the very best.

POLITICALLY CORRECT CHRISTMAS

According to the December 20, 1999 issue of *US News and World Report* (page 10) United States District Court Judge Susan J. Dlott recently dismissed a suit that attempted to bar federal workers from taking Christmas off. The judge stated: "We are all better for Santa—the Easter Bunny, too."

I suppose one could call that "a politically correct Christmas"—or maybe "a judicially correct Christmas."

A few nights ago a well known but somewhat wacky talk show host got real serious about people who want to bring Jesus and other religious notions into Christmas celebrations. In his opinion, they are blue nosed spoilers anti-fun religious zealots, and fanatics who just can't see the really good side of Christmas revelry.

I side with all whose Christmas joy, celebrations, hope, love and peace focus not on the pagan peripherals, but on Jesus the Son of God, Who came down to His world, bringing with Him everything we need for all the best of life.

I enjoy much of the secular stuff: the music, the decorations, the parties and celebrations. But we show immense stupidity when we let all that take the place of the Christ of Christmas, the real Reason for the Season.

He gifts us as no other can—with the gifts of peace, hope, truth, life, joy and meaning.

How about celebrating a spiritually, historically, theologically correct Christmas!

A SONG IN THE NIGHT

The thought of waiting for a song in the night strikes a familiar chord. In all there is a longing for closeness, for someone who cares and who will take away our feelings of loneliness and of a lack of worth—for a song that assures us of meaning and hope for all our living.

The story of the Nativity tells of a song in the night.

The shepherds out in the hills and plains surrounding Bethlehem had a visitation from angels, whose joy knew no bounds. The angels had a song to share with the shepherds—and with us all.

His birth continues to be a song in the night for all ages, taking away fear and loneliness, giving people dignity, courage, hope and love.

Ours could be the night of failure, or of tragic loss. It could be the night that falls when we hear the dread news of disease or disablement, or the loss of job. There are the nights of grief and fear, the nights of guilt and remorse.

In the midst of our personal night there comes a song that tells of a powerful Redeemer, and offers assurance that the night will pass, and that the dawning light of a new day will come.

Out of the night skies the angels sang their magnificent song of good news: "Glory to God in the highest, and on earth peace among men with whom He is pleased!" (Luke 2:14 RSV)

CHRISTMAS— A STATE OF MIND

Mary Ellen Chase said it well: "Christmas is not a date. It is a state of mind."

Well, that calls for some consideration: The state of mind that is Christmas.

First and foremost in such a state of mind is an attitude of anticipation. For some it is the anticipation of the day itself, with all that goes on in the homes of friends and loved ones. For others it is the quiet beauty of the Christmas Eve Service in their churches.

Another Christmas attitude is caring that takes in loved ones and even total strangers. At Christmas, because of the meaning of the first Christmas, we feel more caring, and we want to reach out in love to others, just as God reached out in love toward us in sending His great Gift.

The Christmas state of mind also includes an element of sorrow, of stirred memories of loved ones who are no longer with us—of Christmases past.

And that's not strange at all. The shadow of the cross lay over Bethlehem, and the blood of many a prophet had been shed in preparation for the coming of the Holy Child.

For many their Christmas is a mixture of joy and sorrow, just as in that very first Christmas.

Ms. Chase had it right: "Christmas is not a date. It is a state of mind."

CATCHING UP

Years ago I heard of an African tribe whose members were superb runners. Occasionally they would stop in their tracks and just wait. It wasn't that they were tired. Their explanation was that when one runs so fast, the soul lags behind, and one must wait for the soul to catch up.

Have you ever thought of outrunning, outstripping, outdistancing your soul.

It seems that many in today's society have left their souls far behind them in their mad pursuit of pleasure and sensation. They keep running, and their souls get further and further behind.

An 18 year old man was convicted of brutally raping a three year old girl. I wonder where his soul was when he savaged the child.

A postal worker opened fire on his colleagues, a high school student murdered three classmates as they left a prayer meeting—and many more such incidents just in the past few months all leave me wondering. Where were the souls of the people doing these horrible acts?

Perhaps that's the main purpose of meditation and prayer time, the study of the Scriptures and attending worship faithfully—to let our souls catch up. We dare not run the race of life without our souls.

Properly and worshipfully observed, Christmas can be a natural catchup time for our souls.

ADVENT AND CHRISTMAS VOCABULARY

The Season of Advent takes place every year during the four Sundays preceding Christmas Day. It is a time to anticipate all that Christmas meant in Jesus' time—and all it means today.

To anticipate and truly celebrate one needs a vocabulary for use during the Advent and Christmas Seasons. Words are so important that the One Who came at Christmas is called "The Word" in the first chapter of John's Gospel.

So how's your vocabulary for Advent and Christmas?

A proper one is made up of the most powerful words of the Christian faith. So it's a vocabulary for living as a Christian. Now is the time to sharpen up your vocabulary. It truly does pay to increase your word power—and especially in relation to our God-given faith!

Think of some of the magnificent words and phrases of Advent and Christmas: Messiah, Redeemer, Incarnation, Redemption, Salvation, Son of God, Son of Man, God's Word, Prophecy, the Virgin Birth, Hope, Joy, Peace, Love, Savior and many more.

It is a fact that you and I cannot really understand or enjoy a football game or a contest in just about any worthy sport unless we know quite a lot about the nature of the game—its rules and vocabulary.

Believe it or not, it's the same with Advent and Christmas!

CHRISTMAS CONCEPTS—PREEXISTENCE

If we are to think and celebrate a genuine and accurate Christmas, we need a special vocabulary.

There are some simple Christmas words that all of us can grasp—words such as joy, peace and love.

But we need hefty conceptual words for an understanding that goes deep into God's marvelous realities.

We begin with the word "preexistence." That even sounds deep: "preexistence."

That concept speaks to us of the fact that the Being and Person of Jesus has always been. There never was a time when He was not. We cannot call ourselves preexistent. We came into being at the time of our conception. Jesus, on the other hand, was born into the very world He had created and related to as the preexistent Son of God—in that state and status long before creation.

In John's Gospel, chapter 1, we read this fantastic declaration:

In the beginning was the Word, and the Word was with God, and the Word was God. He was with God in the beginning. Through Him all things were made; without Him nothing was made that has been made. In Him was life, and that Life was the light of men.

John is emphasizing the preexistent Jesus—the Christ Who always has been and always will be.

CHRISTMAS CONCEPTS— INCARNATION

Today's Christmas concept is "Incarnation."

Incarnation speaks of the fact that the eternal Being and Person of Jesus the Son of God entered human form that holy night in Bethlehem.

The most unusual aspect of the Birth of our Lord was not the setting—nor even the fact that angels announced His birth to shepherds and wise men who came from the east following a star and a verse from prophecy. It's even deeper than His being born of a virgin.

The truly fantastic and awesome aspect of the Birth of Jesus is that the eternal God entered human form. He had His reasons for doing so—centering in His desire that He know us and we know Him.

In John's Gospel, chapter 1 we read: "The Word became flesh and made His dwelling among us. We have seen His glory, the glory of the One and Only, Who came from the Father, full of grace and truth." That's incarnation! And that is absolutely awesome.

John opened his first letter by writing: "That which was from the beginning, which we have heard, which we have seen with our eyes, which we have looked at and our hands have touched—this we proclaim concerning the Word of life."

That's incarnation—and that's the heart of Christmas.

CHRISTMAS CONCEPTS— REVELATION

It's interesting that some of the big concepts of our Christian faith may be applied to ordinary matters. Today's conceptual word "Revelation" can be used to describe the ways in which persons open up to reveal their true selves. It's not easy to do that—to let others "in on the know" of who we are, what we believe, our fears and hopes—our faults, failures and dreams.

But that is precisely what God did for us in entering His world. He came to show us what He really is like—to reveal the very essence of His Being—at least as much as we can grasp with our limited intellects.

Revelation is a word we need to understand if we are to comprehend what Christmas is all about.

In ordinary human exchanges, there always will be those who don't give two hoots about the real me or the real you. They are too wrapped up in their own selves.

The same is true of God and His self-revealing. He meets a big "So what?" with many folks who really ought to know better.

In John's Gospel, chapter 1, we read: "Only a few would welcome and receive Him. But to all who received Him, He gave the right to become children of God." (The Living Bible)

Revelation—that's more of what Christmas is all about!

JP

CHRISTMAS CONCEPTS—REDEMPTION

Today's Christmas concept is "redemption"—a word we need to grasp if we are to really "get it" when it comes to a full reality Christmas.

The full story of redemption is the saga of God salvaging at least a remnant of humanity, pulling as many as possible back from the brink of destruction and eternal loss. To describe what God has done in Jesus the Christ we use words like bought and purchased—and we tell of how He suffered and died for us.

Redemption describes God's sacrifice of Himself—how He took our place as condemned sinners who have failed all the tests of holiness righteousness of a just yet loving Creator.

If we believe in Him, His redemptive work applies to us. We are forgiven and cleansed of our sin, we are given power and motivation to overcome it, we are restored to fellowship with God, we are the sure recipients of the gift of life eternal. Nothing can separate us from the love of God in Christ Jesus. We are His forever.

One of the most profound passages in the Bible is found in Romans 3, where Paul wrote: ". . . for all . . . are justified freely by His grace through the redemption that came by Christ Jesus."

Christmas is part of the story of our eternal Redemption.

CHRISTMAS CONCEPTS—RECONCILIATION

One of the sweetest, most beautiful words in any language is the word "reconciliation."

Reconciliation happens when estranged and embittered persons who once were friendly and even loved each other—finally get back together in a spirit of forgiveness and caring—ready to begin their relationship anew.

It is our Christmas concept for today, and rightly so. Reconciliation speaks of how alienated, far from God persons are brought back into harmonious fellowship with our Creator God.

In II Corinthians 5 we read: "Therefore, if anyone is in Christ, he is a new creation; the old has gone, the new has come! All this is from God, Who reconciled us to Himself through Christ and gave us the ministry of reconciliation: that God was reconciling the world to Himself in Christ, not counting men's sins against them. And He has committed to us the message of reconciliation." (NIV)

In Christ Jesus the reconciled become in turn reconcilers—committed to a purpose of fostering peace and reconciling love among persons and even nations.

One of the great hymns of the Christmas Season is "Hark! The

Herald Angels Sing: 'Glory to the newborn king! Peace on earth and mercy mild, God and sinners reconciled.'"

The hymn sings of our big Christmas concept of the day: Reconciliation.

TURNING AWAY FROM CHRISTMAS

We humans have a tendency to turn our backs on the very things we need the most. This includes turning away from the real Christmas, toward what I call "indulgent fantasies."

Christmas offers us the very best and highest of life. A proper Christmas vocabulary is filled with words and phrases related to love, hope, reconciliation, forgiveness, peace and truth.

If we're even a bit keen-minded we know that these are hefty concepts that deal with desperately needed realities for every human being.

And yet, so many simply turn their backs on it all, evidently preferring indulgent fantasies.

Herod, the king of Judah at the time of Jesus' birth, certainly turned his back on Jesus the Messiah of God. He not only thought he could do without Him—he thought he could do away with Him. His intent was to put an end once and for all to what he perceived as the Messiah threat.

Maybe that's it: Some are so threatened by the real meaning and Person of Christmas, they turn their backs on the genuine Christmas, and try to smother out His Presence with an avalanche of secular, self-indulgent fantasies.

But let's not kid ourselves. When we do that we turn away from all that is most needed in our lives.

GET THE SYMBOLS RIGHT!

In all honesty, what are your personal Christmas symbols?

For some the main symbol might be a bottle of booze, for others a charge card. Any symbol of a good time expresses the meaning of Christmas for some. A wrapped gift will do for many.

During one Christmas Season in Minneapolis some teenage girls were oohing and aahing over the display windows in the downtown department stores. The windows were beautiful, and were filled with splendid gifts. Then the girls came to a window depicting the manger scene—with Mary, Joseph and the Christ Child. One of the young ladies cried out, "Imagine that! The nerve! They're even bringing religion into Christmas!"

Many Christmas activities, along with the symbols that express them seem to be playing an avoidance game. There is great determination not to allow Christmas to mean anything beyond their selfish wants and pleasures.

But the realities of Christmas demand symbols that speak of the coming of the Son of God as a Baby born in Bethlehem. There were angels, shepherds, a star and wise men from the east. Lights may speak of the Light of the world. Candles may express the prayers of all God's people who waited and longed for His coming.

Get the symbols right—and we just might get Christmas right.

CHRISTMAS DISINFORMATION

A fairly recent word in our international vocabulary is "disinformation"—which means the deliberate disseminating of falsehoods in order to mislead people.

Shady operators send out loads of disinformation in order to disarm suspicion, make sales, get votes—or whatever. Folks who are experts on dishing out disinformation sound convincing, sincere and full of good will.

There's a lot of disinformation connected with Christmas. It started as early as the days of the prophets, hundreds of years before the birth of the Christ. In Jeremiah 23:32 God tells us: "'Behold, I am against those who prophesy lying dreams,' says the Lord, 'and who tell them and lead My people astray by their lies and their recklessness, when I did not send them or charge them; so they do not profit this people at all,' says the Lord."

From earliest times they have had purveyors of religious disinformation.

When the Wise Men met with crafty King Herod, he dished out disinformation. He made a pretense of wanting to go and worship the new born king—but in reality he was planning to kill Him.

In our time disinformationists try hard to convince us that the real spirit of the so called "Holiday Season" is not religious or spiritual, but heartily pagan. At Christmas time and all times, watch out for disinformation.

CHRISTMASLESS

Consider the word: "Christmasless." It refers to situation in which individuals and families have no resources to celebrate Christmas as many do.

But "Christmasless" may also refer to persons who have no reason to celebrate Christmas.

I have Christian friends who believe it's wrong for them to observe Christmas—and they offer a variety of reasons. The Bible does not teach us to celebrate Jesus' birthday. We're not sure December 25 is the exact date—or even if it happened in the winter. Secular forces have taken over Christmas, and transformed it into a mostly pagan event. And their reasoning goes on.

While I respect their religious convictions, and will not even send them a Christmas card or letter, I decline to share their stance of being Christmasless.

The Bible testifies that Jesus was born in Bethlehem during the reign of Emperor Caesar Augustus, and that angels sang in joyful celebration as they delivered the news to shepherds—who then raced to Bethlehem to get close to the newborn Christ. Wise men came from the East to worship Him and present gifts.

I side with the angels, shepherds and wise men in celebration of God's coming among us in the Person of Jesus of Nazareth. It was a cosmic and earth changing event—well worth our joyful observance.

CHRISTMAS SUFFICIENCY

This time of year people have the word "enough" on their minds—or a similar word, "sufficiency."

What does it take to make just the right Christmas—an "enough Christmas"—a "sufficient Christmas"?

Of course, if you measure Christmas by what you can buy for the family, the gifts and food and fun expenditure—a lot of people will have a tough time of it. They simply do not have enough money to make an "enough Christmas"!

But supposing we concentrate on the great Gift we all received at Christmas: Jesus, the Son of God.

When Jesus is at the center of our Christmas celebrations, there can only be contentment, joy and peace.

What He offers us is sufficient love, sufficient grace, sufficient forgiveness, sufficient hope and sufficient life—in fact, the far more than enough of eternal life.

Jesus is our sufficient Redeemer, our sufficient Friend, our sufficient Lord, our sufficient Teacher.

He is the needed and sufficient Lamb of God Whose sacrifice takes away the sins of the world.

JP

CHRISTMAS CLOSURE

The reported events of Christmas call on us to make a personal closure with the implications of those holy and truly cosmic happenings—a once and for all time embracing of the truths and meanings of the events of Bethlehem and what followed in Christ's life, death and resurrection.

Does the meaning of the word "incarnation" grab you, and do you comprehend its relevance to the Christmas events? If not, then you need Christmas closure.

Do you have that awesome understanding that Christmas is meant to sweep you personally into the arms of God, the way of Christ and a destiny that includes purpose, meaning and eternal life? If not, then you need Christmas closure.

Shepherds and wise men and many others have made their Christmas closure as they accepted and acclaimed what God has done.

One of the most beautiful happenings in the Christmas event is when the aged Simeon, who had been promised he would not die before he saw the Christ, took Jesus in his arms and said: "Sovereign Lord, as You have promised, You now dismiss Your servant in peace. For my eyes have seen Your salvation, which You have prepared in the sight of all people, a light for revelation to the Gentiles and for glory to Your people Israel." (Luke 2:29-32)

Simeon certainly made his Christmas closure.

CHRISTMAS PERIPHERALS

At the beginning of Advent this past year I found myself musing about the facts of Christmas—just the bare facts, without any of the peripherals, good or bad.

What triggered me was a comment I heard just before Halloween. Someone gushed that they preferred Halloween over Christmas because there was less strain and pressure.

My immediate mental response was, "Lady, either you haven't the faintest notion of the true meaning of Christmas—or you've loaded your celebration with so many side activities, the real Christmas simply got buried and hidden from sight under that huge load of mostly nonsense."

Early in Advent we need to sort out the basics from the added baggage. The basics need no critique. Their worth stands for eternity.

The peripherals must be evaluated—and what does not support the core of it all should be trashed, or reassigned to another season.

A genuine and needless Christmas tragedy is when we permit the clutter to obscure the grandeur of the basics—the real facts and meaning. One wonders if some children have even a clue that buried under all that pile of peripherals are such crucial matters as God's eternal love, His incarnation in Jesus Christ, the fulfillment of Divine plans made before creation, along with all the possibilities of a personal and everlasting relationship with God.

JP

CHRISTMAS TRUTH

Christmas puts some folks in a real bind. They are forced by family traditions to keep alive the fantasies of imaginary Christmas personalities.

They know that Santa, Rudolph, Frosty and elves have no substance except in people's heads and emotions. But because it always has been done in their circles, they perpetuate the fantasies of the season for yet another generation of wide-eyed children—kids who some day will learn that they have been had.

It's strange how we ignore truth that is a thousand times stranger, far more wonderful and infinitely more meaningful than any fiction. In its place we insist on prioritizing sheer fantasy, fancified lies.

A fantasized sleigh full of presents somehow has more appeal than the birth of a Baby in Bethlehem back in the days of the Roman Empire.

But what an absolutely fantastic Person was that Baby of Bethlehem—not fantasized, but fantastic. His coming is more exciting than any fictional visitors from either outer space or from the north pole!

God came to earth in the Person of the newborn Child of Bethlehem, to set in motion all kinds of things planned for centuries.

Go for truth in these wonder-filled Seasons of Advent and Christmas.

CONTINUING CHRISTMAS

Please, don't end Christmas on December 26. Once all the gatherings and meals and gifts are out of the way, take some time to think about the wonder of it all.

There's a song I love to hear in this Holy Season:

> I wonder as I wander out under the sky,
> Why Jesus, the Savior, did come for to die
> For poor, ornery people like you and like I—
> I wonder as I wander out under the sky.

Why did He come—especially when He knew full well what He was getting into? The rejection, the scorn, the cross were not surprises. He knew how and why He would suffer. And still He came to us—in what can only be described as the awesome and loving sacrifice of God on our behalf.

You see, Christmas never stops. It is the supreme Gift that keeps on giving—every day and night of the year, through every passage of life, and right into the eternity that lies beyond.

Whether or not we believe it, Christmas does go on forever. The Gift of Christ is so awesome, so complete, effective and life relevant, we need a lifetime to think about it and understand its relevance to the whole of our lives.

Please—whoever you are—don't ever stop celebrating the Gift.

JP

WHOSE BIRTHDAY?

I love this story—apparently a genuine happening!

There was a family in our town who celebrated Christmas every year with a birthday party for Jesus. An extra chair of honor was placed at the table to remind all of the presence of Jesus. A cake with candles, along with the singing of "Happy Birthday, Dear Jesus" expressed the family's joy in the coming of this important member of their family.

One time a Christmas afternoon visitor asked five year old Ruth, "Well, did you get everything you wanted for Christmas?" After just a moment of hesitation, Ruth replied, "No. But then it's not *my* birthday!"

Would that we could all keep that same spirit at Christmas. Disappointments are out. Griping and complaining are unthinkable acts. This is Jesus' Birthday, and we intend to keep the focus on Him. After all, it is *His* birthday!

The Apostle John wrote with Awe:

> **In the beginning was the Word, and the Word was with God, and the Word was God. . . . The Word became flesh and made His dwelling among us. We have seen His glory, the glory of the One and Only, Who came from the Father, full of grace and truth.**
>
> (John 1:1 and 14)

At Christmas there are times when we need to ask, "Whose birthday is this, anyway?"

THE SHEPHERD PROPHECY

One of my favorite Christmas prophetic passages is the Shepherd Prophecy. It's found in Isaiah 40:12: "He tends His flock like a shepherd: He gathers the lambs in His arms and carries them close to His heart; He gently leads those that have young."

This magnificent forthtelling takes on breathless brilliance and clarity when we grasp the fact that the very first announcement of our Lord's Birth was to shepherds out on the hillsides of Bethlehem.

And all that intensifies when we read Jesus' own words:

> **I am the good shepherd. The good shepherd lays down His life for the sheep. . . I am the good shepherd; I know My sheep and My sheep know Me—just as the Father knows Me and I know the Father—and I lay down My life for the sheep.** (John 10:11-14)

But there is more. Jesus came from the tribe of Judah and from the Davidic line—the line of kings. David was the hero king of the land. Flawed and impulsive, yet mighty in power, David is honored even today as the greatest ruler of the united Israel.

He started out as a shepherd. It was David who wrote that magnificent Shepherd Psalm, the 23rd. "The Lord is my Shepherd. . ."

Indeed He is.

JP

WHEN CHRISTMAS HURTS

Undoubtedly there are folks out there who feel pain at Christmas. It could be the hurts of loneliness, illness, separation from loved ones, the death of someone dear, the loss of a job—or just too little of many needs, including money, love, friends, and self-respect.

The customary hoopla of typical Christmas celebrations leave such persons feeling cold, disinterested, hurting. frustrated and often angry.

But in place of such thinking come back to the heart of it all—the Birth of our Lord and Savior, the One Who loves us, came to redeem us, and Who died for us on the cross.

True Christmas—the kind that focuses on the coming of Jesus—gives us the assurance of wholeness, of meeting loved ones again in His eternal abode, of disease and incapacities finally conquered, and loneliness obliterated.

His coming assures us that all the evils of the world are defeated and that all injustices will be made right. Because of Christmas and all its wondrous aftermath, death itself has been overcome, and life abundant and eternal beckons us.

Our hearts should be greatly concerned over persons who hurt at Christmas.

But what it really requires is that all of us turn from the paganism, fantasies and hoopla to the living, reigning Lord Jesus Christ, Who came to us at Christmas.

BAGGAGE FOR THE NEW YEAR

It is very clear that traveling requires a lot of thought about baggage. Most of us tend to take too much with us.

I believe that a very appropriate and essential question is what kind of baggage is each of us lugging into a new year.

What's going along—and what is being left behind.

The "left behind" comes pretty easy: bad memories, failures, broken promises, lost friendships and dumb things we've done. There's a lot of needless stuff that we should shuck right now. Don't take it along. Leave it in the past. One needs to be very intentional about this.

What goes with us?

Baggage for a new year simply must include a savvy, time-tested, whole life, whole reality faith. For sure not the makings of cultic nonsense and spiritualized fantasies, but a whole reality faith centering in God's Gift of Himself. One will not find the knowledge and empowerment for such a faith in any place but in the Word of God, the Holy Bible.

Faith that is whole and healthy, real and truthful, dynamic and related to the whole of life is never excess baggage.

By all means take along the love of family and of close friends—but never leave faith behind!

SOMETHING TO SHOUT ABOUT

Most of us have heard and maybe even used the expression, "Now, that's something to shout about!"

In all truth, for most of us there isn't much in life to shout about. We wish there were more. For the most part life is pretty dull and predictable. Not much excitement.

But the Christmas passages of the Old Testament give us *Someone* to shout about.

In the prophecies of Isaiah, written hundreds of years before Jesus was born in Bethlehem, we read these stirring words:

> **You who bring good tidings to Zion, go up on a high mountain. You who bring good tidings to Jerusalem, lift up your voice with a shout, lift it up, do not be afraid; say to the towns of Judah, 'Here is your God!' See, the Sovereign Lord comes with power, and His arm rules for Him. See, His reward is with Him, and His recompense accompanies Him.** (Isaiah 40:9

The message is clear: In Jesus Christ, because of Who He is and what He has done for us, we really have something to shout about.

In Isaiah 60:5 the prophet tells us what will happen when we finally "get it" in understanding what and Who we have in Jesus: "Then you will look and be radiant, your heart will throb and swell with joy. . ."

ANGELS AND MIRACLES

The reality and power of Christmas hang on the doings of angels and the strange events we call "miracles."

Few people have ever seen an angel. But Mary and the shepherds did. And if we are wise we will be willing to take their word for it.

Many have seen lots of strange happenings—combinations of circumstances the results of which were so wonderful they seemed like miracles. But they didn't contravene any known "natural laws."

Because they happened in a manner that suggests God's activity and presence, we call them "acts of Providence." God often nudges and prods persons and circumstances to the fulfillment of the Creator's will and plans.

But a miracle?

Well, even though we may never have witnessed an authentic, *bona fide* miracle, others have. Matthew, Mark, Luke, John, Peter, James and Paul all testified to the reality of miracles and passed their witness on to us. It is an understatement to say that it is to our best and eternal interests that we accept their testimony.

We have a high stake in the reality of miracles. Our salvation depends on it. Our hope for heaven is contingent on it. Our sense of purpose and destiny in this life evaporates without the miracles of the holy birth, the life, the death and the resurrection of our Lord.

AVOIDING XMAS TRIVIALS AND TRASH

It's essential to take the time to get ready for an authentic Christmas celebration, and to toss out all of what I call "Xmas Trivials and Trash."

The only time I write or say "Xmas" is in relation to the celebrations made up of trivials and trash and lacking anything about the focus of it all, the coming of Jesus into His world.

Remember Him? He is the Holy One of God—promised since the beginning of creation—and finally being born in a small Judean town nearly 2000 years ago. He has been with us ever since—alive, omnipotent and reigning.

During the Xmas season, too many are drawn to the vapid emptiness of fantasy and cutsie stories of non-existent personalities. The mind blasting realities of the actual living and reigning Lord Jesus are far more exciting and meaningful—unless one is very determined to stick with "Xmas trivials and trash."

Here's a suggestion: Go to a Christian bookstore and browse through all the stuff intended to help you celebrate reality and avoid fantasy and other Xmas trash. Buy a book, a recording or two, some ornaments and other decorative pieces that point to Jesus, and acclaim Him as the real "reason for the season."

Get up your determination right now to avoid Xmas trivials and trash and stick with God's magnificent and priceless realities.

GIFTS AND GIFTING

I get a little weary of the laments of some about the commercialization of Christmas. I know people mean well, but they forget one important fact: Christmas is the time for gifts and gifting. That is what Christmas is all about. Indeed, it all started with a Gift—and a well planned one!

Gifts are one of the main features of appropriate Christmas celebrations because of the Gift of Jesus the Son of God, given out of God's loving grace to us humans of earth—who frankly do not deserve Him!

Some like to give unusual gifts. They occasionally turn out to be useless gifts—like the proverbial white elephant.

God's Gift of Jesus is intended to meet our deepest needs, to focus on what we must have in order to survive life here on earth, and to finally enter into His eternal glory.

God's gifts are never useless. Unusual, yes! But merely decorative or even burdensome, never!

There's another angle to real Christmas gifting. While God gave in relation to our needs, He did not limit the meaning and implications to basic needs—but gifted us with all that enriches life, beautifies the soul, and encourages us toward the best in our life endeavors.

"Useful" gifts might evidence some thoughtfulness at Christmas—but life and heart and mind and soul enriching gifts often are the most thoughtful and loving of all.

SEASON OF GIFTING

While Thanksgiving is a national holiday—albeit with religious overtones—I think of it as the fitting entrance or prelude to the Christmas Season. We pause to give thanks for every blessing—and then go head over heels into the joyous celebration of the Season of Gifting.

At some point in our lives we ought to make a transition from viewing Christmas as the Season of *Getting,* to viewing it as the Season of *Giving.*

My hope is that all of us will grow up and take hold of more mature views on Thanksgiving and what follows. It is not "Turkey Day," but Thanksgiving Day. And we have not observed it at all if there is not a genuine giving of thanks to God for all our blessings—no matter how big and wonderful the dinner and the gathering.

In like manner and even moreso, Christmas is not really Christmas if we only scheme and connive in order to be on the receiving end of the love and generosity of others.

We do not celebrate Christmas if there is no giving on our part—gracious and grace filled giving, that takes its cues from God's gifting to the world in His matchless Gift of Jesus.

So let's prepare for these wondrous seasons by reaching for the maturity and actions of faith and understanding.

JP

CHRISTMAS AND SPIRITUALITY

The concept of human "spirituality" presupposes a spiritual dimension to life that overrides every other aspect. In specifying the nature of human beings, "spiritual" takes precedence over physical and mental attributes.

"Spiritual" testifies that we are more than animal. We are the product of a Higher Power Who created us for personal reasons, and Who intends to relate to us in a beneficent manner. And He made us in such a way that we can relate to Him with meaning and intensity.

We'd like to think that our spiritual dimension inevitably pulls us toward the good and motivates us to steer clear of evil and its destructiveness. But in real life situations we quickly learn that we can be pushed either way by various spiritual forces.

In every area of human existence, where good operates, spiritual evil forces seem to intensify their activities. And more often than not, it's something like "Lions 3, Christians 0."

As with all else Christmas was and continues to be a battleground.

If you and I are going to "Christianize" Christmas, and thereby put the emphasis on the lofty, good and sacred, we must gear up for battle.

Hefty thinking and hard work are needed in abundance to make more of Christmas than a Whoopee party.

CHRISTMAS CONTEMPLATION

May Christ's joys and peace, His love and hope fill your hearts and minds throughout the wondrous Seasons of Advent and Christmas—and right into the new year.

If you had been privileged to visit the Christ Child just after He was born, what would you have done? I know that I would have been absolutely captivated. I would have looked on that whole scene with a sense of awe.

I don't think I would have been brazen enough to want to hold the Child—not with the knowledge I have as to His identity and mission in this world.

I think the word is "contemplation"—which means to look at attentively and thoughtfully; to consider carefully and at length; to meditate on or ponder as we seek to grasp the meaning and scope of it all.

We have so much hoopla at Christmas. Excitement is in the air, and I can imagine the activity in homes all over town on any Christmas morning.

But sometime during the Christmas celebration, find a quiet place and contemplate the birth of our Lord Jesus. Meditate on what it all means, what lay ahead of Him, and how He draws us to Himself eternally.

Even an ordinary child merits contemplation. How much more

this Child Who is Lord, Creator, God, King and Savior! One of the most important features of Christmas is its awesomeness. To "get it" requires Christmas contemplation.

CHRISTMAS IN THE OLD TESTAMENT

We sometimes forget that the early Christians did not have the four Gospels, or the letters written by Paul, Peter, James and John. But they had that first portion of the Holy Bible, called The Old Testament—and there they found the prophetic foretellings of Him Who would come as Messiah.

You see—Christmas is in the Old Testament, as well as the New.

Hundreds of years before the birth of Jesus, the Prophet Micah told where the Child was to be born.

> **But you, Bethlehem Ephrathah, though you are small among the clans of Judah, out of you will come for me One Who will be ruler over Israel, Whose origins are from of old, from ancient times.** (Micah 5:2)

And where did we learn of the wondrously close association of light with the coming of Jesus—and why all the lights at Christmas? Again, more than 700 years before the coming of the Light of the world, Isaiah wrote in chapter 9, beginning with verse 2:

> **The people walking in darkness have seen a great light; on those living in the land of the shadow of death a light has dawned . . .**

It's more than a matter of coincidence that without light, there can be no life. And so with Christmas.

CHRISTMAS IS "THE RIGHT TIME"

Yes, Christmas is the right time: For remembering and caring, For giving and forgiving, For sending signals of love and gratitude. Yes, Christmas is the right time!

It's the right time for faith—With faith's symbols all about us, Reminding us that love, joy and peace Are God's gifts for every human heart.

It's the right time for hope—In a world that seems so hopeless, and offers all the makings of despair and gloom; But because He came there is hope abundant—Yes, Christmas is the right time!

It's the right time for thanks—no matter how grieved the heart or Lonely.

It's the right time for change—The time to cast off our fears and follies, And to take to our hearts and lives All the confidence and zest of Christian living.

And it's the right time for receiving—The Word says "'tis blessed to give"—But it also tells us of our need For the love of God, and for His love in others—Yes, Christmas is the right time!

So Celebrate Christmas—the right time—Give yourself over to

Remembering, Caring, Giving and Forgiving—To faith and joyful delight In God's gifts of love, joy and peace!

YES, CHRISTMAS IS THE RIGHT TIME!

CHRISTMAS FOR CHILDREN?

There is a phrase that falls on my ears like one of those shibboleth cliches used to avoid thinking. I'm referring to the nutty refrain, "Christmas is for children."

It's usually said with a self-satisfied, almost pious air—as though the one uttering that drivel is delivering one of the grandest pronouncements of all time. How on earth did this notion ever creep into the celebration of Christmas?

Children did not write the Old Testament prophecies relating our desperate need for a Messiah and the promises of His coming. Nor were those writings directed to just the kids.

The historical happenings of Christmas took place in the world of adulthood. Mary was chosen by God for a touchy assignment. It was traumatic for her and for her fiance, Joseph.

The shepherds in the hills near Bethlehem weren't kids, either. They were adults trying to eke out a living by raising sheep—a chancy operation, to say the least.

The wise men were adults, too. They were looking for something far more significant than toys and games. Neither they nor the star were the trappings of fantasy. In faith they began a long, arduous journey to pay homage to a Child over Whom was cast the tragic shadow of the cross.

Let's face it: Christmas is not kids' stuff. It is meant mainly for adults.

CHRISTMAS PERSPECTIVES

Christmas helps us gain proper perspectives on life.

With some understanding of what Christmas really is all about, our troubles and losses diminish to a size we can handle—especially with God's help.

Because of all that Christmas means we know that all things eventually will work out for our good. We will be healed, made whole and reunited with loved ones who have gone on before us.

No matter what others may think of us, we know that in Christ we are children of God, with high stature, dignity and worth.

Because of His coming, the joys of life are all the sweeter. He has alleviated the pain of parting; He has given us a value system that stands the tests of time and circumstances; He has enriched our most meaningful relationships; He has gifted us with a stature and destiny way beyond anything we could ever imagine, let alone earn or merit.

With all that injecting hope and serenity into our lives, we can only praise God for the Creator's greatness and grace in coming into the world that first Christmas.

To be sure, all the powers of self focus and reality avoidance beckon us to a Christmas of fantasy and pretense.

But God calls us to a deep and meaningful celebration of the full reality of the Creator's grand invasion of planet Earth.

PROFANE AND THE SACRED AT CHRISTMAS

Advent and Christmas confront us with many choices. The most important is deciding whether our celebration will be secular or religious, profane or sacred. We choose the elements that make up our personal observances of the seasons ahead.

The world of commerce and make-believe offers us a vast array of secular trappings that assure us a profane, not sacred celebration.

The Word of God and the Church of Jesus Christ urge us to make it a joyful and sacred celebration—focusing on the realities and implications of the coming of our Savior and Lord, of the incarnation of Almighty God in Jesus of Nazareth.

Granted, many celebrants try to have it both ways. Their approaches are a mix of Yuletide fantasies and the joyful realities of the Holy Birth in Bethlehem. A balance between the secular and profane seems admirable, but for most people the balance tends to tip toward cutsie "Xmas" non-realities. For many, fantasy has more appeal than truth.

The result is an obsession with the fictional figures of the season, candy-coated lies about Santa and his Xmas doings, music that tells of snow and romance—and only a quick, passing nod to the Child of the manger, the Holy One Whose coming was promised through the ages.

The main events of Advent and Christmas give us more than enough reasons for joy and even hilarity in our celebrations.

GOD AND THE SINGLE PERSON

The prophecy of the Virgin Birth is found in Isaiah 7:14: "Therefore the Lord Himself will give you a sign: The virgin will be with Child and will give birth to a Son, and will call Him Emmanuel."

More than 700 years before Jesus was born, God made it clear that an unmarried, single woman would have the honor of giving birth to Emmanuel, "God with us."

Sometimes single persons are regarded by others as disadvantaged and left out of the greater matters of life. God's high regard for single persons is shown in His choice of Mary.

Matthew tells us in chapter 1:18-23

> **This is how the birth of Jesus Christ came about: His mother Mary was pledged to be married to Joseph, but before they came together, she was found to be with child through the Holy Spirit. . . . All this took place to fulfill what the Lord had said through the prophet: "The virgin will be with Child and will give birth to a Son, and they will call Him 'Emmanuel'—which means, 'God with us.'"**

I believe that Mary knew the prophecy, and in her amazement that she should be that chosen person, she responded: "I am the Lord's servant. . . May it be to me as you have said." Then the angel left her.

A "FOREVER" CHRISTMAS

Hang on to the facts and significance of Christmas. Eventually we put the decorations back into storage. But don't even think of doing that with the meaning and sense of it all.

All year long, and throughout our lives, we all desperately need the healing, hope, love and salvation that God sent into His world that first Christmas.

Once we grasp the meaning and power of His Christmas gift, we find ourselves in a state of continuing celebration.

Love came down at Christmas—the love that sets the standards for all our loving—full of the grace of mercy, forgiveness and sacrifice.

Hope came down at Christmas—casting out the gloom of pessimism and defeat, transforming our outlook into a realism that takes God's Word and work fully into account for time and eternity.

Truth came down at Christmas—and in awesome contrast with the lies, exaggerations, deceptions and half truths with which we live so much of the time. We find this truth in the One Who rightfully proclaimed Himself to be the Way, the Truth and the Life.

Indeed, He is all that to us. And that is exactly why the genuine Christmas can never be packed up and stored away. If you have celebrated the real Christmas, then you know that it is forever!

SAVIOR OF THE WORLD

Jesus was foretold in the Old Testament—the Bible of the early Church. They turned to God's Word to discover Who He is and what He has done and why.

One important fact was ignored by people who turned away from the Messiah of God. Or perhaps it is more correct to say that because of this fact of the Christ they would have nothing to do with Him. The fact was and is that He was and is the Savior not just of the nation of Israel, but of the whole world.

Sometimes it is very difficult to share your most priceless treasure with others whom you deem worthless dolts, unsalvageable sinners and godless heathen.

But Isaiah made it clear in chapter 60:

> **Arise, shine, for your Light has come, and the glory of the Lord rises upon you. See, darkness covers the earth and thick darkness is over the peoples, but the Lord rises upon you and His glory appears over you. Nations will come to Your light, and kings to the brightness of Your dawn.**

The coming of the Wise Men, the three Kings, was no coincidence. It's a direct and solemn fulfillment of God's promise through Isaiah: "Nations will come to Your light, and kings to the brightness of Your dawn."

THE SUFFERING GOD

One of the most awesome of all the prophecies about the meaning of the Christmas event is the prophecy of the Suffering God. A forthtelling was given that God was coming into His world to suffer with us—and for us.

That seems hard to believe—especially to those who are convinced that God doesn't care about their suffering and devastation.

But God came in Jesus the Christ to suffer vicariously—and that word means "for us, on our behalf, in our place."

The prophecy is found in Isaiah 53. The prophet wrote:

> **He was despised and rejected by men, a Man of sorrows, and familiar with suffering. Like one from whom men hide their faces He was despised, and we esteemed Him not. Surely He took up our infirmities and carried our sorrows, yet we considered Him stricken by God, smitten by Him, and afflicted. But He was pierced for our transgressions, He was crushed for our iniquities; the punishment that brought us peace was upon Him, and by His wounds we are healed. We all, like sheep, have gone astray, each of us has turned to his own way; and the Lord has laid on Him the iniquity of us all.**

There is sense in which we know absolutely nothing about Christmas until we come to terms with the prophecies of the suffering God.

THE NEW IN NEW YEAR

We say it and mean it, "Happy New Year!" But we suspect that the new year will be more or less a repeat of all our previous years.

Solomon wrote in Ecclesiastes: "Meaningless! Meaningless! Everything is meaningless. . . . Is there anything of which one can say, 'Look! This is something new?'" (1:2

Solomon had the means and wealth to try everything—and I mean every recreation and mind and body adventure that a human being could concoct. But he found it all to be meaningless, repetitious and often just plain silly.

And what did Solomon conclude? He finally wrote: "Remember your Creator in the days of your youth. . . . Fear God and keep His commandments." (Ecclesiastes 12:1,13 With God's help Solomon found that only the person who focuses on God will find meaning in life.

Our walk into the new year and beyond in the company of Jesus is a day by day experience of the new and utterly magnificent. Never mind that before we met Him the wonder went out of life. In Jesus life takes on vibrancy and excitement.

Paul wrote in II Corinthians 5:17: "Therefore, if anyone is in Christ, he is a new creation; the old has gone, the new has come!"

We all need to let God help us put the new in the new year.

JP

THE NUB OF THE MATTER

My youngest grandson, McCleary, takes his celebrations very seriously—whether it's Halloween, Thanksgiving, Christmas or the 4th of July! My daughter told me that when he was out trick or treating this past Halloween, he complained that his candy bag was getting heavy.

As the man came out with candy at the next house, McCleary said to him, "Oh, I don't want any more candy. I've just stopped by for a visit." And he proceeded to do just that—to the amazement of the homeowners and also his parents!

Perhaps unwittingly McCleary understood the nub of the matter—that the people in the house are important for reasons other than the candy we might get from them.

The same goes for Christmas. The nub of the matter is not found in the gifts we give and get—but in the persons who share life with us—and above all, the Person of Jesus our Savior and Lord.

When you think about it, one of the best gifts we can ever offer someone are those of a listening ear and heart—time for visits and phone calls—time to talk about the realities of life, not just the fluff—to communicate caring and sharing on a grander scale than ever before.

You know—that's exactly what God did at Christmas!

THE COVENANT IN PROPHECY

Our Creator never treats human beings as mere slaves or puppets. We see this brilliantly displayed in God's establishing a covenantal relationship with His chosen people—as though we are equals with Him!

God made the first covenant with Abraham, father of the faithful—and He made it clear that the covenant was to be passed on through the line of Abraham right down to the promised Messiah, the Chosen One, Whose coming was assured from of old.

The covenant included the Promise that such a One will come—the Person we know as the Child of Bethlehem, the Son of God and Son of Man, Jesus the Messiah.

In Genesis 12:1-3 we read:

> **The Lord had said to Abram. . . "I will make you into a great nation and I will bless you; I will make your name great, and you will be a blessing. I will bless those who bless you, and whoever curses you I will curse; and all peoples on earth will be blessed through you."**

This was the beginning of a covenant between humanity and God that would stand until Jesus replaced it with what He called at that first Eucharist, "A New Covenant, in My blood." Just as God has covenanted, Jesus has come. Small wonder we sing, "Joy to the world, the Lord is come!"

CHRISTMAS SONGS

Think now. What are the songs that bring the meaning of Christmas to you? Assuming you have the meaning straight, and understand that Christmas centers in the grand event of Christ's coming, what are the songs that say "Christmas" most emphatically?

The romantic and fantasy songs of the season won't do it for anyone who has a firm grasp on the true sense of it all. Songs such as "Frosty the Snowman," "White Christmas," "Winter Wonderland," "I Saw Mommy Kissing Santa Claus" and "Grandma Got Run Over by a Reindeer," are secular and seasonal fun songs at best—*but they're not Christmas songs by a long shot.*

The great musical offerings of Christmas tell the story—reflect on the grandeur and meaning of it all—and press home what Christmas really offers.

Look at some of these wonderful compositions, and then think hard about what each verse or stanza is saying. I'm talking about Christmas music such as "Silent Night, Holy Night," "Joy to the World," "O Little Town of Bethlehem," "Hark! The Herald Angels Sang," "The First Noel" and "As With Gladness Men of Old."

Then there are the great masterpieces of Christmas, with Handel's *Messiah* way out in front.

Be sure you let the real music of Christmas captivate and inform you in this wondrous time.

SHARING CHRISTMAS

By its very nature Christmas is meant to be shared—from the good news of the birth of our Savior to the warmth of love and compassion that seems to grip people in this holy season.

If anyone has trouble figuring out how to share their Christmas, it is probably because they have turned their Christmas celebration into a self-centered event, with the "In" basket piled high and the "Out" basket totally empty. For such barren folks, Christmas is a one way street, and the key word is "Gimmee."

The real Christmas centers on the giving of the greatest Gift the world has ever known. The best Christmas giving are the gifts to people we do not know. And it is done best when they receive such gifts anonymously, so the only person they can thank is God.

How about the gift of our time and energy—in effect, our person? Offer to babysit one evening for that poor family—transport patients to their treatment center for a few weeks—or help out with meals on wheels.

There are hundreds of ways to celebrate a Christmas with the focus where it belongs: On the ways and teachings and commands of the One Who came that night of all nights so many years ago.

Have a great Christmas—but if you don't share it, there really isn't much relevance to the real Happening!.

LIGHTS OF CHRISTMAS

Well, I finally saw it in Christmas lights, spelled out with great effort and expense on the side of a home in nearby Alton, Iowa—the words, "BAH! HUMBUG!"

I thought of knocking at the door and asking if this might be the home of Ebenezer Scrooge. I assume the words are meant in jest.

This is a good time to thank all who go to the trouble and expense to decorate their homes at Christmas. Thank you for the cheer and colored lights in the dark of the night.

I especially want to thank folks out in the country. So many nights I drive the blacktop roads of our area, and am always cheered and blessed by the lights that grace lonely farmhouses and the trees in their yards.

The symbolism of light is tied to Jesus Christ. In a recent Advent worship service the congregation was choosing their favorite Christmas hymns.

Someone called out a number, and when I turned to it I found the hymn that starts out, "The whole world was lost in the darkness of sin—the Light of the world is Jesus."

I looked up and said to the person who made the choice, "You're right. This is a Christmas hymn."

EBENEZER

Some years ago I served as part time Interim Pastor of a church in George, Iowa—Ebenezer Presbyterian Church.

The other day I was talking with someone in another state, and mentioned that I was serving a church bearing the name, "Ebenezer Presbyterian Church." There was a pause, and then the man commented very seriously, "Oh—I suppose it's named after Ebenezer Scrooge." Thinking he was kidding, I said, "O, sure." But he was serious.

Evidently he had never heard of the Biblical references to Ebenezer, which means "stone of help."

In I Samuel 7 it's recorded that Samuel raised a memorial to commemorate victory in a great battle, and it was called "Ebenezer." The Word tells us: "Then Samuel took a stone and set it up between Mizpah and Jeshanah, and called its name Ebenezer; for he said, 'Hitherto the Lord has helped us.'"

An old hymn, "Come, Thou fount of many blessings," has a verse that reads: "Here I raise my Ebenezer, Hither by Thy help I've come; and I hope by Thy good pleasure Safely to arrive at home."

God is our "stone of help"—our Ebenezer—if we will only permit it.

There is a big difference between Ebenezer Scrooge, and the stone of help that marks God's assistance in our lives. We need to make sure we know the difference.

UNDERSTANDING CHRISTMAS

Misunderstandings of Christmas abound.

One little boy made the comment that the reason Mary and Joseph couldn't get into the inn of Bethlehem was because Joseph forgot to make a reservation!

But it isn't just the children who get some funny ideas of the season. Many adults haven't the faintest notion of what the season is all about. So naturally they major on the commercial and secular aspects of Christmas. They simply don't know any better.

Any Christian knows better, and hopefully has adequate understanding of what it all means—of the true events and implications of the Christmas Season.

I'm always pleased when there is even the slightest evidence that people are reaching for understanding. For instance—there was a cartoon that showed three little boys coming to the manger scene bearing gifts. The first two boys brought attractive containers representing the gold and frankincense. The third little boy, however, came to the baby Jesus with a very large box of disposable diapers! Mary could only have wished! The creator of that cartoon had captured love made practical.

That's the best way to celebrate the season—love made practical. That's exactly what God did in the extravagant and yet very practical and life-relevant Gift of His Son.

THE STRANGE PHENOMENON OF PEACE

The central message of Christmas is peace—between alienated humanity and our Creator, and among all the nations, tribes, factions and individuals of the world.

In Jesus the Christ God provided possibilities for peace, if sought in accord with the God ordained principles of grace, repentance, reconciliation, forgiveness and love. Those principles were implicit in the angels' annunciation to the shepherds that holy night. As accurately translated by Eugene H. Peterson in his New Testament translation titled *The Message:* "Glory to God in the heavenly heights—peace to all men and women on earth who please Him."

There is a qualifier: Peace comes to those who get in line with their Creator. It is not a gift to be used for self aggrandizement. Those who seek a magical panacea for peace with no discomfort and no sacrificial participation on their part are facing disappointments. It simply cannot happen.

To enlightened, God-oriented human beings of every race and culture, warfare, animosity, crimes and human violence are anathema. Such events happen, but should not. The horrors of war far outweigh any perceived benefits.

Think now: Do you promote peace in your life? Over and over the Scriptures refer to the Deity as "the God of Peace." If peace is not among your life passions, perhaps you have not found the Prince of Peace.

LENTEN SEASON AND EASTER

BENT CROSS

In the Season of Lent—and especially during Holy Week—the focus is the cross of Jesus and His approach to dying.

The cross is a symbol of God's very best for humanity. It emblemizes Christ's redemptive work—His atoning death, the suffering endured by the Son of God so that we might be delivered from judgment and condemnation.

The cross is a sign of love and grace. It assures us that God is not against us, but for us—that He will not shower His wrath on us, but rather His mercy. There is no greater symbol than the cross for the highest and best for our living and our eternal destiny.

Adolph Hitler took the cross and turned it into a swastika. His was a bent cross, twisted and warped to represent not humanity's best, but our worst. That bent cross ravaged Europe, created the monstrous holocaust in which millions of Jews and other human undesirables were exterminated.

There are more subtle ways to bend the cross—to turn it into a sign of weakness, hate and evil. All kinds of chicanery and savagery have been done under the sign of a cross—most claiming identity with the true cross.

But the cross of Christ is not twisted. If we are honest and open, we can easily distinguish it and all it produces among humanity from the perversions and fruits of a bent cross.

FAITH AS A DOORWAY

Ash Wednesday marks the beginning of the Christian Season of Lent.

Hopefully during the weeks of Lent we all will work at strengthening our faith, as we learn more of the awesome meaning of Jesus the Christ and draw closer to Him.

Have you ever thought of faith as a doorway to the fullest, most complete reality? One of the reasons faith cannot be "proven" is because it deals with such immensities. It is our springboard into the Presence and will of God. Through faith we enter the spiritual, and enhance that basic essence of our very beings.

Without faith we're left with half a loaf at best. We know and understand nothing beyond our five senses, and live very hemmed in and limited lives.

Through their telescopes astronomer's get a glimpse of larger realities. But even so, they always are looking backwards in time as the light of the galaxies makes its way to earth. Through faith we are privileged to glimpse the future, the beyond and all that is yet to come. Just as the astronomer knows he or she is not seeing it all, so we know there is much more than meets even the eye of faith.

May your faith be enlightened and strengthened during the Holy Season of Lent.

A MISSING INGREDIENT

In the aftermath of Holy Week, I understand that some people miss the boat on understanding the Christian faith because they don't have the right perspective on suffering.

As a teenager, my first reaction to the idea of Jesus suffering for me. and taking the guilt and punishment for my sin on Himself, was simply dreadful. That should not happen to Him!

But I was reacting in the same way as the Apostle Peter. **"Never, Lord!" he said. "This shall never happen to You!"** Jesus sternly rebuked Peter: **"Get behind Me, Satan! You are a stumbling block to Me; you do not have in mind the things of God, but the things of men."** (Matthew 16:23)

Peter had the same attitude that prevails today—that suffering simply should not be. Nobody should have to go through it—and especially good people. Suffering is always the enemy, and never serves a useful purpose.

But in Jesus Christ, God accepted horrendous suffering, and transformed it into the means of our redemption, salvation and reconciliation with Him.

To grasp the Christian faith requires that we view His suffering and our suffering as means to good ends, as powerful forces for redemption and reconciliation.

Only then will our walk with Christ be full of sense and eternal hope.

GOD'S BURDEN BEARERS

I am convinced that in the mysterious economy of God certain persons are assigned extra heavy burdens in life.

This should not surprise us. God is not some kind of celestial socialist—or Who, like a fair-minded parent, offers each of His children exactly the same size piece of cake.

It is quite apparent that some get more blessings than others—and some get more burdens and troubles than others!

From the Scriptures we learn that this does not mean God loves or does not love equally. God is simply yet profoundly responding to our individuality in the context of society, and to our various and diverse abilities and needs.

Indeed, He calls us to relate to others in the same manner.

In Galatians 6:2 Paul wrote: "Carry each other's burdens." Then a few lines later he wrote: "For each one should carry his own load. " Well, why doesn't he make up his mind?

The Greek words used for burdens in each of these sentences tell the full story. "Carry your own burdens" uses the word which means "the ordinary pack" of a Roman soldier.

The word used in "Carry each other's burdens" signifies those extra heavy loads which some are called to bear, such as the equipment needed for feeding a platoon of soldiers.

And our responsible response as Christians? Help those who bear those extra loads in every way we can!

THE WEEK CALLED "HOLY"

He called Himself "the Son of Man"—and truly He was and is God's man, the Perfect Person. We can say this about no one but Jesus: "He never sinned. He never committed an act of evil. He lived a life of utter humility and service. His love is the most perfect love the human race has ever seen."

He also is called "the Son of God." We cannot think of Deity without thinking of Jesus. He tells us not only what we should be like, but what God is like.

Jesus is God and the revealer of God. In Him we find the flawless revelation of as much as we could ever know about the nature and aims of the Almighty.

Small wonder we sing hymns and songs of praise that ascribe to Jesus majesty, power, glory, honor, praise and adoration.

So during Holy Week we remember with awesome thanksgiving that Jesus is God's Man—and Man's God.

Did you ever speculate about what it would be like to be all alone on a desert island—and what would be needed most?

In this Holy Week speculate about being alone in this world of sin and troubles—and draw closer to the indispensable, absolutely essential Jesus: God's man and man's God.

P

BLACK FRIDAY—GOOD FRIDAY

I trust that you are aware of the day known as "Good Friday"—the day we commemorate the crucifixion of the Son of God and Lord of Glory, Jesus the Messiah, the Christ.

He died a horrible death. His trials were mockeries. His enemies were vicious and unrelenting. But in all truth He deserved from all human beings nothing but praise and love and adoration and worship.

But they put Him to death. His goodness was just too glorious and real for their stomachs.

Once it was called: *Black Friday.* As Jesus perished on the cross all nature seemed to go wild with protest. The skies grew dark. Earthquakes rocked the land. Storm and fury came forth as though to assail the humanity that would treat the Son of God with such hellish cruelty.

But it is Good Friday, make no mistake about that. Out of it came the makings of our redemption from sin and hell, our forgiveness for all the sins of mind and actions.

As we stand below the crosses of our churches we must say the truth: "He died for me. He suffered for me. Were it not for His holy dying, I would have no claim on God, no assurance of life to come, no peace or hope or help."

Call it "Good Friday" and know the reasons why.

CHRIST AND CULTURE

During Holy Week one of the matters to which we should turn serious attention is the interfacing of Christ and culture, of Christianity and society.

There is abundant evidence that the culture in which we live has a molding and shaping influence on the church—when what is intended by God is the very opposite.

Jesus faced the culture of His time. He clashed with it—He did not mesh or "roll" with it. The confrontation between Jesus and the culture of Judaism and Rome brought about His trial and crucifixion.

A careful reading of the New Testament writings reveals a faith and conduct that were highly confrontational. Neither Jesus nor His close followers bowed or yielded to the dictates, superstitions, traditions, evils and prejudices of culture—and sometimes even society's laws.

They declared their intention to transform culture. It is clear in the New Testament that Jesus and His followers were *counter* culture.

Jesus announced and called in the Kingdom of God as a force that is far superior to anything Rome or Judea had to offer—a force that fully intends to impact and to transform the culture in which it finds itself—be it Galilee, Rome, China, India, the USA, the darkest part of Africa or the most distant western isles.

P

REDEMPTIVE SUFFERING

The theme of Holy Week is redemptive and vicarious suffering. Because "suffering" is qualified by those two descriptors, it becomes a season of joy—a time for praise and thanks because God's Son came to suffer in our place, and to reconcile us to our Creator.

Would that all the suffering on this planet could be transformed into redeeming and reconciling forces. Some can—if persons will see it through, and direct their suffering toward those ends.

Suffering becomes redemptive when by God's design and our head and heart cooperation good is generated by it. Others are helped, destructiveness and hate are muted or ended, people are reconciled to each other and there is a discernible triumph of God's good.

The anguish, frustration, suffering and deprivation all over the world hold millions in their grip—with misunderstandings, fear, hate and violence in abundance.

But there also are those who long for it all to give way to healing, reconciliation and works that are truly redemptive. Pray that the world's suffering may be transformed with God's help into redemptive and reconciling forces. And we need to be sure that attitudinally we regard any suffering we are called to endure not as hopeless, unjust and unfair—but as potential creative and redemptive forces for good.

You're right—it's not easy. But the alternative is empty and fruitless cynicism and despair.

JESUS IN FOCUS

Some years ago a young lad in our congregation gave me a cutout of letters mounted on a board of contrasting color. It is still on my desk, and some visitors have a tough time figuring it out. When you look at it casually all you see is a jumble of jagged pieces of wood, some long, some short, some vertical and others horizontal.

Stare at it long enough and eventually the name of Jesus comes into focus, and you wonder why you didn't see it from the very beginning. It's a kind of optical illusion, and very appropriately symbolic of the presence of Jesus in our lives.

We often fail to see our Lord's handiwork in our daily living. Unless we look very carefully we see neither pattern nor presence—only a jumble of spaces and pieces.

Then, when thought and intentional searching take over our minds we see the patterns and presence of our Lord in our daily doings. He is with us. There is nothing in our lives that is of no concern to Him, and He intends to help us weave a patter of purpose and meaning in our living.

Often all it takes is an open mind, and we'll see Jesus. But if we are not expecting Him, for sure we will never see Him. And if we do not *want* to see Him, we likely will not.

When life seems like just a jumble of meaningless pieces going in all directions, step back—and look for Jesus. For sure He is there.

P

ASH WEDNESDAY

Ash Wednesday is the beginning of the Holy Season of Lent. It's given that name because we are at the beginning of a time for sober reflection about some of the deepest aspects of our faith—including the sufferings of our Lord Jesus for our sin and folly.

We take sin too lightly. We laugh it off or shrug it off as though it is of no consequence. But it is. And one of the consequences of our sinful acts of life is the crucifixion of the Lord of Glory. Some of us have caught on to the fact that in a true sense we were at Calvary. We helped erect the cross and nail the Him to it because of our sins for which He died. The writer of the Book of Hebrews cautions us:

It is impossible for those who have once been enlightened, who have tasted the heavenly gift, who have shared in the Holy Spirit, who have tasted the goodness of the word of God and the powers of the coming age, if they fall away, to be brought back to repentance, because to their loss they are crucifying the Son of God all over again and subjecting Him to public disgrace. (Hebrews 6:4-6)

According to this passage there is a sense in which we can bring even more shame and pain on our Lord Jesus by our perversity and straying from the faith.

Ash Wednesday is a day of mourning for our sins and their terrible impact on our Savior. Then, as we move through the Season of Lent, we ought to deepen our understanding of genuine faith. Only then can we truly share His resurrection.

THE ANSWER TO DEATH

It's sad when Christians who have attended church for many years and always on Easter Sunday, still do not understand that Jesus is the answer to death.

Indeed Jesus gives us the only answer that makes any sense and gives the needed comfort and hearty encouragement we all must have as we near those dreadful portals that willy nilly lead us out of this life—and into either silence and oblivion forevermore, or eternal life in the Kingdom Realm of our Lord God.

I have no doubt whatsoever about the outcome of my life and the glory that death will lead me into. I believe that Jesus willingly went to His death on that first "Good Friday" back in 29 A.D. He would not have suffered and died if that had not been His planned intent.

Jesus viewed His death by crucifixion as the main part of the work that He in concert with the whole Godhead had agreed on. His holy mission was to accomplish humanity's salvation by the means and power of His self sacrifice.

And I believe that His death on that cross, along with His Easter resurrection, are all that you and I need for absolute assurance of a better and eternal life to come. For the Christian death holds no fear. Its power has been broken by Jesus the Mighty One.

I truly hope that's where you are as you move through Easter celebrations and toward your own demise.

THE SOURCE OF HOPE

Have you ever been in a situation where with all your heart you wanted to encourage someone to hang on to hope—and you found yourself at a loss for words? You simply could not offer one reason why they should have any hope.

A lot of folks mutter what amount to empty phrases, pious platitudes, or phony cheerfulness. If they have any sensitivity at all, they know immediately how hollow their words sound in the hearing of those who long for words of hope in the midst of suffering and desperation.

During Holy Week we need to remember that Jesus and Jesus alone is Hope Personified. When hope seems utterly unavailable, we will always find it in Him.

Indeed, the Holy Scriptures speak of Christ as our hope—not only for individuals, but for nations. Matthew 12:21 tells us: "In His Name the nations will put their hope."

In the Bible the word "hope" means more than a slim expectation and weak confidence in better things in the offing. It is redolent with the certainties we find only in Christ Jesus. It is utterly confident expectation that He will deliver completely on what He has promised.

I pray that for all of us this Holy Week and ever after will be full of the hope that only Christ can give.

HOLY GROUND

The expression "holy ground" is right out of the Word of God. It refers to those times and places when we are standing with or before God in a special way. His interests are especially paramount, and His concern for the matter at hand is unusually heavy.

I am convinced that human suffering constitutes holy ground. The very places and times of suffering generate awe and reverence for the pain, humiliation and torture inflicted on people.

I have so many memories of being in places where terrible suffering took place. It takes a great deal of insensitivity to walk through the horrific exhibits of the holocaust memorials and not be brought to tears and driven to prayer. Holy ground.

The bedside of someone in pain is always holy ground. Hospital rooms are often places of forced jocularity and attempts at humor. But they also are holy ground. Walk and talk with care.

The same as true of individuals who are experiencing emotional problems. Personal struggles of every kind are holy ground. Walk with care as you deal with them. You are on holy ground.

In all truth, every worthy human endeavor is holy ground—including marriage, friendships and all relationships that call for tenderness and responsibility. We are wise to treat all the most precious experiences of life as holy ground.

HOLY WEEK—AND THE UNHOLY

Have you managed to uncover the awesome truth that precisely because there is so much of the unholy and evil at work in the world, the greater is our need of knowledge of and access to that which really is holy?

Whether or not one believes in the existence of devils, it's pretty obvious that the world is chock full of deviltry.

But if we will think, look and learn there are some beautiful life offerings of the holy, the sacred.

From Palm Sunday to Resurrection Sunday is Holy Week. For quite a few of us it will be passe and just a passing event, holding little relevance for us. That's because we have allowed it to be so through our ignorance and negligence.

In our lives there is an awesome need to balance the impact of the unholy with the holy. Violence and immorality of every kind assail our senses daily. All those impressions and what they do to us need to be balanced off by an even greater familiarity with the holy.

Holy Week is about the massive and always contemporary impact of a Man Who alone deserved the titles "Son of God" and "Son of Man." He is our prime resource for resolving the enormous conflicts and destructive influences that are the daily fare of humanity. What He taught and what He did are the most worthwhile models of high and holy service that we could ever follow for our own living.

Go for the holy as you seek to keep the unholy at bay.

MOMENTS OF ETERNITY

Lent is a wonderfully special time to think about moments of eternity. Life goes so fast. Sometimes it seems like a fast-forwarding video tape—just zipping by.

But have you ever been so captivated by a happening of seconds or minutes that you wished you could hold on to it forever? It was more than precious—it was like a moment of eternity.

I like that phrase. It was introduced by William Congreve, a writer who lived from 1670-1729. In his play, *The Old Bachelor,* he wrote, "Eternity was in that moment."

Have you ever felt that way about some happening you have experienced? Eternity was in that moment. It seemed that everything that makes life worthwhile and good was enclosed and expressed by that beautiful experience.

We may find moments of eternity in worship. We may find them in a loving relationship. We find them sometimes in a play or a symphony, a great poem or novel—or in just being quiet by a lake. Eternity is in many moments of our life—but we will not experience and recognize them unless we are on the lookout, and filled with expectation.

A child is born, a friend comes through for us, we accomplish something meaningful to ourselves and others, we gain insight and discernment about important concerns of life—of these we may say in all truth, "Eternity was in that moment."

RESURRECTION AFTERMATH

In His post-resurrection appearances, Jesus first spoke to Mary Magdalene. He appeared to Peter, then to two followers on the road to Emmaus. Then He came twice to the disciples in the upper room, and then to seven of them who had gone fishing in the Sea of Galilee. Finally He appeared to Paul who was heading for Damascus to deal harshly with the followers of the Way.

On what did Jesus major in these appearances? Relating and relationships. That's right!

He made His Presence felt and known by the disciples. He related to them, spoke with them and ate with them. He rebuked Thomas for his doubting and Peter for his denials.

He charged them with Kingdom work, and among His final words was the promise: "And surely I am with you always, to the very end of the age." (Matthew 28:20)

He promised them more than power, more than discernment, more than help and comfort—He promised them His Presence, His companionship.

It's true that the Church, your church, came into being for the purpose of worship. But it also was founded to promote companionship—and relating with each other with Jesus as the most significant party in that relating.

How are you doing at relating to Him, and with Him to others—and how is your church doing?

THE DAY OF THANKS

IT'S NOT "TURKEY DAY"!

Inevitably every year we hear someone refer to Thanksgiving Day as "Turkey Day"—thereby revealing a major shortcoming of their souls.

"Turkey Day" hardly calls for prayers of thanks. Maybe a silly "gobble-gobble" but not thanks.

Believe it—there is much more to Thanksgiving than turkey and all the trimmings. It's a day to add it all up and celebrate the blessings God has so graciously permitted us to have—no matter how many tough times we've been through.

There are despondent souls who honestly believe they have nothing for which to give thanks. Gratitude is out because they have had such harsh experiences, are lacking so many things, have lost so much and have been treated so terribly by others. One or two I have known heave a big sigh and tell me that they just don't have the heart or motives for thanksgiving.

That is really too bad. Imagine someone without one bit of motivation for gratitude! That person just has to be one of the most shallow, faithless and graceless souls on the face of this earth—and may not even know it.

Every person has been on the receiving end of blessings and so has a debt of thanks. Remember those blessings. Then tell God you are grateful—and everyone else who has helped you along life's way.

CALL IT BY ITS RIGHT NAME

As our nation approaches Thanksgiving Day it's time for my annual plea that it not be referred to as "Turkey Day."

What kind of person would devote a whole day to thinking turkey? There's a bird to honor! Dumber than a dodo! But delicious!

Isn't it amazing how we're encouraged by the forces of darkness to substitute appetites for the spiritual exercise of giving thanks for God's great blessings.

There are many more reasons for thanks than the turkey on the platter—along with all the rest of the food on the table.

Part of the problem is that the giving of thanks is not a natural human attribute. We have to work at developing a gratitude attitude. I fear that some never quite make it. Probably in part this is due to sheer ignorance about *Whom* to thank as well as the *reasons* we have for offering our thanks.

Parents often chide their children about "the magic words"—"please" and "thanks." Apparently some fairly old kids need some chiding, too.

Between now and that annual Thanksgiving Thursday practice saying the magic word. It's "thanks"—the day is "Thanksgiving"—and the One Whom we thank is the God Who has given us all things. Tell Him you are really grateful. And mean it!

THINKSGIVING

A proper and rewarding celebration of Thanksgiving requires a prior celebration of what I call "Thinksgiving." We have to *think* if we are going to *thank.*

Without some real deep thinking that special day will be a meaningless holiday. You'll eat yourself silly, gab with the relatives, watch some games on TV—and that's it. Thanks takes thinks. Are you up to it?

One of the saddest of all character traits is ingratitude. Most of us have known people who haven't a breath of gratitude toward God or anyone else.

One of the most revealing incidents in the life of our Lord is when He healed ten lepers of their dread disease—an affliction that kept them isolated from the rest of the community.

Dr. Luke wrote:

> **One of them, when he saw he was healed, came back, praising God in a loud voice. He threw himself at Jesus' feet and thanked Him—and he was a Samaritan. Jesus asked, "Were not all ten cleansed? Where are the other nine? Was no one found to return and give praise to God except this foreigner?"** (Luke 17:12-18)

You know—I have a feeling Jesus really was not surprised. Gratitude is *not* doing the what comes naturally.

THANKSGIVING PRAYER

The very word "Thanksgiving" calls for prayer on that day. So please—be sure that someone offers a meaningful prayer of thanks before you dig in and dine.

Here's one I prepared for the people of a church I once served:

Our heavenly Father—be present with us as we share this wonderful Thanksgiving dinner. In our minds and hearts may we receive it as a sign of Your bountiful blessings—and may we share it with gratitude for this and all Your gifts.

We give thanks for all who prepared this meal and brought us together. We thank You for loved ones—both here and far away. We give special thanks for all who have shared their love with us and who have gone on to be with You.

For the health we have enjoyed, we give You thanks.

For a faith to live by, for work and friendships, for church and home, we express our deepest gratitude.

As we dine, keep us mindful of the many who are in need throughout the world—and give us a sense of responsibility toward them. Grant us the motivation and wit to find ways to share our bounty with them.

Now, Holy God, give us the spirit of lively conversation and all the warmth of loving relationships as we partake of this food. We pray in the Holy Name of Jesus. Amen.

WILD TURKEYS!

The other day I was traveling on a gravel road in South Dakota. It wound through a woodsy area, right alongside a river. I came around a curve and there before my eyes were seven wild turkeys. When they saw me coming they winged and hopped over the brush line and into the woods.

Never in my life have I seen a wild turkey out in its natural element, and that group of seven made up a truly beautiful sight.

Abundant wildlife give us one of the great blessings of living in this part of the country. The song line that reads, "Where the coyotes howl, and the wind blows free," certainly describes the border area of Iowa and South Dakota.

For sure that event will be on my Thanksgiving list—giving thanks for how close to nature we can be out here in the Midwest.

I must confess that the sight of those big wild turkeys brought to mind Thanksgiving Day. We are authentic traditionalists, and turkey has always been the main fare at the big dinner.

In early history there were those who would have made the Wild Turkey the national symbol, rather than the eagle. Another thing to be thankful for. It would have seemed odd and somehow repugnant to dine on our national bird!

THANKSGIVING AND HARVEST TIME

Fall is Harvest Time. Again the earth has produced crops in abundance, and there is a sense of fruition and completion.

There are life parallels to Planting Time and Harvest Time. Seeds are sown, nurture and care are given—and then the reward of harvest.

The Bible uses the metaphors of sowing and reaping to teach what life is really all about. There is good seed and the harvest of good crops. But if we sow seeds of evil, the harvest will be abundant and calamitous evil.

Chapter 10 of the Book of Hosea gives us a remarkable example of the metaphors of springtime and harvest, of sowing and reaping.

> **Sow for yourselves righteousness, reap the fruit of unfailing love, and break up your unplowed ground; for it is time to seek the Lord, until He comes and showers righteousness on you. But you have planted wickedness, you have reaped evil, you have eaten the fruit of deception.**

The Apostle Paul delivers that remarkable harvest statement in Galatians 6:7: "Do not be deceived: God cannot be mocked. A man reaps what he sows."

Along with all who are alive, you and I know the joy of sowing. We all are sowers. But there always is the question: What will the harvest be?

THANKSGIVING LIST

Most of us know about making a Christmas list. When we were children we might have been encouraged to make such a list in order to give our parents some ideas about what we wanted.

And would it not have been wonderful if they had given us the whole list?

Now many of us make lists for gifts to our children and grandchildren, and beginning in early fall we pester them for suggestions as to what they want for Christmas.

But how about a Thanksgiving List? I'm talking about a setting down on paper the things and relations and happenings for which to give thanks to God in this Season of Thanks.

Perhaps in regard to Christmas lists we heard the admonition, "Now don't make it too long or too unrealistic!"

But Thanksgiving lists ought to be long, and if they are not, something may be wrong with our "thanks equipment."

"Think and Thank!" are the watchwords for the celebration of the Day of national gratitude. Our minds may be so cluttered with ingratitude and bitterness that thinking of reasons for thanks will be difficult—and too time consuming. But work on it. Otherwise you'll not be celebrating Thanksgiving at all—and it might add up to just another time to pig out.

THANKSGIVING PREPARATIONS

The cooks of the households know all about the preparations required for those fantastic meals they will set before their loved ones on Thanksgiving Day. But there are other preparations in which every person should be involved.

It's an obvious requirement that in order to offer thanks to God we must have a great deal of understanding of matters, relationships and successes for which we ought to be thankful. Thanksgiving preparations require a review of our life circumstances—where we began, where we have come and how.

Then there is the even more important concern about the matters that might make our thanks fall on the deaf ears of God—deaf because we have unconfessed sin, hate and prejudice we have not dealt with, hurts and harm we might have caused to others—and generally an unclean and unredeemed soul.

I've always viewed Thanksgiving as the time to get ready for Christmas—which to me is the far more significant and greater occasion. You and I cannot appreciate, much less understand Christmas, until we have come to terms with God's reasons for coming into His world.

You see—His focus was and is on us—individually and collectively. He intends to offer us the one and only way of salvation—

and to receive His magnificent Gift, we have to understand why we need it.

And those blessings constitute our main reasons for thanks!

THANKSGIVING ATTITUDES

During Thanksgiving week I can well imagine that all over the area families are making plans and preparing for the annual family food binge.

As is my annual custom during this time, I'll again make my plea that people not refer to this highly meaningful celebration as "Turkey Day."

Of course, if that is all it means to a person, then go for it. But the wise among us know that it is meant to be much more than a day of opulent dining. It is a day of personal and national Thanksgiving!

I've met a few people in my years of living who have insisted they have *nothing* for which to be thankful. Whatever difficulties they have experienced in their lives loom so large and seem so overwhelming they miss the more subtle, but nonetheless very authentic reasons for thanks.

The truth is, every person alive has reasons to mourn and give themselves over to regret and sorrow in this or any other holiday season. If we concentrate on the tough times that have been and simply ignore the blessings of the present, we're setting ourselves up for a life of misery.

It's also true that folks who can't think of any reason for thanks make lousy company at holiday times—or for that matter, any time!